US politics today

Politics Today

Series editor: Bill Jones

US politics today

Edward Ashbee
and Nigel Ashford

Manchester University Press
Manchester and New York

distributed exclusively in the USA by St. Martin's Press

Copyright © Edward Ashbee and Nigel Ashford 1999

The right of Edward Ashbee and Nigel Ashford to be identified as the authors of this work has been asssserted by them in accordance with the Copyright, Designs and Patents Act 1988.

Published by Manchester University Press
Oxford Road, Manchester M13 9NR, UK
and Room 400, 175 Fifth Avenue, New York, NY 10010, USA
http://www.man.ac.uk/mup

Distributed exclusively in the USA by
St. Martin's Press, Inc., 175 Fifth Avenue, New York,
NY 10010, USA

Distributed exclusively in Canada by
UBC Press, University of British Columbia, 6344 Memorial Road,
Vancouver, BC, Canada V6T 1Z2

British Library Cataloguing-in-Publication Data
A catalogue record for this book is available from the British Library

Library of Congress Cataloging-in-Publication Data applied for

ISBN 0 7190 5463 X *hardback*
　　　0 7190 5464 8 *paperback*

First published 1999

06 05 04 03 02 01 00 99   10 9 8 7 6 5 4 3 2 1

Typeset in Photina
by Servis Filmsetting Ltd, Manchester
Printed in Great Britain
by Biddles Ltd, Guildford and King's Lynn

Contents

Tables

Preface and acknowledgements

The collapse of the Soviet bloc left the United States as the world's only 'super-power'. Despite the growing importance of the European Union during the 1990s, the US plays a crucial part in shaping politics, economics and culture across the globe. As such, it deserves close scrutiny.

US politics today surveys American institutions and current debates. The book:

- assesses the ideas and ideologies underpinning the US political system;
- offers an introduction to the institutions of government, most notably the presidency, Congress and the federal courts;
- considers the role of parties and interest groups;
- examines the factors shaping the outcome of presidential and Congressional elections.

US politics today owes much to our students and colleagues at both Denstone College and Staffordshire University. However, we are also indebted to others. Edward Ashbee in particular would like to acknowledge Ellie Dwight's generous and patient support. John Dumbrell's many incisive comments were a great help. Daniel Gregson and Esther Jubb read draft chapters. Phil Hosay and the staff of the Multinational Institute of American Studies at New York University created an environment in which a number of the ideas and arguments in the book took shape. Nigel Ashford wishes to record his gratitude to all his friends in Washington, DC for their discussions on US politics over the years, and in particular to Frank and Ann Lavin for their hospitality. We should, however, stress that responsibility for errors and omissions remains ours alone.

Edward Ashbee and Nigel Ashford
Denstone College/Staffordshire University

February 1999

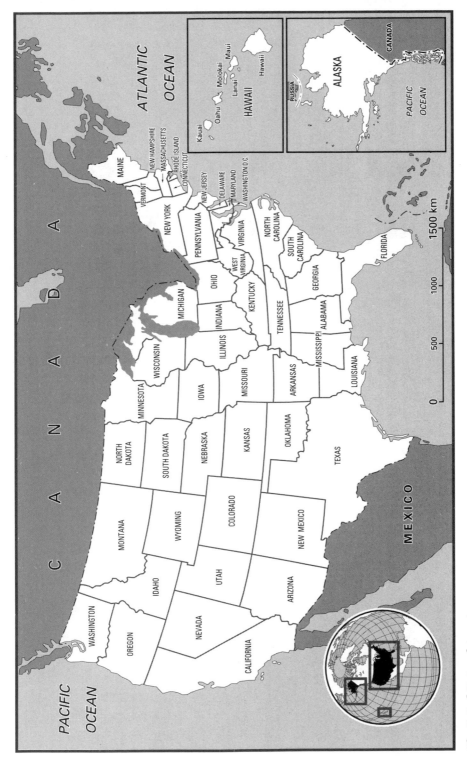

The United States of America

Part I

Diversity and consensus

1

Differences and divisions

The US has a population of over 265 million. It spans much of a continent. Even if the states of Alaska and Hawaii are excluded from the picture, it extends across four time zones. Los Angeles is 2,445 miles from New York City. The Mississippi River is 2,340 miles long.

In contrast with the countries of the 'Old World' in Europe, the US is a relatively youthful nation. The first permanent settlement of Europeans was established at the beginning of the seventeenth century. Since then, the nation has been transformed by a process of westward expansion, Civil War, industrialisation, and the absorption of successive waves of immigrants.

Although the US was, at the time of its founding, a relatively homogeneous society dominated by the descendants of English settlers, it now has a *multiethnic* and *multicultural* character. The contemporary US, some observers argue, should be seen as an amalgam of different identities and interests. They emphasise the many fissures and cleavages, particularly those that are derived from race, ethnicity and region. Although a number of commentators welcome this diversity as a source of vitality, others fear that the divisions are such that they will lead to *Balkanisation* and the eventual break-up of the US. Arthur Schlesinger Jr, a distinguished historian and former adviser to President Kennedy, has, for example, warned of 'the fragmentation of the national community into a quarrelsome spatter of enclaves, ghettos, tribes' (1992: 137–8). This chapter surveys contemporary American society and outlines the basis for these claims.

Race

About 12.6 per cent of the US population is black or *African-American*. Some 55 per cent of the black population still live in the southern states, where their ancestors once worked as slaves. Others are the grandchildren and great-grandchildren of those who sought the 'promised land' in the North. From the

First World War onwards, millions migrated to the northern cities. They were drawn by the promise of industrial employment, and the chance to escape the rural poverty and segregation laws of the South. Blacks now constitute 39 per cent and 75 per cent of those living in Chicago and Detroit respectively.

Race: the American dilemma

Many immigrants thought in terms of religious, economic and political freedom. About 1.5 million Africans were, however, brought across the Atlantic in leg and neck irons. They were mostly destined for the southern states such as Virginia, Georgia and Maryland.

Although slavery came to an end in 1865, when the South was defeated in the Civil War, southern blacks faced continuing discrimination. Until the reforms of the 1960s, public facilities were *segregated* and many blacks were unable to vote. There was a gulf between the democratic ideals that constituted the American creed and political institutions structured around racial oppression. Gunnar Myrdal, a Swedish sociologist, termed this *the American dilemma*.

Amid all of this, black Americans are sometimes portrayed as passive victims. However, despite endemic racism, slaves and their descendants made an enduring mark on American life and society. For a brief period – in the aftermath of the Civil War – blacks in the southern states gained *political* rights. They were elected to state legislatures and the US Congress, although they lost these positions as whites regained their dominance in the region.

There were also a number of black *economic* success stories. Madam C. J. Walker made her fortune from beauty salons. John Merrick founded the North Carolina Mutual Insurance Company. Blacks also 'voted with their feet'. In the early years of the century, large numbers migrated from the South to northern cities. The growing black electorate in cities such as Detroit and Chicago created the conditions in which blacks could organise and again win political representation. In 1928, Oscar DePriest, a Republican, was elected to the House of Representatives. Others supported Marcus Garvey's radical 'Back to Africa' movement. Black *culture* also began to gain recognition as the Harlem Renaissance took shape. Novelists, poets and jazz musicians carved out a distinctive black culture in uptown New York City that influenced black and white Americans alike.

In the 1950s and 1960s the civil rights movement, led by figures such as Martin Luther King and the Reverend Ralph Abernathy, began to gain substantive victories. Against a background of Cold War pressures, the Montgomery bus boycott of 1955–56, the 'freedom rides', sit-ins and marches compelled federal legislators to act. The 1964 Civil Rights Act and the 1965 Voting Rights Act finally brought segregation to an end and allowed African-Americans to vote freely.

To what extent is the US now a racially equal society? Liberals emphasise the continuing hold of *institutionalised* discrimination. The disparities between whites and blacks – in terms of poverty, educational attainment and jailings –

suggest to them that federal government action is required. They call for large-scale public investment in the inner-city districts, and a further extension of affirmative action programmes so as to ensure that minorities are proportionately represented on higher education courses and in senior management positions. Conservatives – and black nationalist organisations such as the Nation of Islam – adopt a different approach. They argue that although government regulations prevent individuals building up their own business enterprises, many of the former obstacles to black progress have now been eliminated. The black communities, they argue, need to rediscover the entrepreneurial spirit, and address the problems of illegitimacy, criminality and drug abuse within their own communities.

Further reading

Carnoy, M. (1994), *Faded Dreams: The Politics and Economics of Race in America*, New York, Cambridge University Press.
Rueter, T. (1995), *The Politics of Race: African Americans and the Political System*, Armonk, M. E. Sharpe.

There are important differences in the social and economic circumstances of the races. In 1995, almost 30 per cent of the black population lived below the poverty level. Just over 11 per cent of white families faced similar difficulties. The infant mortality rate for blacks is twice that for whites. In 1996, over a quarter of African-American teenagers failed to graduate or successfully complete their studies at high school. Blacks are disproportionately likely to be victims of crime. Significant numbers are also offenders. One in three black men, aged between twenty and twenty-nine, is in jail, on parole, or otherwise under the supervision of the criminal justice system (Esler 1998: 112).

Race is also important because it informs social and political opinions. There are significant differences between black and white attitudes. African Americans are the Democrats' most loyal constituency. In the 1996 presidential election, 84 per cent of black voters supported Bill Clinton. In contrast, only 44 cent of whites who voted in the election backed the incumbent president. Furthermore, whereas a large proportion of whites support the death penalty, polls suggest that it is endorsed by less than half of the black population. A clear majority of African-Americans believe that the federal government should set basic national standards in the provision of welfare and other forms of social assistance. Less than a third of the population as a whole share this opinion.

The degree of polarisation between blacks and whites was evident when O. J. Simpson, the black sports star and film actor, was acquitted of murder in October 1995. The verdict was hailed by many blacks and condemned by many whites. It is also evident in the differences of attitude towards Louis Farrakhan, leader of the Nation of Islam, a radical black separatist organisation. Farrakhan attracted controversy because of the vehemently antisemitic and anti-white character of his public statements and those of his close aides. Despite these, he is viewed favourably by over 40 per cent of black men and almost a third of black women. However, he is dismissed by the population as a whole. Only 7.7 per cent regard him favourably.

White attitudes should also be considered. While there is evidence to suggest that racial prejudice may have either diminished or taken a less overt form, it is still evident. A 1991 survey suggested that racial stereotypes were widely accepted. Almost half of whites agreed that 'blacks tend to be lazy'. A clear majority endorsed claims that blacks 'prefer welfare'. Almost half said that they were 'unintelligent' (Smith 1995: 39). Sentiments such as these have at times been translated into votes. David Duke, a former Ku Klux Klan leader, who still maintained many of his earlier opinions, stood as a candidate in the 1992 Republican presidential primaries. He gained 11 and 7 per cent of the vote among Republican primary voters in Mississippi and South Carolina respectively.

Mississippi Burning

Director: Alan Parker (1988)

Starring: William Dafoe, Gene Hackman, Frances McDormand

Mississippi Burning traces the FBI investigations that followed the murder of three civil rights activists in 1964. It is a powerful drama and a damning indictment of southern racism. The film has, however, been much criticised. African-Americans are confined to walk-on parts. Civil rights organisations such as the Southern Christian Leadership Conference, which directed many of the protests against the Jim Crow laws, are neglected.

Ethnicity

Although hostility towards the black population bound whites together during America's formative years, they should not be seen as a homogenous bloc. The white 'race' is constructed from different ethnic – or cultural – groupings. This is because the US is a 'nation of immigrants'.

About 16 per cent of the white population claim English ancestry. They are WASPs – White Anglo-Saxon Protestants – who have traditionally constituted the American governing elite. A further 7 per cent have Scottish, Welsh, Scots-Irish or other British origins.

British settlers were the first permanent 'immigrants' in mainland North America. In May 1607, a settlement was established in Jamestown, Virginia.

Despite many hardships, it survived by exporting tobacco. Thirteen years later, the Pilgrim Fathers landed at Plymouth Bay, in what was to become Massachusetts. In contrast with the Jamestown settlers, who were commercial adventurers, the Puritans hoped to build a self-governing Christian commonwealth.

Native Americans

By the 1840s, the US was committed to conquering much of the continent. The *manifest destiny* of the nation was to occupy all the lands from the Atlantic to the Pacific.

For the Native Americans, or 'Indians', the westward shift led to the final destruction of tribal societies and their nomadic way of life. Despite occasional victories – most notably the rout of General Custer and his soldiers at the Little Big Horn in 1874 – Indian resistance was crushed. The tribes were not only outgunned. Mass slaughter led to the near extinction of the buffalo herds on which they depended. The capture of Geronimo in 1886 symbolised their final defeat.

Today, the remnants of Native American society are to be found on the reservations. The largest – the Navajo nation – stretches across parts of Arizona, New Mexico and Utah. Some of those living on the reservations have made a living by offering goods and services such as fireworks and gambling that are prohibited elsewhere under state law. There are also earnings from tourism. Some – most notably the Navajo – have sold coal and uranium mining rights.

Despite these initiatives, reservation dwellers face severe problems, including economic hardship and unemployment. In 1996, 31.2 per cent of American Indians lived below the poverty level. (Bureau of the Census 1997: 51)

Further reading

Catlin, G. (1989), *North American Indians*, New York and London, Penguin.
Stoutenburgh, J. (1990), *Dictionary of the American Indian*, New York, Wings Books.

During the seventeenth and eighteenth centuries, these beginnings evolved into stable and ordered communities. Much of the eastern seaboard was settled. The population were British colonists, but a separate and distinct American identity was beginning to emerge. Although there were significant differences between the northern 'Yankees' and the southerners, this identity formed a basis for rebellion against British rule, and the Declaration of Independence was published in 1776. The War of Independence followed, culminating in the defeat of the British forces at Yorktown in 1781. The first US president, George Washington, took office in 1789.

Although WASPs formed the backbone of the new nation, others followed. During the nineteenth and early twentieth centuries, millions of migrants made the journey from Europe. Before the Civil War (1861–65), they were largely drawn from countries such as Ireland, Germany and Sweden. After the war, it was the turn of those from eastern and southern Europe.

Between 1845 and 1854, three million people crossed the Atlantic. In 1907 alone, 1.3 million arrived in the US. Why did they make the journey? The answer is that both 'push' and 'pull' factors were at work. 'Push' factors are the pressures that encourage migrants to abandon their country of origin. For example, in Poland, peasants were forced from the land because of competition from more advanced forms of agriculture in western Europe and the US. Their difficulties were compounded by a high birth rate, the occupation and partition of the country by neighbouring powers, and the anti-Catholicism of the German government. However, 'pull' factors also played their part. The Poles were drawn to the US by the promise of employment in industrial cities such as Chicago, Buffalo and Pittsburgh. At the same time, the transatlantic journey became less arduous and costly. The advent of the steamship cut the crossing time to weeks rather than months, and intense competition between shipping companies reduced the fares.

There were broadly similar pressures in other European countries. The failure of the potato crop led to mass famine in Ireland. From 1847 until 1855, over 100,000 emigrated annually. In 1851, emigration reached a peak of 221,000. In the US, the men found employment in construction projects, such as canals and railroads, along the East coast. Women worked in the textile industries.

The US offered more than a regular wage. Although immigrants often encountered *nativist* resentment from those who had been in the country for many generations, America represented freedom. It promised economic freedom to those who had been adversely affected by the process of economic change. In Europe, the displaced artisan (or skilled independent craftsman) faced only unemployment or absorption into the ranks of the industrial working class. In the US, he might rebuild a business of his own. The commercial history of the US is adorned by individual success stories. German-American artisans established companies such as Steinway & Sons, the piano makers, and Levi Strauss, the clothing manufacturers. For other migrants, there were hopes of religious liberty. Sects such as the Amish and the Mennonites sought the freedom to live independently of others. They survive to this day as autonomous communities in states such as Pennsylvania and Ohio. The US also offered political freedom and civic rights. In Europe, Jews faced discrimination. In the years before the First World War, there were violent antisemitic massacres in Poland and Russia. After the war, prejudice against the Jewish communities was sustained as the newly formed Slav nations began to establish themselves.

However, from 1921 onwards, admissions to the US were severely restricted, and skewed towards those from northern Europe. This policy lasted until the 1965 amendments to the Immigration and Nationality Act abandoned the system of quotas for particular nations and established 'family reunification' as the defining criteria for entry. As a consequence of reform, the number of immigrants has risen dramatically, and they have again become a significant element within American society. In 1990, the foreign-born constituted 7.9 per cent of the American population. In 1995, 720,461 legal immigrants were admitted. The majority of the new immigrants are from the Americas (particularly Mexico) and Asia, but there are growing numbers of other nationalities.

These official figures are, however, an underestimate. Illegal immigrants should be added to the picture. Studies suggest that 4.3 million are now resident in the US, of whom about half have settled in the border states of California and Texas. Illegal immigration has inevitably become a defining political issue in these states, and in November 1994, the voters of California passed Proposition 187 ending non-emergency state benefits, such as health care and education, to 'undocumented aliens'.

Hispanics

There has long been a Hispanic or *Latino* presence in the US southwest. Their numbers grew significantly from the 1880s onwards when Mexican labourers came to border states such as Texas and California in search of work. There has been renewed growth in recent years following the liberalisation of immigration laws in 1965. By 1994, there were 27 million Hispanics, representing a 28 per cent increase since 1990. The rise can be attributed to immigration and a relatively high birth rate.

To an extent, Hispanics share the problems facing the black communities. In March 1994, for example, 11 per cent were unemployed compared with a figure of 6 per cent for non-Hispanic whites. Almost a third are in poverty, and in 1993, median family income was only $23,670.

It would, however, to wrong to make generalisations. As the *US Bureau of the Census* emphasises, the term 'Hispanic' refers to speakers of Spanish and therefore describes different races, nationalities and ethnicities. There are important cleavages within the Hispanic population. In 1993, for example, poverty rates were 17 per cent among Cubans and 35 per cent for Puerto Rican families. There are also variations in the economic, cultural and political relationship between the Hispanic communities and the wider population. In California, there have been tensions which were reflected in the passage of Proposition 187. Passed in November 1994, the measure sought to deny non-emergency state benefits to illegal immigrants. It was supported by 63 per cent of 'Anglos' and opposed by 69 per cent of Hispanics. In Texas, however, cities such as Houston seem to have been restructured around a 'Tex-Mex' identity. They have, for example, adopted bilingualism in the schools and significant numbers of Hispanics have won public office. Furthermore, although the Hispanic vote across the US as a whole is now overwhelmingly Democratic, there are signs that minority politics in Texas are being 'normalised'. There is serious competition for the Hispanic vote, and the state's Republican Governor, George W. Bush, attracted 49 per cent of the Hispanic vote in November 1996.

Immigration has been on such a scale that – despite continuing WASP pre-dominance – it reshaped the culture and character of the US. This is evident in four ways:

1 Immigration has fractured the geography of many American cities. To this day, New York City has a Chinatown, Little Italy and El Barrio. More recent immigrants have also made their mark. The Atlantic Avenue district in Brooklyn, a borough of New York City, is predominantly Arabic. The Brighton Beach area is now known as 'Little Odessa' following an influx of Russians. Hispanics constitute 39.9 per cent and 27.6 per cent respectively of the populations of Los Angeles and Houston.

2 Mass immigration led to religious diversity. Although the early settlers were brought together by a shared commitment to the Protestant faith, they belonged to different churches. Some brought Anglican traditions with them. Many – particularly in New England – were committed to Puritanism. Some sects, such as the Shakers and the Amish, isolated themselves from the external world. Other faiths were reshaped by outsiders. In the South, for example, the evangelism that characterised black forms of worship left a distinct cultural mark on the white churches.

   Since the mid-nineteenth century, the US has progressively become a less Protestant and more pluralistic nation. Immigrants from eastern and southern Europe, and recent immigrants from Central and South America, brought Roman Catholicism and Judaism with them. A 1994 survey revealed that 24 per cent of the American population is Catholic, and that there are over three million Jews. Other faiths are also growing. In 1990, for example, Islam had over half a million adherents. They were drawn from both immigrants and the native-born black population.

3 Although there has been a steady process of assimilation into the American mainstream, and many of the ethnic neighbourhoods have lost their distinctive character, ethnicity still offers a basis for self-identification. Indeed, in recent decades, there has been a renewal of commitment to cultural organisations and festivals. Denver holds an annual *Oktoberfest*. In Savannah, the schools are closed on St Patrick's Day (Dinnerstein *et al.* 1996: 266). The annual St Patrick's Day parade in New York City attracts about 150,000 participants.

4 Ethnicity has political significance. In many states, an ethnically balanced ticket is essential for electoral success. In Minnesota, every state governor between 1925 and 1976 had a Scandinavian background. Since the mid-nineteenth century, the Irish vote has had to be courted in cities such as New York and Boston. There was, from 1916 until 1969, a Jewish 'seat' on the US Supreme Court bench. Today, some Republicans fear that the growing Hispanic vote, and its increasingly close alignment with the Democrats, could fatally damage their party's long-term electoral prospects.

Fears such as this are fuelled by predictions that the ethnic mix will change significantly over the next half-century. Projections suggest that by 2050, whites will have almost been reduced to minority status. The proportion of African Americans will only rise marginally to about 13.6 per cent. However, there will have been a dramatic increase in number of Hispanics or *Latinos*. At present, 10.6 per cent of the US population is of Hispanic origin. By 2050, they will constitute a quarter of the country's population. Asians and Pacific Islanders will account for a further 8.2 per cent. Some conservatives, most notably Peter Brimelow, believe that these shifts will have dramatic consequences for the US. He asserts that Hispanic immigrants may eventually seek the break-up of the US. He warns that 'throughout the lifetime of my little son, American patriots will be fighting to salvage as much as possible from the ship-wreck of their great republic' (1996: 268).

Underclass and overclass

Most Americans belong to the middle class. However, US society is marked by significant socio-economic divisions. There are those who are separated from the remainder of society by being permanently 'locked' into poverty. Inner-city neighbourhoods or 'ghettoes' – such as Harlem or the Bronx in New York, the Chicago South Side, and the Watts neighbourhood of Los Angeles – have become synonymous with the most severe forms of urban deprivation. Members of the *underclass* have few job-based skills, and are either unemployed or underemployed. Blacks, Hispanics and other minorities are disproportionately represented in its ranks.

The 'underclass' is a contested concept. Many who use the term have drawn on the work of Charles Murray, a conservative commentator, who has tied it to cultural as well as economic dimensions. It has become associated in the popular mind with criminality, drug abuse, a high teenage pregnancy rate, the collapse of family structures, and welfare dependency. Few, however, dispute that although economic opportunities opened up during the 1990s, there is still a pervasive sense of isolation and helplessness in many of the inner cities. As Cornel West, a noted black social commentator, puts it: 'we have created rootless, dangling people with little link to the supportive networks – family, friends, school – that sustain some sense of purpose in life' (1993: 9).

Urban poverty is explained in different ways. Liberals stress economic factors and emphasise the decline of manufacturing industry. Some also point to the way in which inner-city neighbourhoods lost their vitality as more affluent, predominantly white, families moved out to the suburbs. The solution to the urban crisis, they argue, lies in federal government intervention and increased funding for inner-city regeneration, education, and welfare provision.

Conservatives accept that economic factors play a role, and they suggest that deregulation would create the conditions for urban renewal. However, they also emphasise the need for cultural change. Welfare reform, a strict law and order policy, inner-city enterprise zones where business initiatives would be actively encouraged, and a market-based school system would, they assert, encourage responsible behaviour, self-reliance, and entrepreneurship. Conservative commentators argue that the 1996 Welfare Reform Act, which ended the principle of welfare as an entitlement, represented a first step along this road.

The 'underclass' entered the popular vocabulary some years ago. However, a number of observers have now also begun to talk of an *overclass* or 'a new national elite'. It is an economically and socially privileged grouping – between about 5 and 10 per cent of the American people – that consists of those with advanced degrees and their families. Members of the 'overclass' have views and interests that mark them out from other sections of the population. For example, their need for domestic staff, particularly nannies, has led them to support open immigration (Lind 1996: 139–80).

Regional identities

The regions are associated with different traditions and cultural identities. The Yankee Northeast was shaped by its Puritan roots. Although the character of states such as New Hampshire and Maine is still defined by their forests, lakes and mountains, the region was also the locus of the American industrial revolution. Cities such as Lowell in Massachusetts owed their origins to the textile mills. By 1846, they were producing almost a million yards of cloth a week. As time progressed, the tools and techniques used in the textile mills were applied to other industries. Machine shops and factories were established. In 1851, when the first World's Fair was held at the Crystal Palace in London, Americans won more prizes for their industrial products, compared to the number of entries, than any other nation. On the basis of such achievements, the Northeast increasingly became economically, socially and politically predominant.

The identity of the Midwest is more difficult to define. It is popularly associated with agriculture, the small town and *isolationist* attitudes. For many, the character of the region has been captured by the Minnesota writer, Garrison Keillor, in his stories about the fictional Lake Wobegon. However, the Midwest is not homogeneous. Agriculture is divided between corn, wheat and dairy production, and the culture of the region was shaped by German, Scandinavian and British settlers. The Midwest also includes the industrial belt around the Great Lakes, cities such as Detroit, and the metropolis of Chicago.

The West includes states such as Arizona and New Mexico. They were among the last to be brought into the US, and still retain a sense of the 'frontier' about them. Much of the terrain is arid and dramatic. There are large-scale, albeit impoverished, Indian reservations. The character of Utah has been shaped by Mormon settlers. Las Vegas is the gambling capital of the US. On the

West coast, California has – from the 'gold rush' of 1849 onwards – been seen as a land of opportunity.

The Empire Wilderness

Robert D. Kaplan paints a particularly bleak portrait of America as a divided nation in his 1998 book, *The Empire Wilderness* (New York, Random House). The US will, he argues, continue to fragment as social and economic trends, that are already evident on the West coast, become institutionalised. The wealthy are retreating into 'standardized corporate fortresses, privately guarded housing developments, (and) Disneyfied tourist bubbles'. At the same time, others are being confined to 'isolated suburban pods and enclaves of races and classes unrelated to each other'.

Among the different regions, the South traditionally had the most distinct cultural character. In the years before the Civil War, it was structured around 'King Cotton', the plantation (although the small farm was, in practice, more representative) and slavery. Tensions between the South and the North grew as the century progressed. Abolitionists in the North called for an end to slavery. Northern manufacturers insisted upon protective tariffs, although these threatened the interests of the cotton trade.

For southerners, the election of the Republican candidate, Abraham Lincoln, as president in November 1860, seemed to symbolise the determination of the North to impose its will upon the entire nation. His victory led eleven southern states to *secede* from the US and establish the Confederate States of America as an independent nation. Although Lincoln was, despite his opponents' fears, prepared to accept the maintenance of slavery, he could not countenance the dissolution of the US. In the Civil War that followed 620,000 were killed.

The northern victory in April 1865 led to the abolition of slavery, the temporary occupation of the southern states, and the long-term hegemony of the North. However, the white South progressively rebuilt itself. Its political representatives dominated Congressional committees for the greater part of the twentieth century. From the 1890s, segregation was imposed across the South, confining blacks to certain occupations and restricting their access to public facilities. Bogus 'tests' and rigged state constitutions were used to remove their right to vote. These forms of institutionalised racism – known as 'Jim Crow' laws – were only brought to an end in the 1960s.

Although some observers talk today about the 'homogenisation' of the nation, regional contrasts persist. Carl Degler notes that the South is still marked by greater 'rurality'. Living standards are lower than the national average. Although there is a significant African-American population, there is less ethnic and religious diversity than in other regions. Conservative thinking has a more entrenched hold (1997: 14–22).

However, although these regional differences remain, many of the disparities take a different form to those that existed in the past. In earlier decades,
manufacturing industry defined the character of both the Northeast and the
Midwest. However, these regions have been subject to long-term structural
decline. For this reason, they have sometimes been dubbed the *Rustbelt*.

In contrast, there have been high levels of growth in the *Sunbelt* states of the
South and the West. The network of interstate highways built during the
Eisenhower years transformed hitherto isolated rural communities. The federal
government funded other infrastructural projects. Many defence installations
were located in the Sunbelt states. The space programme was based in Houston
and at Cape Canaveral. These projects, the low cost of land, and the relative
weak character of trade unionism encouraged the development of new industries. In the 1980s, employment in the South and West grew by 26.3 per cent
and 29.8 per cent respectively.

The economic disparities between the regions inevitably led to population
shifts. Some cities and states in the Northeast and Midwest have experienced
either low or negative population growth. Between 1990 and 1996, the population of Pennsylvania grew by only 1.46 per cent. Connecticut's population
fell by 0.39 per cent. However, during the same period, the population in the
southern and western states grew substantially. For example, the population of
Arizona rose by 20.8 per cent.

However, although there are these trends, it is important not to succumb to
over-generalisation. Parts of the South and the West were seriously hit by the
recessions of the early 1980s and 1990s. At the same time, there was some
recovery in areas such as New England and in the Great Lakes, where the construction of industrial robots began to take the place of automobile production.

Extremists

There are other fissures and divisions. Although its scale should not be exaggerated, there is a cleavage between those who accept the *legitimacy* of the political
system – the right of the federal government to rule – and those who reject it.
During the 1960s and 1970s, some far left groupings and black nationalist
organisations, such as the Weathermen and the Black Panthers, defied government authority and resorted to violence. However, in the 1990s, their place has
been taken by far right networks such as the militias and 'patriot' organisations.

The militias are armed paramilitary groupings. In 1995, observers identified
militia activity in at least forty states, involving, they estimated, somewhere
between ten and thirty thousand individuals. They are tied by a network of individuals and organisations to the more long-established and broad-based Patriot
movement.

The US has, in their eyes, been abandoned by its own leaders. Those leaders
serve the interests of international forces and are committed to the imposition of
a dictatorial world government. Militia publications assert that secret military

preparations are already being made by these forces. There will be a surprise attack against the American people, who will then be reduced to the status of serfs. Those within the Patriot movement have more developed ideas about the character of the conspiracy that is being directed against US citizens. Some see it as directed by liberals and world institutions such as the United Nations. Others are anti-semitic and talk of a 'cabal' of Jewish bankers and communists.

Because the militias and the Patriot movement see the federal government and those who act on its behalf as *illegitimate*, they commemorate acts of 'armed resistance' against government forces. In particular, they remember the FBI's 1992 shoot-out with a white supremacist in Ruby Ridge, Idaho. They also cite the federal government's 1993 confrontation with a religious cult – the Branch Davidians – in Waco, Texas. This culminated in the deaths of 86 men, women and children, and is used to show the need for 'self-defence' by armed citizens.

Although groupings such as the militias are on the fringes of American politics, their growth reflects a shift in the popular mood. Some conservatives have, for example, begun to talk of the federal government as a 'regime', suggesting that it is *illegitimate*. At the same time – and this is explored in later chapters – there is a widely shared sense of disenchantment with, and suspicion towards, the formal political process. This is evident at an anecdotal level in the popularity of conspiracy-based films and TV programmes such as *The X-Files*. It can also be seen in the electoral turnout figures. In the November 1996 elections, administrative reforms had made it easier for the public to register as voters. Nevertheless, less than half the adult population cast a ballot. Only about 49 per cent of eligible Americans voted. This was the lowest level of voting since 1924 and the second lowest since 1824.

Furthermore, the influence of groupings such as the militias can be exaggerated. They are a small and unrepresentative minority. The April 1995 Oklahoma City bombing created a climate in which far-right organisations were regarded with hostility and suspicion by the general public. In a poll, 78 per cent of respondents said that they did not believe individual citizens had the right to arm themselves and resist the federal government. A similar proportion, 73 per cent, believed that the federal authorities had been right to use force against the Branch Davidian cult in Waco (Golay and Rollyson 1996: 135–6).

Gender

Many political observers talk in terms of a 'gender gap'. They are referring to *attitudinal* differences between men and women. The gap can be seen in terms of *partisan identification*. Polls suggest that 39 per cent of women, but only about 30 per cent of men define themselves as either 'weak' or 'strong' Democratic Party identifiers (Bureau of the Census 1997: 287).

Although the scale of the gender gap should not be exaggerated, it is rooted in economic and cultural shifts. The decline of manufacturing industry and the growth of the service sector have led to a shrinkage in the number of traditionally 'male' forms of employment.

> For American men of all races, the past twenty years have been marked by declining or stagnant wages for the majority, by the collapse of a market in jobs paying high wages for a strong back, and by the steady collapse of the patriarchal family, with father as the breadwinner and mother as the caregiver. (Edsall 1997: 138)

As employment has become more insecure and traditional certainties have been eroded, men have been drawn towards conservatism. In contrast, women have been subject to different pressures. Although often short-term and part-time, job opportunities have opened up. The proportion of women in civilian employment has grown steadily, from under 38 per cent in 1960 to 59.3 per cent in 1996 (Bureau of the Census 1997: 403). There has also been a shift in education and training. By 2006, men will only constitute 44.2 per cent of those with degrees (Bureau of the Census 1997: 191). At the same time, there has been a significant rise in the proportion of female-headed, single-parent households. In 1993, for example, 23.3 per cent of children lived only with their mothers. A high proportion of women are both workers and domestic carers, and many look to government as a source of support.

Culture wars

There is a further cleavage in contemporary American society. It is, in part, the product of the gender gap, but it has also been shaped by growing levels of mobility, exposure to urban modernity, the specific experiences of different generations, and religious affiliations.

Among some groups, traditional attitudes have weakened. Moral *relativism* -the belief that different 'lifestyle choices' have equal validity – has gained increasing acceptance. This is reflected in the TV viewing figures. *NYPD Blue* and *Ellen* came thirteenth and thirtieth respectively in the 1996–97 TV ratings. There are now fewer traditional households in the US. In 1996, 32 per cent of all births were to unmarried women. About a third of the nation's children live with a parent or parents who have never married. Ideas about sex roles and responsibilities drawn from feminism and the women's movement have gained currency. The gay movement – perhaps the most visible repudiation of moral traditionalism – is entrenched in cities such as Los Angeles, San Francisco and New York.

However, a significant proportion of Americans still regard themselves as moral traditionalists. They stress the importance of the conventional family. The institutions of marriage and family are, they assert, not only rooted in biblical teaching, but also represent an important building block for a stable and ordered society. Although they disagree about the extent to which government can or should 'legislate morality', there is agreement that homosexuality, attempts to devalue the marriage vow, and illegitimacy are immoral. Attitudes such as these have won considerable support, particularly within the

Republican Party. Campaigns to curb 'value-free' school sex-education courses, pornography on the Internet, and TV programmes such as *Roseanne, Murphy Brown, Ellen,* and *NYPD Blue* that seem to condone immorality, have been widely endorsed.

Conclusion

The US is a diverse and heterogeneous society. Some radicals and liberals see the country's ethnic, racial and gender differences in positive terms and as a basis for *identity politics.* They call for the maintenance and extension of policies such as affirmative action. In its most rigorous form, this attempts to ensure 'equality of outcome' by setting numerical goals – or 'quotas' – so that women and minorities are more fully represented in senior management positions or on educational courses. Many liberals also stress the importance of multiculturalism and diversity in education. School pupils, they assert, should be taught to understand and appreciate the different cultures from which the US is constructed.

For their part, conservatives and some more traditional liberals argue that such policies are socially divisive, and will lead to the fragmentation of the US as a nation. In place of policies such as multiculturalism and affirmative action, they instead stress the beliefs, principles and traditions that bring Americans together. These are explored in Chapter 2.

References and further reading

Alsop, R. J. (1997), *The Wall Street Journal Almanac 1998,* New York, Ballantine Books.
Brimelow, P. (1996), *Alien Nation,* New York, HarperPerennial.
Bureau of the Census (1997) *Statistical Almanac of the United States 1997,* Washington, DC, US Department of Commerce.
Degler, C. N. (1997), *Place Over Time: The Continuity of Southern Distinctiveness,* Athens, University of Georgia Press.
Dinnerstein, L, Nichols, R. L. and D. M. Reimers (1996), *Natives and Strangers: A Multicultural History of America,* New York, Oxford University Press.
Edsall, T. B. (1997), 'The cultural revolution of 1994: Newt Gingrich, the Republican Party, and the third Great Awakening', in B. E. Shafer *et al., Present Discontents: American Politics in the Very Late Twentieth Century,* Chatham, Chatham House.
Esler, G. (1998), *The United States of Anger,* London, Penguin.
Fuchs, L. H. (1990), *The American Kaleidoscope: Race. Ethnicity, and the Civil Culture,* Hanover and London, Wesleyan University Press.
Golay, M. and C. Rollyson (1996), *Where America Stands 1996,* New York, John Wiley.
Henwood, D. (1994), *The State of the USA Atlas,* London, Penguin.
Lind, M. (1996) *The Next American Nation: The New Nationalism and the Fourth American Revolution,* New York, The Free Press.
Pomper, G. M. (1997), *The Election of 1996: Reports and Interpretations,* Chatham, Chatham House.

Schlesinger, A. M. Jr (1992), *The Disuniting of America: Reflections on a Multicultural Society*, New York, W. W. Norton.
Smith, R. C. (1995), *Racism in the Post-Civil Rights Era*, Albany, State University of New York Press.
West, C. (1993), *Race Matters*, Boston, Beacon Press.

American politics and the Internet

One of the best starting points for exploring the subject is the website offered by the American Studies Resources Centre. Based at John Moores University in Liverpool, it provides information about conferences and courses in the UK. It also incorporates links to other sites in both the US and UK. These include the three branches of government, the parties, and pressure groups such as the National Association for the Advancement of Colored People (NAACP). There are also links to sites offering information about historical events such as the Vietnam War.

http://www.americansc.org.uk

The University of Keele's Department of American Studies website also offers links to a range of other sites and search engines:

http://www.keele.ac.uk/depts/as/ashome.html

An exhaustive set of links to political organisations and institutions in the US and other countries can be found at:

http://www.ulster.net/~btuchman/links.html

2

A shared culture

Chapter 1 outlined the claims of those who assert that the US is a divided and fractured nation. However, their arguments represent only part of the picture. Despite the fissures, there are also unifying ideas and principles that draw Americans together into a common nationality. They define what it means to be an 'American'. This chapter surveys these beliefs.

Principles

In most European countries, citizenship is generally derived from an individual's parentage or place of birth. People are born into a certain nationality. However, being an American rests on the acceptance of particular beliefs and principles. As G. K. Chesterton, the British novelist and essayist, wrote: 'America is the only nation in the world that is founded on a creed.' The creed, ethos or *ideology* has a number of components. These include the 'American dream' and principles such as self-reliance, democracy and freedom.

The American dream

The 'American dream' is the belief that individuals are – with sufficient commitment and application – capable of almost unlimited achievement. Hard work and initiative will, it is said, bring material rewards because the US offers boundless opportunities and possibilities. Whatever their former circumstances, individuals can begin again. They can, in a sense, be reborn. James Truslow Adams, a historian, refers to 'that dream of a land in which life should be better and richer and fuller for every man, with opportunity for each according to his ability or achievement' (Fossum and Roth 1981: 6). In 1993, President Bill Clinton talked in similar terms: 'The American dream that we were all raised on is a simple but powerful one – if you work hard and play by the rules you should be given a chance to go as far as your God-given ability will take you' (Hochschild 1995: 18).

The American dream is a recurrent theme in American literature. In the nineteenth century, Horatio Alger wrote over 130 novels celebrating America as a land of opportunity and advancement. In 1925, F. Scott Fitzgerald's book, *The Great Gatsby*, was published. It tells the story of Jay Gatsby, who accumulates a fortune through his own efforts. His past is an irrelevance.

The dream also takes a political form. It expresses itself in the belief that individuals can, like President Abraham Lincoln (1861–65), rise from 'log cabin to White House'. President James A. Garfield, who was assassinated shortly after taking office in 1881, is another celebrated example. He was born in a pioneer home in Ohio, distinguished himself in the Civil War, rose to be Speaker of the House of Representatives, and later gained the Republican nomination for the presidency. Other presidents have been hailed in similar terms. Following the presidential election of 1992, President Bill Clinton talked of his own progression from Hope in rural Arkansas to the White House.

Statistical evidence suggests that the dream is remarkably resilient. It has survived all the economic uncertainties of the twentieth century. A 1994 study revealed that 74 per cent of those who were asked agreed with the statement, 'In America, if you work hard, you can be anything you want to be.' In her study, *Facing Up to the American Dream*, Jennifer Hochschild concludes that Americans are 'close to unanimous in endorsing the idea of the American dream' (1995: 55).

The dream has a hold because it is, at least to some extent, rooted in the realities of life. Some individuals and families *have* begun with little and accumulated vast sums. Andrew Carnegie (1835–1919) was born in Scotland. He was sent to the US at the age of thirteen, and initially laboured in the mills for a salary of $1.20 a week. He eventually became a wealthy steel magnate. Today, figures such as Bill Gates of Microsoft, and Ross Perot, who built up a Texas computer company and contested the presidency in 1992 and 1996, seem to show that the dream is still a reality.

However, although the dream is widely accepted, and despite the existence of individual entrepreneurs who appear to represent its fulfilment, there are those who have questioned its validity as a description of American society. Some have argued that the process of moving upwards is a much more brutal process than the depictions of the American dream generally suggest. For example, at the end of the nineteenth century, the novelist Jack London saw the US as a savagely competitive society in which only the fittest survived. The dream has also been represented as a way of disguising the realities of American life. The late Christopher Lasch, a *communitarian* theorist, argues that in the nineteenth century, it was thought that wealth and property should be broadly distributed. If ownership was concentrated in only a few hands, the propertyless would coalesce into a 'degraded laboring class' (1995: 7). Society would be polarised between the classes and perhaps torn apart.

Lasch suggests that – ironically – the belief that the US offered boundless opportunities for upward mobility established itself and displaced these thoughts of a property-owning, republican democracy just as opportunities for individual advancement were drying up. At the end of the nineteenth century, the 'frontier' – unclaimed territory lying beyond the areas settled by Europeans – was 'closed'. By this time, all US territory had been occupied and taken into ownership. The closure of the frontier 'forced Americans to reckon with the proletarianization of labor, the growing gulf between wealth and poverty, and the tendency of each to become hereditary' (1995: 73). Since then, however pervasive its hold, Lasch claims that the dream of upward social mobility has been a myth. It has, however, persuaded successive generations that they should accept American society as it is constituted and not seek radical change.

Self-reliance, individualism and laissez-faire

The American dream promises opportunity and reward to those who have initiative and work hard. There is, however, a corollary. If individuals fail to advance, and are, for example, unemployed or in poverty, it is regarded, to a very large extent, as their own responsibility. There is a widely shared commitment to the principles of individualism and self-reliance. Individuals should not look towards the government. Instead, they are expected to provide for themselves, and there is a degree of impatience with those who fail to do this.

The national emphasis upon self-reliance is tied to laissez-faire or free-market economics. There is a belief that companies and individuals should be left to make their own economic decisions, and that the government should play only a minimal role. A cross-national survey of public opinion conducted in 1985–86 showed some significant differences. Whereas 81 per cent of British people believed that the government should spend more on old-age pensions, only 47 per cent of Americans held the same opinion. Eighty-five per cent of British people agreed that it was the responsibility of government to provide health care. Only 40 per cent of Americans concurred.

American faith in self-reliance and laissez-faire is such that attempts to establish a labour or social democratic party, committed to extending government ownership, control and provision, have always foundered. These efforts reached a peak in 1912, when Eugene V. Debs, a socialist and trade unionist, made the third of his four bids for the presidency. However, he gained only 6 per cent of the vote. In contrast, the socialist parties that emerged in the European countries at the turn of the century, had, by the end of the First World War, become parties of government.

Why did American socialism fail? The pervasiveness of the American dream, and its at least partial basis in economic reality, provides much of the answer. The US offered greater opportunities for personal advancement than could be found in other nations, and in comparison with Europe, class barriers seemed much less rigid. Some have argued that the 'frontier' also had a role. The process of continuous expansion westwards, and the availability of free or cheap land through the Homestead Act of 1862, provided an escape route for those who were discontented. It constituted a 'safety valve' that released social tensions. There are also, however, other reasons why socialism failed to establish itself. Many socialists were first-generation immigrants who lacked roots in American society. The cultural divisions between different ethnic groupings formed a barrier to working-class unity. Socialist calls for the regulation of business were co-opted by others – such as urban reformers – and absorbed into Progressivism, a much broader modernising movement.

Democracy and freedom

Democracy and freedom are further elements within the American creed. Indeed, during the Cold War years, the nation was seen as a beacon of both by many of those opposing Soviet rule in eastern Europe and Asia. At its simplest, the concept of democracy implies rule by the people, or, at least, a majority of the people. However, this can be interpreted in different ways. The US is a *representative* democracy. This means that those who serve in government, whether at federal, state or local level, should be subject to periodic election. This extends further than in many other representative democracies. Many positions that are taken by appointees in the UK and other European countries – including judges and sheriffs – are occupied by elected officials in the US. However, although those who are elected to office serve on behalf of those they represent, they are, once elected, expected to exercise their own conscience and judgement. Representatives cannot be instructed or *mandated* to vote in a particular way by their electors.

Freedom rests on the belief that barriers should not be placed upon individuals and groups. The American creed offers freedom from restraint, particularly from those restrictions imposed by government. It is not, however, absolute, insofar as the freedom of others must be considered. In the words of the nineteenth-century political philosopher, John Stuart Mill, freedom means 'pursuing our own good in our own way, so long as we do not attempt to deprive others of theirs, or impede their efforts to obtain it'.

This conception of freedom can be contrasted with contemporary left-wing liberal, social democratic and socialist conceptions of freedom. These suggest that free-market economies generate wide disparities of income, and that, in practice, freedom from restraint only offers opportunities to those with significant financial resources. The Left argues instead for a conception of freedom that goes well beyond this. There are, for example, calls for 'freedom from want' and 'freedom from ignorance'. Welfarist notions such as these were widely accepted in Europe during the three decades following the Second World War. However, critics charge, they are, in reality, an assertion that the government should provide particular services or goods for all, and that they should be funded from taxation. Because of this, it is said, such 'freedoms' would constrain individual choices and should not be regarded as freedoms at all.

Rights and obligations

Commitment to freedom leads to a stress on the rights of the individual. Some of the most important rights are enumerated in the Bill of Rights – the first ten amendments to the US Constitution – and have particular importance. They include freedom of speech and religion, the right to 'bear arms', and freedom from 'cruel and unusual punishments'.

Individual rights such as these are regarded as God-given. The Declaration of Independence spoke of people 'being endowed by their Creator with certain unalienable rights' (see Chapter 3). Furthermore, political philosophers such as John Locke, who influenced the thinking of the Founding Fathers, talked of 'natural rights'. These existed in the *state of nature* that, they believed or supposed, preceded the emergence of governments. The role of government was to protect these rights, which were retained by the people.

Contemporary attitudes towards authority have given individual rights an added importance. There is a profound suspicion and hostility towards government, particularly at federal level. There is a widely shared belief that many of those elected to office, and the bureaucrats who work on their behalf, consider and pursue only their own interests. This is evident in the University of Michigan's National Election Studies. The numbers prepared to trust the federal government 'most of the time' fell from 57 per cent in 1958 to 30 per cent in 1996. As a corollary, the proportion of the American population believing that 'quite a few' government officials are 'crooked' rose from 24 per cent in 1958 to 52 per cent in 1992 (Center for Political Studies, University of Michigan 1995–98). Rights represent an important line of defence against further encroachments on the freedom of the individual by Washington, DC.

The emphasis that American citizens place on rights marks the US out from the countries of Europe. Many Americans believe that there is a private sphere which is sovereign, and into which the government cannot intrude. For example, in a 1990 cross-national survey of attitudes towards the compulsory wearing of car seat belts, 82 per cent of West Germans accepted that they should be required by law. Only 49 per cent of Americans concurred.

The stress on rights is sometimes depicted as excessive individualism. 'Rights talk' ensures that controversies often become clashes between competing absolutes. American citizens assert their own individual interests and disregard those of others. There is a reluctance to compromise. This is, in turn, reflected in the 'legalisation' of popular culture as individuals increasingly resort to lawyers and the law.

Furthermore, some observers suggest that the assertion of self-interest associated with a stress on rights has been compounded by the erosion of earlier notions of communal and civic obligation. The idea that citizens had responsibilities to others was undermined as the US became a predominantly industrial nation and traditional communities – based around small, intimate groupings of families and neighbours – were broken up.

However, the argument has been countered. Thomas Bender accepts that many traditional rural communities were lost, but he draws attention to the survival – albeit in a different form – of small communities represented by families, friends, work groups and other networks (1993: 135–6). There is evidence to support this. There is still a strong sense of obligation to fellow citizens. This is, for example, evident in *volunteerism*. Even today, many towns have a part-time volunteer fire department. Peter Drucker notes that almost every other adult works for at least three hours a week as a volunteer with a social-sector organisation (quoted in Lipset 1997: 277–8).

Equality

When the American colonists declared their independence from the British Crown in 1776, Thomas Jefferson proclaimed that 'all men are created equal'. Commitment to equality represents another element within the American creed. However, in contrast with the ideologies of the Left which stress equality of income, reward or outcome, America offers a different form of egalitarianism. The American conception of equality is structured around a number of characteristics:

1 There is an equality of regard for each individual. This stems from an absence of deference. Visitors to the US are often struck by the informal character of American culture, and the relatively unrestrained way in which strangers address each other. Even in the eighteenth century, a foreign observer noted that the American 'dictionary' was 'short in words of dignity, and names of honor'. Similarly, when Mrs Frances Trollope, an Englishwoman, visited America in 1830, she complained about the 'coarse familiarity, untempered by any shadow of respect, which is assumed by the grossest and lowest in their intercourse with the highest and most refined'.
2 The ideology of Americanism also rests on *equality of rights*. There is an insistence that basic rights – especially those enshrined in the first ten amendments to the US Constitution – apply to *all* citizens, regardless of income or status.
3 The American creed also proclaims *equality before the law*. All, whatever their rank or station, are subject to the rule of law. There would be no scope for the arbitrary judgements that had marked out the regimes of Europe. Even the president is bound by court rulings. In 1974 – during the final days of the Watergate drama – the US Supreme Court compelled President Richard Nixon to release tape recordings he had made of his personal conversations. In 1998, President Bill Clinton had to answer questions before a Grand Jury.

However, although a commitment to these forms of equality is at the heart of American thinking, realities have been very different for significant numbers of Americans. At the time of the Declaration of Independence, about half a million blacks, constituting 20 per cent of the population, were held as slaves. Segregation and institutionalised oppression did not come to an end until the mid-1960s. Other groups have also endured discrimination. In the nineteenth century, Native Americans faced what some call genocide as they lost their land, economy and culture. During the Second World War (1941–45), Americans of Japanese descent were regarded as potentially disloyal and held in detention camps across California.

Patriotism

National symbols and the rituals of citizenship constitute a further element within the American creed. Visitors to the country often comment on the flying of the flag outside American homes. Statistical surveys invariably reveal a high level of loyalty and patriotism. A 1990 Gallup study reported that only 11 per cent of Americans would like to emigrate if the opportunity became open to them. In contrast, 38 per cent of British citizens, 20 per cent of the Japanese, and 30 per cent of Germans, said that they would rather live abroad (Samuelson 1997: 259).

Religion and moralism

Religion plays a pivotal role in American life. In a 1995 survey, 69 per cent of those asked said that they belonged to a church or synagogue. Forty-three per cent had attended a service in the preceding seven days. The different faiths strengthen and reinforce the hold of the American creed.

Many early settlers were Puritans, and their beliefs left a powerful ideological legacy. Alexis de Tocqueville, the French nobleman and writer who visited America in 1831–32, and is still widely regarded as a commentator on American political culture, concluded: 'I think I can see the whole destiny of America contained in the first Puritan who landed on those shores.' As Max Weber was later to emphasise in his classic 1904–05 study, *The Protestant Ethic and the Spirit of Capitalism*, Puritanism was structured around values that corresponded with the development of commerce, private enterprise and capitalism. It emphasised the virtue of self-reliance, thrift, deferred gratification, hard work, humility and ambition, all of which represent components of the American creed.

Puritanism also had a relatively democratic character, insofar as it was, in contrast to the Roman Catholic and Anglican churches, structured around the congregation. The preacher was the servant of the church membership rather than its master. Religion thereby infused American culture with the democratic egalitarianism that became one of its defining hallmarks.

Puritanism also left another ideological legacy. Seymour Martin Lipset terms it 'utopian absolutism'. As he puts it, Americans 'tend to view social and political dramas as morality plays, as battles between God and the Devil, so that compromise is virtually unthinkable' (1997: 63). This ties together with the emphasis on individual rights, so as to infuse American culture with the feeling that there are clear and unambiguous answers to questions of policy and philosophy.

Although Puritanism had a firm grip on the early New England communities, there has always been – as Chapter 1 established – a multiplicity of faiths and sects. However, although there are theological differences between the churches, they have all – to a greater or lesser extent – inherited the basic beliefs of the early settlers. The insistence upon capitalist values, a broadly democratic structure, and a belief in absolute good and evil are still evident. They all bolster the American creed and add to its influence. For example, Jennifer Hochschild notes that religion plays a particular role in holding poor African-Americans under the 'spell' of the American dream (1995: 168). She argues that the churches confirm the values associated with the creed, and serve as a prop, giving spiritual and emotional assistance, thereby helping individuals realise their aspirations.

Ideologies and the American creed

Although the principal tenets of the American creed are widely endorsed, there are – within the framework of the creed – two broad approaches to politics, society and the economy. Those on the Right regard themselves as conservatives. The Left is associated with liberalism.

At first sight, there appears to be a significant gulf between conservatism and liberalism. Certainly, there has, at times, been considerable bitterness between the two camps. Michael Dukakis was the Democratic Party's candidate for the presidency in 1988, and his defeat was widely attributed to the ability of the Republican campaign to depict him as a liberal, and to demonise the liberal tradition.

However, despite the ferocity of the rhetoric that is sometimes employed, both liberalism and conservatism are structured around the American creed. In practice, there are similarities as well as differences between the two forms of thinking.

Liberalism

The meaning of the term 'liberalism' has changed over the past century. Classical liberalism – the liberalism that was associated with the founding of the US and its development during the nineteenth century – is very closely tied to the principles of Americanism. Both emphasise laissez-faire, minimal government, and basic freedoms. Indeed, writing in the 1950s, Louis Hartz portrayed the US as a liberal society. In other words, other doctrines – such as conservatism – were subsumed within the broader framework of liberalism.

However, in twentieth-century America, 'liberalism' has increasingly been used in another way. It now refers to the belief that government – particularly the federal government – should manage the economy and society. Liberals talk of a 'positive' or 'affirmative' role for government. They assert that government can succeed, where private enterprise had failed, in generating full employment and eliminating poverty. Liberal policies are directed towards these goals, and include redistributive taxation, the regulation of business, and the use of government spending to increase overall demand levels. The New Deal of the 1930s holds an important place in liberal thinking. It dramatically expanded the federal government's role and authority. Work schemes, most notably the Tennessee Valley Authority (TVA), offered employment and reinvigorated the wider economy. Although attempts at regulating conditions of employment through the National Recovery Administration had to be abandoned, the 1930s established the federal government – and the president in particular – as 'the manager of the economy'. Although the New Deal was not, despite the rhetoric of critics, a form of socialism, it was a halfway revolution.

The 1960s and 1970s added to 'New Deal liberalism'. In 1965, President Lyndon Johnson called for a 'War on Poverty'. He talked of making the US a *Great Society*. There was a growing belief that the federal government should commit a much greater level of financial resources to the alleviation of poverty and deprivation. Programmes such as the Job Corps for unemployed young people and Head Start for pre-school children were established. Furthermore, it was increasingly argued that those in poverty should no longer simply be the object of social policy. They should be involved, through political mechanisms, in determining their own fate. These ambitions were never, however, fulfilled. Johnson's 'Great Society' liberalism was discredited by the administration's evident inability to win the 'War on Poverty' and US involvement in Vietnam.

Liberalism was also influenced by the sexual revolution of the 1960s. Traditional institutions such as marriage and the family were increasingly questioned. The rise of the women's and gay movements placed feminism, calls for abortion on demand, and the campaign for homosexual rights on the liberal agenda. During the same period, other social movements also emerged, and their ideas were similarly incorporated into the liberal *paradigm*. For example, the 'black power' and 'black liberation' movements pushed race to the forefront of liberal thinking.

In the foreign and defence policy sphere, liberalism was associated with hostility to American military intervention in Vietnam and Cambodia. It became increasingly tied to a broader opposition to the role of the US in the Cold War. For example, liberal concerns inspired the 'nuclear freeze' movement of the early 1980s. Its supporters argued that the US should not add to, or modernise, its stock of nuclear weaponry.

However, there have always been limits to the radicalism offered by the liberal vision, and it has remained within the broad parameters of the

American creed. Although some liberals point to what they see as the excessive power of corporate interests, American liberalism remains committed to the private ownership of companies and businesses. It should therefore be distinguished from socialism. As Michael Foley notes, liberals believe that 'it is possible to achieve substantial change while still conforming to the general ethos of capitalism' (1991: 118). In essence, US liberalism represents an attempt to open up opportunities – the American Dream – to all, including those who have been long disadvantaged by prejudice and discrimination. In liberal eyes, the contemporary US does not live up to the promise offered by Americanism. As Foley puts it, liberals 'seek not the repudiation of American values, so much as their full realisation' (1991: 102).

Liberalism proved increasingly unable to address problems such as economic decline, growing criminality, and welfare dependency and it has been in retreat since the 1970s. Although some liberals continued to believe in what their opponents dubbed 'tax and spend' policies, others have accepted much of the conservative agenda established during the Reagan years. There is a growing willingness to question the efficacy of government. For example, many of today's liberals acknowledge that welfare provision has to be much more limited and selective than in the past. Increasingly, they accept that there are limits to the powers and abilities of government. President Bill Clinton is himself committed to this form of 'neo-liberalism'.

Conservatism

American conservatism is structured around four principal themes. First, although there are tensions between those who back *free trade* and supporters of *protectionism*, modern conservatism has inherited and integrated classical liberalism's commitment to laissez-faire and minimal government. Furthermore, since the late 1970s, the conservative belief in small government has fused with *supply-side economics*. 'Supply-siders' assert that reduced rates of taxation and a process of *deregulation* – the phasing out of laws restraining business activities – will generate much higher levels of economic growth. The conservative commitment to 'small government' is thereby justified as both a question of principle and on the grounds that it offers economic prosperity.

Second, there is a fear that traditional institutions such as marriage and the family are in decline. During the 1980s and 1990s, groupings such as the Moral Majority and the Christian Coalition established themselves as important components of the conservative movement. They were tied to 'Judeo-Christian' values. Abortion is regarded as murder. There is deep hostility to the many films and TV programmes which, they assert, depict immoral forms of behaviour – such as homosexuality or promiscuity – in a positive or uncritical way. According to William J. Bennett, Secretary of Education during George Bush's presidency, there are fourteen thousand references to sex in the programmes watched by the average TV viewer over the course of a year (1992: 104).

Furthermore, conservatives argue, today's public schools not only fail to teach basic skills, but do little to instil a respect for morality and tradition.

Third, conservatives emphasise law and order. They assert that there is growing lawlessness and criminality, and that the security of the citizen requires a firm response by those in authority. Conservatives stress the need for punishments structured around the principle of deterrence.

Fourth, conservatism is associated with an assertive foreign and defence policy. From the late 1940s onwards, conservatives accepted that the US had to take the leading role in containing the forces of communism. The end of the Cold War has, however, led to divisions. Some conservatives – most notably

---

Liberalism and conservatism

According to polling conducted during the 1996 presidential election, about 33 per cent of the adult population describe themselves as 'conservative' and 20 per cent call themselves 'liberal'. A large proportion – 47 per cent – think of themselves as 'moderates' (Bennett 1997: 27). There has been a long-term decline in the proportion of self-declared liberals. In 1988, for example, about a quarter of the adult population embraced the term.

It is clear, however, that large numbers of people do not associate themselves with formal ideologies. Instead, their thinking is derived from elements within both liberalism and conservatism. There is support for some traditionally liberal concerns. Large numbers – particularly in the suburbs – want to see greater federal and state government action to protect the environment. They would like smoking prohibited in public places. They accept that women should be able to take paid employment, and not simply be mothers and wives. A growing proportion also reject discrimination against homosexuals.

There are, however, limits to these expressions of social liberalism. People do not, for example, want their children exposed to violence on television. While they endorse gay rights, they draw the line at open expressions of homosexuality in the armed forces. At the same time – intermeshed with these broadly liberal ideas – many people are committed to economic policies drawn from the conservative tradition. They support low levels of taxation and reduced government spending.

Those who think in these terms are now estimated by one pollster to represent 35–40 per cent of the electorate. They are to be found, in greater numbers, in the Northeast and West, rather than the South or Midwest.

Writing in the *Atlantic Monthly*, Christopher Caldwell has suggested that the roots of President Clinton's political successes lie in his ability to structure his speeches and policies around the feelings and aspirations of this section of the American population. Correspondingly, although other factors, most notably the state of the economy, were crucial in both 1992 and 1996, Republican presidential candidates were also defeated because the Republican Party tied itself to the traditional social values of the South and neglected important groups within the voting population (1998: 72).

Patrick J. Buchanan, who sought the Republican Party's presidential nomination in 1992 and 1996 – have argued that the US should no longer act as the 'world's policeman'. In the months that preceded the Gulf War of 1991, he opposed American military involvement. Other conservatives reject this approach. In place of Buchanan's *isolationism*, they assert that the US still has important strategic interests in Europe, the Middle East and Asia. It must therefore continue to engage with the wider world. A third current of opinion within the conservative camp has inherited the optimism and sense of global vision that characterised some Cold War liberals. The US, they argue, has a particular role to play in promoting democratic values and laissez-faire principles across the globe.

Although contemporary American conservatism incorporates beliefs that its critics regard as intolerant or authoritarian, such as an insistence on 'family values', it is also, like liberalism, a direct restatement of the American creed. Indeed, conservatives regard themselves as the most resolute guardians of American values. They assert that the creed has lost much of its former hold. Conservatives and those influenced by conservative thinking suggest that it has been largely abandoned. This is evident in four ways:

1　The US has become an *entitlement* society. American people have come to expect secure jobs and rising living standards, regardless of individual effort.

> Sixty or seventy years ago, Americans by and large subscribed to the notion of the 'rugged individual' ... Now the spirit has shifted. If something's wrong, it's someone else's fault. Government, business, the schools, or the courts are responsible. Or we are brought down by racism, sexism, ageism or some other 'ism'. What is now called 'victimology' has become widespread and respectable. (Samuelson 1997: 16)

2　Although the US has an ideological commitment to the principle of laissez-faire, the federal government increasingly played an *interventionist* role. The New Deal and the Great Society extended the boundaries of its activities. While the conservative revolution during President Reagan's years in the White House began a process of 'rolling back' government, government spending remained between about 20 and 22 per cent of the country's Gross Domestic Product (GDP) throughout the 1980s and 1990s.

3　Although the American creed rests on the principle of individual liberty and the curtailment of government power, restrictive laws have been introduced. Conservatives see gun-control legislation as particularly intrusive. They also assert that it represents a strengthening of government and a threat to the fundamental rights of the citizen.

4　Conservatives also suggest that the American commitment to equality of opportunity has been undermined by the race and gender-based programmes introduced since the late 1960s. They oppose 'quotas' and other forms of affirmative action which seek to ensure that minorities and women are more fully represented in higher education and company management structures. Conservatives are similarly critical of 'redistricting', which, until curtailed by the US Supreme Court, redrew the boundaries between electoral areas so as to enlarge the number of black and Hispanic-majority ('minority–majority') districts.

Shared values

The ideology of Americanism is widely accepted. It brings many otherwise diverse groupings together. The assertions of those who talk in terms of fissures and tensions – which were outlined in Chapter 1 – can be countered. Although, for example, race is a significant cleavage within contemporary American society, survey evidence also suggests that whites and blacks share many basic values. The black poor are socially and economically isolated, and might be expected to reject the American creed. However, as Jennifer Hochschild argues, although there are pressures and tensions, they subscribe to mainstream American values to a greater extent than the black middle class (1995: 72).

Nor should ethnic differences be overemphasised. The process of assimilation led to the absorption of the different ethnicities. Indeed, the process of integration, absorption and assimilation took such an all-encompassing form that American society came to be known as a *melting pot*. This term was coined by a playwright, Israel Zangwill. In 1908, he described America as 'God's Crucible, the great Melting Pot where all the races of Europe are melting and reforming . . . German and Frenchman, Irishman and Englishman, Jews and Russians – into the Crucible with you all! God is making the American.' As Zangwill saw it, the US brought together the immigrant groupings from across the globe and fused them together so as to construct a new nationality.

The mechanisms of assimilation have included the public (or state) schools, intermarriage and war. In the nineteenth and early twentieth centuries, the schools had a largely Protestant ethos, taught in English and insisted upon 'American' forms of behaviour. Traditionally, the English language was essential for those seeking to move up the social and occupational ladder. The children of immigrants grew up as Americans, and, in many instances, married someone from a different ethnic background. Although many schools now teach in minority languages as well as English, the breaking down of neighbourhood barriers through intermarriage continues today. Nearly a third of Hispanics are married to non-Hispanic whites. Thirty-six per cent of native-born Asian husbands have white spouses.

The two world wars also contributed to the assimilative process. Some groups rallied to the flag because the nation was threatened. Others sought to abandon their identity because they had family ties with the enemy country. For example, US participation in the First World War (1917–18) led many German-Americans to close down their clubs and newspapers, and anglicise their names. They sought social 'invisibility'. Following the Second World War, the Cold War and fear of communism bound Americans together. In particular, it drew in the 'white ethnics' whose homelands had come under Soviet domination.

Many past regional contrasts have also been eroded, as geographical mobility has increased and the communications industry assumed first a national and second an increasingly global character. In particular, the southern states have lost much of their former distinctiveness.

Furthermore, the gender gap should not be overstated. Although there are some differences, men and women subscribe to the same core values. Many women, for example, join with men in opposing affirmative action programmes. A 1995 survey suggested that 40 per cent of women and 51 per cent of men disapprove of such policies (Golay and Rollyson 1996: 60). Furthermore, although they have received scant attention, many other 'gaps' – such as the 'gap' between rural and urban voters – are considerably larger (Ashford 1996: 66). Attempts to depict the 'baby boom' generation, the sexual revolution of the 1960s and 1970s and the rise of countercultures as a break with Americanism are also difficult to sustain. Although some aspects of these countercultures represented an affront to established values, the post-war generation accepted the fundamental tenets of the American creed, particularly its commitment to self-reliance and upward mobility. Indeed, feminism, black politics, and gay activism have lost much of their former radicalism. They have not only been absorbed by corporate structures, but have become integral to some marketing strategies.

Conclusion

The US is characterised by social diversity, but it is also a nation of *shared values*. As Alexis de Tocqueville noted, Americans 'are unanimous upon the general principles that ought to rule human society'. Many of these 'general principles' are still evident today.

References and further reading

Ashbee, E. (1998), 'Immigration, national identity and conservatism', *Politics*, 18:2, May, 73–80.
Ashford, N. (1996), 'Angry white males', *Talking Politics*, Autumn, 64–8.
Bender, T. (1993), *Community and Social Change in America*, Baltimore, Johns Hopkins University Press.
Bennett, A. J. (1992), *American Government and Politics 1992*, Godalming.
Bennett, W. J. (1997), *The Devaluing of America: The Fight for our Culture and our Children*, New York, Summit Books.
Caldwell, C. (1998), 'The southern captivity of the GOP', *The Atlantic Monthly*, June, 35–72.
Center for Political Studies, University of Michigan (1995–98), *The NES Guide to Public*

Opinion   and   Electoral   Behavior   (http://www.umich.edu/~nes/nesguide/nes-guide.htm), Ann Arbor, University of Michigan Center for Political Studies.

Foley, M. (1991), *American Political Ideas*, Manchester, Manchester University Press.

Fossum, R. H. and J. K. Roth (1981), *The American Dream*, Durham, British Association for American Studies.

Golay, M. and C. Rollyson (1996), *Where America Stands 1996*, New York, John Wiley.

Hochschild, J. L. (1995), *Facing Up to the American Dream: Race, Class, and the Soul of the Nation*, Princeton, Princeton University Press.

Lasch, C. (1995), *The Revolt of the Elites and the Betrayal of Democracy*, New York, W. W. Norton.

Lipset, S. M. (1997), *American Exceptionalism: A Double-Edged Sword*, New York and London, W. W. Norton.

Samuelson, R. J. (1997), *The Good Life and its Discontents*, Vintage Books.

3

The US Constitution

The defining features of the American political consensus were outlined in Chapter 2. It has, however, a further characteristic. Although there is considerable cynicism towards the politicians who serve in Washington, DC, there is also a deeply rooted and widely shared belief in the fundamental structures and principles around which the American political system is constructed. There is, in particular, a well-established faith in the US Constitution, the document upon which the US was founded.

While the Constitution is often at the centre of political controversy, that debate is about the interpretation of the principles upon which it rests rather than the fundamental worth of those principles. Proposals for reform are nearly always put forward as a means by which the spirit of the Constitution can be more fully implemented.

This chapter outlines the principal features of the US Constitution, considers the institutions that were created on the basis of it, and surveys the debates about the meaning of the Constitution today.

Origins of the US Constitution

For much of the eighteenth century, the thirteen American colonies were ruled by Britain. The colonists had, however, many grievances. In particular, they demanded 'no taxation without representation'. It was a protest against the ability of the British Parliament, in which they were not represented, to levy taxes upon them.

Resentments had intensified during the 1770s. Britain had granted monopolies that restricted the importation of certain goods, such as tea, into the colonies. This raised their price. The strength of American feeling was dramatically illustrated in 1773 when the rebels raided British vessels and threw imported tea into Boston harbour. The incident became known as the Boston Tea Party. The colonists' other grievances included imprisonment without trial and the quartering of soldiers in people's homes without their permission. In a celebrated speech to the Virginia legislature, which symbolised a shift from protest to rebellion, Patrick Henry said, 'give me liberty, or give me death'.

The overthrow of an established system of rule is a radical, indeed revolutionary, act. It was justified, in 1776, by the Declaration of Independence:

> We hold these truths to be self-evident, that all men are created equal, that they are endowed by their Creator with certain unalienable rights, that amongst these are life, liberty and the pursuit of happiness. That to secure these rights, governments are instituted amongst men, deriving their just powers from the consent of the governed. That whenever any form of government becomes destructive of these ends, it is the right of the people to alter or abolish it, and to institute a new government. (Foley 1991: 31)

The Declaration was the work of Thomas Jefferson. His argument had a number of stages:

1 All people – not only Americans – have certain natural rights, most notably 'life, liberty and the pursuit of happiness'. These rights are granted by God and cannot be taken away or 'alienated'. They are 'unalienable'.
2 The purpose of government – the reason why it is created – is to protect these rights. There is a social contract between the people and government in which the people accept a duty to obey the government. In return, those in government have an obligation to protect the people's rights.
3 The people have the right to withdraw that consent, and have the right of rebellion if the government fails to protect their rights.
4 King George III and the British Parliament had, through acts of oppression, broken their side of the social contract. The people had been denied their 'unalienable' rights. The American colonists could therefore justifiably break their side of the contract and deny the British authority on American soil.

These principles legitimised the American Revolution. The Declaration put forward a list of twenty-seven specific grievances against the British Crown to demonstrate the ways in which the rights of the colonists were being denied. Because the rebels believed that there were only reclaiming what they regarded as the rights and liberties of the 'freeborn Englishman', their actions have been described as 'a conservative revolution'.

There is some controversy about the ideas that influenced Thomas Jefferson. Some suggest that his thinking was derived from the writings of the seventeenth-century English philosopher John Locke. Locke emphasised the importance of liberty and spoke of a social contract between the people and government. He used the phrase 'life, liberty and property' to describe the most important natural rights. However, other historians claim that Locke's influence has been exaggerated, and they see the Declaration of Independence as an attempt to re-create the tradition of 'civic republicanism' established in classical Greece and Rome.

The British were finally defeated in October 1781 at Yorktown. The American Revolution – or War of Independence – had brought colonial rule to an end. However, in the wake of military success, the Americans had to create a new constitution and build their own forms of administration. In 1781, they adopted their first constitution, the Articles of Confederation, and established a system of government based upon it.

The Articles of Confederation (1781)

The thirteen former colonies – now independent states – initially created a system of government based upon a very weak national government. Each state maintained 'its sovereignty, freedom, and independence', but the Congress – in which each state had one vote – had only limited powers. Important decisions and changes to national law required the backing of nine of the thirteen states. There was, furthermore, no separate executive branch. Decision making was inevitably a slow, cumbersome and uncertain process.

The powers of the national government were limited for two reasons. First, there was a reaction against the strongly centralised character of British rule. Second, there was a desire to respect the different traditions of the individual states. However, the Articles and the Confederation established on the basis of these, were subject to growing criticism:

1 Trade was the responsibility of the states. They imposed tariffs against each other so as to protect their own immediate commercial interests. There were also difficulties enforcing contracts between the citizens of different states. Such restrictions held back the economic development of the nation.

2 There were periods of turmoil when the country seemed to be falling apart. The Congress established under the Articles of Confederation and the different state governments could not enforce their own decisions or impose their own authority. During a period of economic depression, the state of Massachusetts imposed property tax increases so as to pay off debts incurred during the war. When the taxes were not paid, farms and homes were seized. In 1786, many farmers took part in Shay's rebellion as a protest. Some of them blocked the courts in Massachusetts. The rebellion was put down by the state militias, but only with difficulty.

3 There were fears that foreign powers would seek a foothold for themselves within the new Republic. Britain, France and Spain all had colonies else-where on the North American continent, and there were concerns that

some of the states might be tempted into alliances that would break up the Confederation.

Because of these criticisms, a constitutional convention of delegates from the states was called in Philadelphia to modify or amend the Articles. However, a new constitution emerged from its deliberations.

The Philadelphia Convention (1787)

The debate at the convention between the fifty-five delegates (who became known as the 'Framers', Founders, or 'Founding Fathers') came to revolve around two models of government. The Virginia Plan rested on a strong national government while the New Jersey Plan offered a weak national government and left power largely in the hands of the states.

The result was a compromise between the different political forces at the convention.

1 The larger states favoured a strong national government which assigned representation on the basis of population. However, the smaller states feared that they would have little influence over such a government. The result became known as 'the Great Compromise'. Numbers in the House of Representatives would be based on a state's population. This favoured the larger states. However, the Senate was based on equal representation of two Senators for each state, regardless of size or population. This helped to protect the interests of the smaller states.

2 There were differences at the convention between populist democrats and sceptics of democracy. It was agreed that some form of democracy was required to act as a check on the abuse of power by the executive, but it was feared that unchecked majority rule might neglect the basic rights of the individual citizen. These concerns grew because of events in Pennsylvania. It had a directly elected, unicameral and strong legislature. As a consequence, it was said, liberties had not been protected, Quakers had lost the vote, and opponents of the war had faced sanctions. The convention therefore sought to place constraints on the will of the majority. They agreed that only the House of Representatives would be directly elected by the people. Both the president and the Senate would be indirectly elected. The judiciary would be appointed.

3 There were tensions between free states and the slave states. Many in the northern states wished to abolish slavery, but the five southern states would have refused to join the US if slavery had not been permitted. As a consequence, slavery was not addressed in the Constitution, although there was a provision that, for the purposes of representation, slaves would be counted as three-fifths of citizens. This was at the insistence of the free states, who wanted to limit the political influence of the slave states.

4 There was also a debate between advocates and opponents of a strong, centralised executive branch of government. Some of the Founders, most
notably Alexander Hamilton, argued that there had to be 'energy in the
executive' so as to unify the nation. They called for a single executive that
would have far-reaching powers. Others feared, however, that the placing of
so much power in the hands of a single figure would lead to tyranny. They
therefore agreed upon a single executive – the president – but restricted the
powers of the office. They were concentrated in foreign policy-making where
swift and decisive action might be required. In the domestic sphere, the
powers of the executive branch were to be more limited.

Adopting the Constitution (1789)

The Constitution was eventually accepted – or *ratified* – in 1789. However, there
was a fierce debate and initially only nine out of the thirteen state legislatures
ratified the document. Debate raged between supporters of the new
Constitution, known as the Federalists, and its opponents, the Antifederalists.

The supporters of the new Constitution argued that it would create a system
of government that had strength and cohesion but would not threaten the fundamental rights and liberties of either the states or the people. They wrote a
series of newspaper articles in its defence, which became known as the
Federalist Papers. The two principal authors were James Madison and
Alexander Hamilton, assisted by John Jay, who all wrote under the pseudonym
of 'Publius'.

The Antifederalists feared that the Constitution would lead to an overcen-
tralisation of power in the hands of the federal government, and this would
inevitably threaten the independence of the states and the rights of the citizen.
Although the Antifederalists lost the debate, the concerns that they expressed
still resonate in American politics today. So as to secure majorities in some of
the states and to win the agreement of those states that had voted against
ratification, ten amendments were added in 1791 so as to satisfy opponents.
They became the Bill of Rights.

Principles of the Constitution

The Constitution had six defining principles. First, it offered a form of government based upon the representation of the people. Indeed, the Constitution
rested upon the belief that a government's right to rule – its *legitimacy* – depends
upon the consent of the governed. Second, however, the representation of the
people takes a constrained form. The Constitution promised a 'republic' that
would be responsive but also responsible. The Founders not only distrusted the
tyranny of elite minorities, but were also suspicious of majority rule. They
believed that a majority could infringe or deny the rights of minorities. They

therefore hoped to ensure that government could act only when there was a widely shared consensus on a clearly and widely accepted public good. The Constitution not only sought to exclude hasty or impulsive decision making. It was informed by an *anti-majoritarian* spirit.

The Constitution was structured, third, around a separation of powers. Political systems involve legislative, executive and judicial responsibilities. These terms refer to the making, implementation and interpretation of the law. The Constitution established that the three functions would be carried out by separate institutions: Congress, the presidency and the federal courts. The three branches of government were assigned different powers, methods of election or appointment, and terms of office.

Fourth, the Constitution rested on *checks and balances*. The Founding Fathers built conflict between the branches of government into the fabric of the Constitution. They sought to ensure no single branch could become too power-ful. The Constitution therefore requires that almost all decisions must have the endorsement of more than one branch. For example, presidential appoint-ments for the most important positions in the executive branch have to be made with 'the advice and consent' of the Senate. Similarly, the Supreme Court has the power of *judicial review*. It may strike down any law or action undertaken by the two other branches of government if it deems them to be unconstitutional.

The Constitution was based, fifth, on *federalism*. The powers of government are divided between national and the individual state governments. In the US the national or federal government is granted certain specified – or *enumerated* – powers. Its responsibilities include foreign policy, defence, foreign trade and commerce between the states. As the Tenth Amendment emphasised, all other powers and responsibilities lie with the states or the people.

Last, the Constitution acknowledged the rights of both the people and the states. As the Declaration of Independence proclaimed, the purpose of govern-ment was to protect individual rights. However, the Founding Fathers disagreed about the way in which these rights could be secured. The majority believed that rights were protected through the structure of the Constitution. Only limited, enumerated powers had been granted to the federal government. Furthermore, the states had their own constitutions, and these incorporated bills of rights. However, the strength of opposition from the Antifederalists led to the adoption of ten amendments known as the Bill of Rights in 1791. It is usually recognised as part of the original Constitution.

Structure of the Constitution

The Constitution consists of one single document of only seven thousand words. It is divided up into sections or *Articles*. These mostly consider the powers, responsibilities and character of the three different branches of govern-ment.

Preamble

The introduction to the Constitution has two key features. First, it begins with the phrase 'We the People', thereby establishing that it is the people who have the power to create, and by implication also end, the new Constitution. Second, the Preamble identifies the broad purpose of the new federal government. It is to 'establish justice, insure domestic tranquillity, provide for the common defence, promote the general welfare, and secure the Blessings of Liberty'.

Article I: Congress

Congress, the national legislature, was to be the principal source of law and policy. *The Federalist* stated that 'in republican government, the legislature necessarily predominates'. Its role is outlined in Article I. The right to levy taxes, the 'power of the purse', is assigned to Congress so as to ensure its supremacy. The president was viewed in more limited terms. He was to be a check on a potentially overpowerful Congress. His leadership responsibilities were largely confined to the making of foreign and defence policy. Early presidents, with the exceptions of Thomas Jefferson, Andrew Jackson and Abraham Lincoln, accepted the restrictions on their role. It was not until the twentieth century that the president came to assume the prominence he has today.

Congress was given a *bicameral* structure. It was, in other words, divided into two chambers. The Senate and the House of Representatives were to be elected in different ways and with different and sometimes overlapping powers. The House of Representatives was designed as the popular, directly elected chamber. Its members are elected every two years and in single member constituencies – or *districts* – so as to ensure its responsiveness and answerability to the electorate. It can be regarded as the equivalent of the House of Commons in the UK. Every state was guaranteed at least one Representative or 'Congressman', but otherwise representation was based on the population of a particular state. The Senate is the upper chamber. It was intended to represent the individual states and have a more thoughtful and deliberative character. It would act as a check on the more populist House. Every state, regardless of size, is entitled to two Senators. Originally they were elected by state legislatures, but since 1913 have been elected by the voters of the state. Senators are elected for six-year terms, and a rolling system of election was adopted so that one-third of the Senate is subject to re-election every two years. This was established so as to ensure that the Senate would not surrender to the 'passions and panics of the moment' to which the House would be prone.

Article I also specifies the enumerated powers of the federal government and the limits upon them. It was to collect taxes, borrow money, regulate interstate commerce, declare war, maintain an army and navy, and run the post office. At the same time, the states were not allowed to act in matters which were the exclusive responsibility of the federal government. The states could not, for example, issue their own currency or place tariffs on trade. These powers were assigned to Congress.

Article II: the president

The president is elected for a four-year term by an electoral college, originally composed of elder statesmen chosen by the different state legislatures. They are now chosen by the voters in each state, although the College has not played a significant political role since 1888. From 1951 onwards, the president has been restricted to two terms of office.

The Founders believed that the executive branch of government should be headed by a single person, so as to ensure that the federal government had direction and that foreign policy had the necessary degree of purpose and coherence. However, they also wanted to prevent the president becoming pre-dominant. He was assigned important defence and foreign policy powers. These included his position as commander-in-chief of the armed forces and his ability to negotiate treaties with other countries. However, his domestic powers were more limited. He had a responsibility to ensure that the laws were carried out. He was also given the right to veto bills. This was included as another check on the populist and impulsive tendencies of the House of Representatives. A vice-president was also to be elected. He was to take the president's place in the event of death or incapacity, but his powers were otherwise ill-defined and unspecified.

Article III: the Supreme Court

Article III offers only a partial guide to the role of the Supreme Court. It simply states that 'the judicial power of the United States shall be vested in one Supreme Court'. The responsibilities that are identified include the resolution of conflicts between state governments. It was only later, through a process of evolution, that the Supreme Court established the power of judicial review and the right to declare a law or action undertaken by the federal or state government unconstitutional.

Article IV: federalism

The principal purpose of Article IV was to encourage closer co-operation between the individual states. For example, it laid down in the 'full faith and credit clause' that each state should recognise the laws of every other state. Article IV also allowed for the admission of new states to the US, and guaranteed that every state should have a republican (or representative) form of government.

Checks and balances

By the legislative branch on the executive

1 The Senate confirms the major presidential appointments
2 Congress controls executive budget and appropriations (expenditures)
3 Congress passes or rejects all legislation requested by the president
4 Congress can impeach and remove the president for 'high crimes and misdemeanours'
5 The Senate ratifies foreign treaties signed by the president with a two-thirds majority
6 Congress can override a presidential veto by a two-thirds majority in both houses

By the legislative branch on the judiciary

1 The Senate has to approve all judicial appointments
2 Congress can create new lower courts
3 Congress can change the number of judges
4 Congress can impeach and remove judges for misbehaviour

By the executive branch on the legislature

1 The president can propose legislation
2 The president can veto bills passed by Congress
3 The president can call special sessions of congress

By the executive branch on the judiciary

1 The president appoints all federal judges

By the judicial branch on the legislature

1 The Supreme Court can rule an act unconstitutional
2 The Supreme Court interprets laws passed by Congress

By the judicial branch on the executive

1 The Supreme Court can rule presidential actions unconstitutional
2 The Supreme Court can rule against the executive in cases
3 The Supreme Court can issue or refuse warrants to allow police search

Article V: amending the Constitution

The process of amendment was made intentionally difficult. It was to occur only when there was a large and considered 'supermajority' throughout the country. A constitutional amendment must be proposed by either a two-thirds

---

The Bill of Rights

Amendment I: Limits on Congress
Congress shall not make any law establishing a religion or limiting freedom of religion, speech, assembly or petition.

Amendments II, III and IV: Limits on the Executive
The executive shall not limit the right to bear arms (II), place soldiers in people's homes (III), or search and seize for evidence without a warrant (IV).

Amendments V, VI, VII and VIII: Limits on the Judiciary
Serious trials shall be with a grand jury; immunity is provided against testifying against oneself; an individual cannot be prosecuted for the same offence twice; and no property can be taken without appropriate compensation (V). Courts shall provide a speedy trial and ensure the right of the accused to face his chargers (VI), trial by jury (VII), and not impose excessive bail or punishment (VIII).

Amendments IX and X: Limits on the National Government
The listing of rights should not imply that these are the only rights the people have (IX). Any powers not explicitly given to the federal government remain with the states or the people (X).

---

majority in both houses of Congress or by a special constitutional convention that would have to be convened by two-thirds of the state legislatures. Any amendment arising from Congress or the convention has then to ratified by three-quarters of the states.

No constitutional convention has been held, and only twenty-seven amendments have been passed in the entire history of the US. Ten of these were the Bill of Rights, which were adopted just four years after the Constitution was written, and they are generally regarded as a part of the original Constitution. Other subsequent amendments extended the right to vote, added to civil rights, increased the power of the federal government and made limited alterations to the institutions of government:

1 The amendments forming the Bill of Rights were intended to offer greater protection to individual citizens and the states against the power of the federal government. By limiting the actions of government and recognising liberties, they are based on a negative conception of rights.

   The First Amendment is widely known. It protects freedom of speech and religion. The Second Amendment guarantees the right to bear arms and is, today, controversial. The Ninth Amendment, perhaps the most neglected, states that the people retain any rights not specifically listed. The Tenth Amendment seeks to limit the powers of the federal government still further by stating that all powers not explicitly granted to the federal government shall remain with the states or the people.

> ### *The People v. Larry Flynt*
>
> *Director:* Miloš Forman (1996)
>
> *Starring:* Woody Harrelson, Courtney Love
>
> How far should freedom of speech, guaranteed under the First Amendment, extend? Does 'speech' extend to all forms of expression? *The People v. Larry Flynt* explores these themes.
>
> Larry Flynt publishes pornographic magazines. The film traces his battles in different state courts where he faced obscenity charges. It also reconstructs his biggest confrontation with the law. This came when *Hustler*, one of his magazines, printed a cartoon ridiculing the Reverend Jerry Falwell, a leader of the Christian Right. Falwell sued, and was awarded substantial damages for 'emotional distress'. As the film shows, the case eventually reached the Supreme Court. The Court ruled that if such damages were allowed, freedom of speech and the First Amendment would be in jeopardy.

2 A series of later amendments established that the right to vote could not be denied on grounds of race (15th), granted the vote to women (19th), the citizens of Washington, DC (23rd), those over eighteen (26th), and ended laws that tied the right to vote in federal elections to the payment of poll taxes (24th).

3 The recognition of civil rights was extended with the abolition of slavery (13th), and the assurance that all citizens were entitled to 'the equal protection of the laws' (14th). These amendments were initially regarded as an extension of civil liberties to those who had been excluded from American citizenship. Over the years, however, these amendments have come to be understood in a different way. They have become an instrument by which 'civil rights' have been extended. In contrast to the 'shall nots' laid down in the Bill of Rights, these amendments have been used to ensure that the government 'shall' undertake a particular action.

4 The Sixteenth Amendment, adopted in 1913, allowed the federal government to raise an income tax. The Eighteenth Amendment prohibited the sale of alcohol across the US, but after thirteen years of Prohibition was repealed in the Twenty-first amendment. These amendments added to the powers of the federal government.

5 Other amendments have reformed the institutions of government. The most significant of these restricted the president to only two terms of office (22nd), and established that all Senators should be directly elected by the people (17th). Passed in the wake of public resentment about congressional privileges, the Twenty-seventh Amendment states that Congressional pay rises cannot take effect immediately. Instead, members of Congress must wait until after the next election so that voters have the opportunity to pass judgement.

The US Bill of Rights and the Internet

A number of interest groups that are campaigning to uphold the constitutional rights of the individual – as they are seen from the different political perspectives – can be found on the Internet. The Heritage Foundation website provides links to a network of conservative organisations that campaign around constitutional rights and liberties:

http://www.heritage.org

The American Civil Liberties Union (ACLU) site offers links to a large number of broadly liberal organisations:

http://www.aclu.org

Assessing the Constitution

The goal of the Founders was to create a government that would be effective but limited. It would be efficient in undertaking its responsibilities, but would at the same time respect and protect the rights of both the citizen and the states. Subsequent debates around the Constitution have examined the extent to which these goals have been achieved. Whereas some assert that the federal government is relatively powerless, others claim that it has become overbearing.

Too weak

Those who call for active forms of government, mainly liberals, argue that the system prevents government from successfully resolving the many pressing economic and social problems facing the nation. It lacks effective power. There is, they say, a need to close the gap between rich and poor, protect minorities, and confront the threat of environmental catastrophe. However, the Constitution has developed in such a way that the 'energy in the executive' required by Alexander Hamilton has been crushed. The critics claim that:

1 In practice, checks and balances have created *gridlock*. Decisions cannot be made because there is insufficient agreement between institutions. In contrast with the countries of western Europe, the US has, they argue, been unable to impose effective gun control or establish comprehensive health-care provision because decision making requires such a widely shared consensus.
2 The co-ordinating role that parties used to play in bringing members of Congress and the president together, and easing the tensions between them, has been undermined by the declining importance of the political parties.
3 By distributing power, the American system of government lacks account-

ability. Power is so widely distributed that it is difficult for citizens to identify who is responsible for any particular action or decision.

4 The dispersal of power offers numerous opportunities to block decisions. This enables wealthy and self-interested elites to veto progressive reforms such as the creation of comprehensive healthcare provision.

The Committee on the Constitutional System, a body of political reformers, claimed that:

> The separation of powers, as a principle of constitutional structure, has served us well in preventing tyranny and the abuse of high office, but it has done so by encouraging confrontation, indecision and deadlock, and by diffusing account-ability for the results. Because the separation of powers encourages conflict between the branches and because the parties are weak, the capacity of the federal government to fashion, enact and administer coherent public policy has diminished and the ability of elected officials to avoid accountability for govern-mental failures has grown. (Committee on the Constitutional System 1987: 3)

Those who believe that the political system is too weak have put forward a number of proposed solutions. These seek to strengthen the presidency and increase the internal cohesion of the parties. They suggest that:

1 The president should be able to appoint members of Congress to the Cabinet so as to establish a closer, and less confrontational relationship between the two institutions.
2 The president should have the power to dissolve Congress and demonstrate through an election whether the people endorse him or his Congressional opponents. This would allow a particular issue to be resolved in a decisive way.
3 There should be one six-year term for the president. He would not, then, have to think in terms of immediate electoral popularity, and this would strengthen his bargaining position.
4 The president and Congress should be elected together on the same ticket in every district. This would ensure that a single party had control of both Congress and the White House.

Too strong

There are those, however, who have asserted that government has become too powerful and intrusive. They are mostly conservatives. They argue that the federal government is now much more interventionist than the Founders intended. They point to high levels of taxation, the federal government's role in regulating business, and its growing involvement in state responsibilities such as education and social policy. In simple terms, the federal government has become too big, too expansive and too expensive. In contrast with liberals, conservatives complain that the federal government does too much rather than too little. Why has the Constitution failed to check the growth of federal government? Conservatives identify three factors:

1 'Special interests' have come to dominate the decision-making process. Many political decisions therefore reflect narrow sectional interests and are not for the public good. Some conservatives point, in particular, to the way in which trade unions and some producer groups have been able to secure legislation, such as the minimum wage or other barriers to entry in a particular trade, that exclude newcomers and confer monopoly privileges. The process of government is now controlled by the 'factions' that James Madison deplored.
2 The federal government has, through financial incentives and legislation that led to an expansion of its role, gained control and influence over many responsibilities that were the traditional prerogative of the states. The Tenth Amendment, which placed the principal responsibilities of government on to the states, has been forgotten.
3 The federal judiciary has abused judicial review. It has enlarged its own powers at the expense of elected institutions. In the interests of social equality, the Court has also allowed government interventionism and curtailed individual freedom of action. It has colluded in destroying the powers and prerogatives of the states.

Conservative critics therefore propose a number of amendments to the Constitution or seek to establish a different understanding of its Articles and amendments.

1 They back an amendment which would impose term limits on members of Congress. In most of the proposals, federal legislators would be restricted to twelve years. This represents six terms in the House and two Senatorial terms. Such a reform, they assert, would begin to re-create a 'citizen legislature' that would be much more closely tied to the people it purports to represent.
2 The Balanced Budget amendment would require the federal government to balance its revenues and expenditures. It would only be able to borrow in times of war or other emergencies.
3 The Tax Limitation amendment would limit the amount that the federal government could tax as a proportion of the Gross National Product (GNP), or require a supermajority of 60 per cent if taxation levels were to be raised.
4 There would be a stronger emphasis upon the Tenth Amendment by all three branches of government and a recognition of *states' rights*.
5 Some conservatives have also called for curbs on the role of the federal courts. For example, Patrick Buchanan, who sought the Republican presidential nomination in both 1992 and 1996, has argued that federal judges

should be subject to reconfirmation by Congress every eight years. Buchanan also calls for a Constitutional amendment, allowing Congress to set aside Supreme Court rulings if there is a two-thirds majority in both houses and the president is in agreement (1990: 356).

Conclusion

American society has changed beyond recognition since the late eighteenth century. A contrast can be drawn between 1776, when the Declaration of Independence was published, and the 1990s. The population of the US has multiplied from 3.5 million to 263 million. The country now encompasses a significant proportion of a continent. Its economy has been transformed. An agrarian nation is now a leading industrial power. As Chapter 1 established, a relatively homogenous society of settlers with English roots now has a diverse and multicultural character.

The fact that the US Constitution has survived over two hundred years without being fundamentally altered shows its essential strength. It has adjusted to the diversity and complexity of contemporary American society. It is striking that few commentators believe that the Constitution requires radical change, and even those most critical of the current political system still claim that the principles it embodies remain valid. The Constitution's resilience can, in part, be explained by the relevance of the principles associated with constitutional democracy to both agrarian and industrial societies. It can also be attributed to the amendments that have have been adopted. The most important amendments modernised those sections that were most deeply rooted in late eighteenth-century thought. The survival and strength of the Constitution can also, however, be explained by the Supreme Court's role in reinterpreting it. The Court is surveyed in Chapter 4.

References and further reading

Buchanan, P. J. (1990), *Right from the Beginning*, Washington, DC, Regnery Gateway.
Committee on the Constitutional System (1987), *A Bicentennial Analysis of the American Political Structure*, Washington, DC, Committee on the Constitutional System.
Foley, M. (1991), *American Political Ideas*, Manchester, Manchester University Press.
Lowi T. J. and B. Ginsberg (1992), *American Government: Freedom and Power*, New York, W. W. Norton.

American politics – resources

Anthony Bennett publishes an annual survey of US government and politics. Further details and copies of the survey can be obtained from Dr Bennett at Chapel House, Charterhouse, Godalming, Surrey, GU7 2DE.

Part II

The institutions of government

4

The US Supreme Court

Does a woman have a right to an abortion? Should it be illegal to burn the American flag? Should universities be allowed to favour women, blacks and other minorities in the provision of university places? Can a doctor assist in the committing of a suicide? What rights should be given to a suspect in a criminal case? All these questions have been resolved by judges on the Supreme Court bench rather than the elected branches of government.

The Court rules on issues such as these because the federal courts have the power of judicial review. If an appropriate case is brought before them, they can assess the *constitutionality* of any law passed, or action undertaken, by either the federal government or the state governments. Laws and actions can be declared null and void if the Court concludes that they are unconstitutional. Although judicial review is not specifically identified in Article III of the Constitution, Supreme Court Chief Justice John Marshall (1801–35) claimed the right when ruling in the case of *Marbury v. Madison* (1803). It has been accepted and unchallenged ever since.

The Court also has other functions. First, it adjudicates when there is a conflict between the different branches and levels of government. It decides, for example, on the responsibilities and powers of the executive and legislative branches of government or determines whether a matter is the responsibility of the state or federal government. Second, the Court interprets the laws passed by Congress. Legislation can lack clarity and precision and is, as a consequence, open to differing interpretations.

There are nine members of the Supreme Court bench. There are also 'inferior' or lower federal courts, and 525 judges preside over ninety-five district courts. There are thirteen courts of appeal, or circuit courts, with a corps of 159 full-time judges (Ragsdale 1996: 412): the Supreme Court is the final court of appeal. These courts only consider cases arising under federal law. The states have their own judicial systems which interpret and apply state laws.

This chapter surveys the appointments process, and assesses the significance, sources and limitations of the Court's powers. It asks whether America has 'government by judiciary' or if the Court is, as some have claimed, 'the least dangerous branch'. It also looks at other debates. What approaches should judges on the Supreme Court bench adopt in making their rulings? Some call for judicial activism, and argue that the Court should use its powers in a proactive way to change American society. Others, however, favour judicial restraint. The chapter also asks if the Court should be considered a judicial or political institution.

Appointing the judges

All federal judges are appointed by the president with 'the advice and consent of the Senate' (Article II section 2). Although there are no official criteria, a number of considerations have emerged (McKeever 1997: 119–25):

1 An appointee is almost always associated with the same party as the president.
2 The president will usually appoint those who share his political and judicial philosophy. Franklin Roosevelt altered the direction of the Court's decisions by appointing judges who believed that government had an interventionist role to play. During the Reagan era, the Justice Department was particularly thorough in the selection of judges. It chose conservative judges who would have little sympathy with either affirmative action or the rights of criminal suspects.
3 There is a tradition of 'senatorial courtesy' in the making of district court appointments. If the senators representing the state where the appointment is to be made belong to the same party as the president, they may either propose or veto a nominee.
4 Judges are expected to be legally qualified, have practised law, and have had judicial experience. The American Bar Association, the professional body for lawyers, always gives ratings for potential appointees, although some conservatives believe that it has a liberal bias.
5 It is now accepted that there should be at least one woman, a black, and a Catholic on the Court. Thurgood Marshall, the first African-American, was appointed in 1967. Sandra Day O'Connor, appointed by Reagan in 1981, was the first female Justice on the Supreme Court. Between 1916 and 1969, there was a 'Jewish seat' on the Court (McKeever 1997: 124).
6 Although difficult to prove, there is evidence to suggest that a judicial nominee must hold a certain attitude towards abortion. It would be difficult for a Republican president to make a pro-choice appointment, or for a Democrat to select a pro-life candidate. Even if the president himself does not have strong convictions, there will be a powerful lobby within his party.

Presidential nominations have traditionally been accepted by the Senate, but confirmation cannot be assured. Eleven have been rejected and other

The US Supreme Court – December 1998		
	Date appointed	*President in office*
Chief Justice		
William Rehnquist	1971	Nixon
Appointed as Chief Justice in	1986	Reagan
Associate Justices		
John Paul Stevens	1975	Ford
Sandra Day O'Connor	1981	Reagan
Antonin Scalia	1986	Reagan
Anthony Kennedy	1987	Reagan
David Souter	1990	Bush
Clarence Thomas	1991	Bush
Ruth Bader Ginsburg	1993	Clinton
Stephen Breyer	1994	Clinton

Liberal		Centre		Conservative
Stevens	Breyer	O'Connor	Rehnquist	Thomas
Ginsburg	Souter	Kennedy	Scalia	

Source: Adapted from McKeever 1997: 29.

nominations had to be withdrawn or postponed. However, only five of these rejections were in the twentieth century (Ragsdale 1996: 422–3). In 1969 and 1970, the Senate opposed two of Nixon's nominees, Clement Haynesworth and G. Harrold Carswell, on the grounds of alleged racism. In 1987, Reagan nominated Robert Bork, a former law professor, a justice of the DC Court of Appeals and a leading advocate of judicial restraint. A widespread public campaign was organised against him, and the Senate defeated the nomination by fifty-eight to forty-two votes. A further nominee for the post, Douglas H. Ginsburg, withdrew his nomination in 1987 after admitting to having smoked marijuana. President Bush won a narrow victory in 1991 when he nominated Clarence Thomas, a conservative black judge, to replace Thurgood Marshall. There was strong opposition on ideological grounds, echoing the arguments against Bork, and there were also claims of sexual harassment by a former assistant, Anita Hill. Thomas described his televised interrogation by the Senate Judiciary Committee as a 'high-tech lynching', but he was narrowly endorsed by fifty-two to forty-eight votes. Clinton had little trouble in his nominations of centrist liberals, Ruth Bader Ginsburg and Stephen G. Breyer, who were appointed in 1993 and 1994 respectively.

Although the appointment of justices is an important presidential power, appointees do not always act in the way a president expects. President Eisenhower nominated Earl Warren, who, as a former governor of California, was regarded as a cautious moderate. However, to Eisenhower's chagrin, he proved to be a judicial revolutionary. Similarly, today, although Republican nominees are in a majority on the Court, their rulings are often much more centrist than conservatives would wish.

Judges are appointed for life, subject to 'good behaviour'. They have only been removed in the most exceptional circumstances. To further protect the Court from political pressure, their salaries cannot be reduced during their period of office.

The number of justices is not specified in the Constitution. Originally there were six, and the number varied between six and ten during the course of the nineteenth century. However, since 1869, it has remained at nine. However, the number of lower-level judges has changed as the demands upon the courts have grown. For example, President Carter nominated 257 judges to the district and circuit courts, and Reagan proposed 291 (Ragsdale 1996: 424).

Hearing cases

In a limited number of areas the Supreme Court can consider cases directly. It has *original jurisdiction*. These are specified in the Constitution, and include cases involving two or more states, the US and a state, and foreign diplomats. However, the majority of cases are *appellate* cases, in which the Court may, at its discretion, consider appeals against decisions made by lower courts, US Courts of Appeal, state supreme courts and the US Court of Military Appeals. The Court receives over seven thousand petitions every year and considers between only 3 and 4 per cent of them.

When the oral arguments have been put, the Court meets in private, and the judges make their decisions with the assistance of law clerks, or assistants. The Court is presided over by the Chief Justice, but his powers are limited and he is not always in the majority. A vote is taken, and a majority is required if a lower court is to be overridden. The decision is then announced, together with a written opinion. Opinions can take three forms: the majority opinion, which explains the basis for the Court's decision, a concurring opinion, which agrees with the decision but bases it on different legal grounds, and dissenting opinion.

This allows a minority to express its reasoning for opposing the decision. All the opinions are subject to considerable examination and debate. Around 40 per cent of cases are unanimous.

The other federal courts, apart from the Supreme Court, should not be neglected. District courts consider almost 300,000 cases a year. Their rulings generally have only a limited impact on public policy, although there are exceptions. It was, for example, a federal district judge in Arkansas who dismissed Paula Jones's claim of sexual harassment against President Clinton in 1998.

How much power?

Some commentators believe that the courts are too powerful. Raul Berger made the claim in *Government by Judiciary* (1997). He asserts that the Supreme Court has made rulings that go far beyond the Constitution. Others argue that the federal courts have only limited power. Borrowing a phrase from Alexander Hamilton, Alexander Bickel claimed it is *The Least Dangerous Branch* (1962).

Key rulings

Those who stress the powers of the Court point to the scope and scale of its judgements. It has reshaped American society and politics. Much of its history has been associated with three broad and often interlinked constitutional questions. These are the relationship between government and the economy, federalism and equality, and the rights of the citizen.

Government and the economy

As the US became an industrial society, there were increasingly vocal calls for government intervention in economic affairs. The federal and state governments, it was said, should alleviate poverty and the urban problems. Monopolies should be restricted. Working hours should be regulated. The slums and tenement blocks should be cleared.

What role does the US Constitution assign to government? During the late nineteenth and early twentieth centuries, Court decisions reflected the view that it was severely limited. In *Lochner v. New York* (1905), the Court ruled that the state of New York did *not* have the power to regulate working hours for bakery workers. Their ruling rested on the principle of 'substantive due process' in the Fourteenth Amendment. It was understood to protect the right of an employer to hire workers without external interference.

This limited, laissez-faire interpretation of the government's role was challenged by the activist interventionism of the New Deal era. Several key elements of President Franklin Roosevelt's economic programme were struck down by the Court. In May 1935, in *Schechter Poultry Corporation v. United States*, the Court declared that the National Industrial Recovery Act was unconstitutional. The Act had extended the powers of the federal government to regulate businesses by interpreting the interstate commerce clause very broadly. The Court would not permit this. Roosevelt's agricultural programme, which also added to the powers of the federal government, was similarly deemed unconstitutional in *US v. Butler* (1936).

Roosevelt responded in 1937 by seeking to enlarge the Court beyond the existing nine members to fifteen. His 'court packing' plan would have enabled him to have gained a majority which would have been sympathetic to the New Deal. However, the proposal met firm resistance in Congress. It was seen as an attack on the separation of powers. However, the Court modified its approach. Both Washington state's minimum wage laws and the 1935 National Labor Relations Act, which upheld the rights of trade unionists, were deemed constitutional. The Court's apparent change of heart was described as 'a switch in time that saved nine'.

Since then, the Court has been cautious in challenging presidential and Congressional actions in the economic field, and there are some who claim that the Court has thus surrendered its obligations under the Constitution by failing to limit the federal government to its enumerated powers.

Federalism and equality

The Constitution sought to limit the federal government's authority. However, despite this, there was uncertainty about rights of the states during the early years of the US. Under Chief Justice John Marshall, in *McCulloch v. Maryland* (1819), the Court established the principle of national supremacy over the states by recognising the right of the federal government to set up a national bank. Congress, the Court said, had 'implied powers' that went beyond the exact wording of the Constitution. Furthermore, the federal government was not subservient to the individual states. Instead, it had its own independent powers and responsibilities.

Four decades later, in *Dred Scott v. Sandford* (1857), the Court, headed by Chief Justice Roger Taney, moved in a different direction. It declared that the Missouri Compromise, an Act of Congress that had allowed former slaves to be free in the new border territories created by westward expansion, was unconstitutional. The Court insisted that the slave, Dred Scott, who had been taken to a free state and had claimed his liberty, be returned to his former owner. The ruling endorsed slavery and curtailed the rights of the federal government. It contributed to the outbreak of the Civil War.

From then on, federalism and civil rights were intertwined. In the aftermath of the Civil War (1861–65) and the defeat of the southern states, the Constitution was amended. Slavery was ended. In 1868, the fourteenth amendment granted citizens 'the equal protection of the laws'. However, after Reconstruction had come to an end in 1877, white rule progressively re-established itself across the South. Blacks were excluded from voting and – under the guise of the 'separate but equal' doctrine – segregation was imposed. The Supreme Court accepted its constitutionality. In 1896, the Court declared in *Plessy v. Ferguson* that the segregation laws 'have been generally, if not universally recognized as within the competency of state legislatures in the exercise of their police powers' (Tindall and Shi 1989: 476).

Fifty-eight years later, the Court took a different view. In September 1953, President Eisenhower appointed the former Governor of California Earl Warren as Chief Justice. Despite expectations that it would pursue a conservative course, the Warren Court (1953–69) brought about a judicial revolution. The Court's rulings were pervaded by a spirit of judicial activism. In 1954, in *Brown v. Board of Education (Topeka, Kansas)*, the Court reversed the Plessy judgement and declared that segregated schooling was unconstitutional. The relegation of black children to separate schools conveyed a message of inferiority and caused psychological damage. It was a denial of 'equal protection'. A year later, the Court demanded that the desegregation of southern schools should proceed 'with all deliberate speed'.

Earl Warren was succeeded as Chief Justice by Warren E. Burger. Although in some respects more cautious than the Warren Court, the Burger Court (1969–86) extended the 'civil rights revolution'. Although the southern states were finally desegregated a decade after the Brown ruling, the US remained a racially divided and unequal society. In both the South and the North, blacks and whites lived in different areas and districts. Even in the absence of restrictive laws, neighbourhood schools were predominantly white or black. Furthermore, blacks were under-represented in higher education, business and the professions.

In 1971, in *Swann v. Charlotte-Mecklenburg Board of Education*, the Court ruled that school students should be taken by bus to different schools across a city so as to ensure a broad racial balance in each school. The Court also considered affirmative action. Such programmes are derived from a conception of equality based not on opportunity but on outcome. Their supporters assert that disparities of income and achievement between the races, ethnic groupings and genders are, in themselves, evidence of institutionalised discrimination. In their most rigorous form, affirmative action programmes include numerical admissions quotas so as to increase minority representation in a certain field of employment or on a particular educational course. In *Griggs v. Duke Power Company* (1971), the Court outlawed selection tests that were not obviously job-related and produced different pass rates between the races. In making the judgement, Chief Justice Warren Burger focused on 'the *consequences* of employment practices, not simply the motivation' (Thernstrom and Thernstrom 1997: 430). In *Regents of the University of California v. Allan Bakke* (1978), the Court did not accept the full affirmative action argument.

Nevertheless, it ruled, albeit by a narrow majority, that although racial considerations were not to be the only consideration, educational institutions could
include race as a factor when recruiting students. Subsequently, in 1980, in
Fullilove v. Klutznick, the Court endorsed racial *set-asides* that awarded a fixed
proportion of federal government construction contracts to minority-owned
firms.

The civil rights era created the conditions for the emergence of the women's
movement. Feminism established itself on the political and judicial agenda.
Against this background, the Burger Court ruled in *Roe v. Wade* (1973) that a
woman had an unfettered right to an abortion in the first three months of a
pregnancy. States were allowed to impose only limited restrictions in the second
trimester so as to protect the mother's health. In the final trimester, when the
foetus may be viable outside the mother's womb, states may introduce laws
restricting abortion, except when the women' s life or health are at risk. Prior
to *Roe*, abortion regulations varied greatly between the different states and the
ruling circumscribed their ability to make their own laws. The ruling led to the
mass mobilisation of both the pro-life and pro-choice movements.

The Court also pursued other forms of equality. These contributed to a
further erosion of the states' traditional prerogatives. In *Baker v. Carr* (1962),
the Court ruled that the districts used for elections to Congress and the state legislatures had to be equal in terms of population size. Prior to the *Baker* ruling,
there had been significant differences in the population of different constituencies, due either to movements in population (which favoured the rural areas),
or to the deliberate manipulation – *gerrymandering* – of boundaries so as to
favour the majority party. However, as critics asserted, the judgement removed
the right of state legislatures to determine electoral districts. Furthermore, they
observed, the principle of mathematical equality clashed with the US
Constitution, which allowed for representation in the Senate on the basis of territory, not population.

Chief Justice William Rehnquist (1986–) is a conservative. He favours a
much more restrictive conception of discrimination based on individual
instances of unfair treatment. He also backs 'states' rights'. However, although
he is supported on the bench by figures such as Antonin Scalia and Clarence
Thomas, conservatives failed to gain a clear majority on the Court during the
Reagan and Bush era. Some of those appointed in this period turned out to be
judicial moderates. Then, in the 1990s, when President Clinton had the opportunity to appoint Stephen Breyer and Ruth Bader Ginsburg to the bench, conservative hopes of securing a Court committed to a constitutional
'counter-revolution' were finally dashed. As a consequence, although conservative arguments have shaped a significant number of rulings, there is no
clearly dominant bloc on the Court. The Court does not have a consistent character. Instead, the composition of the majority and the minority changes
according to the issue under consideration.

Affirmative action programmes have been progressively circumscribed since the *Griggs*, *Bakke* and *Fullilove* rulings. It has not, however, ruled that they are unconstitutional. The roll-back began in 1989 when the Court ruled in *Richmond v. J. A. Croson* that state and local governments could only adopt a system of minority set-asides for contracts if they were addressing specific instances of discrimination. They were to be 'strictly reserved for remedial settings' (Thernstrom and Thernstrom 1997: 437). Other Court rulings imposed further constraints on affirmative action programmes. *Wards Cove Packing Company v. Antonio* (1989) looked again at company employment policies. It narrowed the grounds on which discrimination could be claimed, and at the same time broadened the basis on which employers could justify the use of particular selection tests and hiring practices. In 1995, *Adarand v. Pena* applied the arguments that underpinned the *Croson* ruling to the award of federal government contracts, and permitted minority set-asides in only narrowly prescribed circumstances. The Court had similar concerns about racial redistricting. In some states, the boundaries between electoral districts had been drawn so as to ensure that there were black or Hispanic majorities. This was intended to increase the overall level of minority representation in Congress. However, in *Shaw v. Reno* (1993) and *Miller v. Johnson* (1995), the Court rejected redistricting plans in which race was the 'predominant factor'.

There has been a partial, but limited, pull-back from the assertion of abortion rights in *Roe v. Wade*. The basic framework established by the *Roe* ruling has, however, remained intact. In July 1989, in *Webster v. Reproductive Health Services*, the Court upheld the constitutionality of a Missouri law prohibiting the use of state facilities and personnel in the performance of an abortion. Three years later, in June 1992, *Planned Parenthood of Southeastern Pennsylvania v. Casey* permitted states to impose a waiting period before an abortion is carried out, and required unmarried women, aged under eighteen, to gain the consent of a parent or judge (Hinkson Craig and O'Brien 1993: 329–41). In *Garcia v. San Antonio Metropolitan Transit Authority* (1985), the Court allowed the federal government to regulate the wages paid by the city authorities to local bus workers. It was a centralising judgement. Ten years later, in 1995, the Court appeared to stress the constitutional limits on the role of the federal government. In *US v. Lopez*, the Court declared the Gun-Free School Zones Act unconstitutional. Washington, the Court argued, did not have the power under the interstate commerce clause of the Constitution to restrict the possession of a gun in the vicinity of a school (McKeever 1997: 45). Appropriate legislation was, the judges asserted, a matter for the individual states.

The rights of the citizen

The Bill of Rights establishes the basic liberties of the individual. However, the federal courts have also played a role in determining the practical meaning of those rights. A succession of cases focused on the rights of suspects in criminal cases. *Gideon v. Wainwright* (1963) laid down that all defendants had a right to

Factors influencing the Supreme Court

Attempts to assess the factors shaping Supreme Court rulings must inevitably be speculative. Although both majority and minority opinions are published, the Court's proceedings are confidential.

Nevertheless, some tentative conclusions can be drawn. A number of influences are evident. First, there are internal factors. As has been noted, the justices regard their role in legal, not political, terms. They are bound by the wording of the Constitution. They are guided by past precedent – the principle of *stare decisis*. Their understanding the judicial process is also important. Whereas some are strict constructionists, others argue that the Constitution should be interpreted and reapplied to twentieth-century conditions. Jurists, they argue, should be more concerned with the spirit than the text of the Constitution.

External factors should, however, also be considered. Although members of the Court are not subject to election and are therefore sealed off from the other branches of government and public opinion, they do appear to be swayed by wider opinion. This takes three forms:

1   When a case is being considered, interest groups submit *amicus curiae* briefs to the Court. These argue in support of a particular outcome. In 1978, the *Bakke* case, that considered the constitutionality of affirmative action, attracted fifty-eight such briefs (McKeever 1997: 83).

2   The Administration also 'lobbies' the Court. It is represented by the Office of the Solicitor-General which is located in the Department of Justice. The Office will ask the Court to review particular cases and also submits *amicus curiae* briefs. It has a high success rate, both because its staff will have more expertise than other litigants and because they have a relatively close working relationship with the Court. When, during the Reagan years, *amicus curiae* briefs were submitted, the Court concurred with the opinion stated in them in 67.5 per cent of cases (Ragsdale 1996: 434).

3   The Court has shifted its ground in response to changes in the public mood. In 1942, it backed the internment of Japanese-Americans as a necessary wartime measure. The Brown ruling (1954) should be seen against the background in which the armed forces had already been integrated and groupings such as the NAACP had begun to campaign against segregation. Similarly, *Roe v. Wade* (1973) emerged at a time when the women's movement and feminist arguments were beginning to gain acceptance.

an attorney. To ensure this, the states would pay the expenses of those on a low income. Three years later, *Miranda v. Arizona* (1966) established that criminal suspects must be read their rights upon arrest. The ruling was derived from the protection of the right against self-incrimination in the Fifth Amendment.

Since the days of the Warren Court, there has been much less of a readiness to extend the rights of the accused. Instead, the ability of the authorities to secure a conviction has been much more of a consideration. In 1991, in *Fulminante v. Arizona*, the Court ruled that even if a confession is obtained by coercion, it does not necessarily invalidate a conviction based upon it.

The rights of the convicted have also been circumscribed. In two 1989 cases (*Penry v. Lynaugh* and *Stanford v. Kentucky*), the Court ruled that it was constitutional to extend capital punishment to the mentally retarded and to juveniles who committed murder (McKeever 1995: 283). The ability of the Court to consider appeals based on an alleged denial of constitutional rights by the state courts was also reined in. The most conservative judges on the Court, Antonin Scalia and Clarence Thomas, have taken the view that the Constitution, and therefore the Supreme Court, could not forbid 'the execution of an innocent man who has received, though to no avail, all the process that our society has traditionally deemed adequate' (Roberts 1995: 155).

Sources of power

The Supreme Court has, then, had a far-reaching impact on American politics and society. There are a number of reasons why it is so powerful:

1 The Court has wide jurisdiction. The supremacy clause of the Constitution (Article VI Section 2), which establishes the Constitution and the laws of the US as the supreme law of the land, and the evolution of judicial review, mean that the Court can apply its judgement to any law or governmental action. By 1995, the Court had declared more than 125 acts of Congress unconstitutional (Wetterau 1995: 201). Its interpretations have reshaped and changed the accepted meaning of many others.
2 The president, Congress, executive departments and agencies, and states can be overruled. The Supreme Court's 1974 ruling that President Richard Nixon's *executive privilege* did not extend to the tape recordings of his conversations in the White House led to his resignation.
3 The Court's judgements can only be reversed through the process of constitutional amendment. Only five amendments have been passed so as to overrule Supreme Court decisions (Wetterau 1995: 201).
4 The Court has immense authority and prestige. Although the southern states obstructed the implementation of the *Brown* ruling, the Court's right to decide on constitutional questions is almost always unchallenged, even by those who disagree with their decisions.
5 Because Supreme Court judges serve for life, or until they chose to retire, they are, in contrast with those who are subject to periodic re-election, protected from the pressures of public opinion. They can therefore make unpopular rulings, such as the *Brown* judgement, without fear of electoral consequences.
6 The Court can decide which cases it considers and is under no obligation to

examine every case that is brought to its attention. On average, the Court accepts only about ninety cases a year out of seven thousand or more. The right to hear a case is called the power of *certiorari* ('to make more certain').

7 The federal courts have a wide range of remedies available to correct what are considered wrongs. One federal judge insisted on the improvement of prisons in Alabama, at a cost of $40 million per annum, on the grounds that the conditions in them constituted a 'cruel and unusual' form of punishment prohibited under the Eighth Amendment.

8 The federal courts also play an important role in American life because it is a *litigious* society. Americans resort to the courts to resolve conflicts and to protect what they regard as their rights. Many issues are taken to court, providing countless opportunities for judicial decision making. One in every four hundred Americans is a lawyer.

9 The courts offer an access point for interest groups. Groups that have failed to achieve their goals in the political arena will frequently seek to achieve them in the courts. Interest groups have, furthermore, backed individuals bringing cases. The civil rights movement and the pro-choice groups have both used this strategy successfully. When not directly involved, interest groups will also submit briefs – *amicus curiae* ('friend of the court') – to the courts in support of a particular ruling. In some years, there have been over three thousand of these (Wetterau 1995: 206).

10 As government has become more and more involved in every aspect of life, the range of issues considered by the courts has been extended. They have, in particular, been involved in judging the constitutionality of growing government intervention in the economy.

11 Other institutions may avoid reaching a decision. They thereby assign responsibility for the issue to the courts. When the two houses of Congress and President Clinton could not agree how to proceed with a balanced budget amendment to the Constitution, some sections of it were worded in a loose and imprecise way so as to maximise support for the measure. If it had become law – and it failed the necessary two-thirds majority in both chambers – it would undoubtedly have had to be considered by the courts.

Constraints on power

Although some observers argue that the federal courts play an immensely influential role, others emphasise the limits and constraints on their powers.

1 They are limited in their ability to enforce their rulings. They are dependent upon the compliance of those whom the ruling affects, or require the backing of the executive branch. It was this that led Alexander Hamilton to describe the federal judiciary as 'the least dangerous branch' because, in contrast with the other branches of government, it has the power of neither

'the sword nor the purse'. The events that followed *Brown v. Board of Education* in 1954 illustrate this. Although the ruling called for desegregated schooling, the process of implementation required the use of troops. There was hostility from white crowds and the state authorities in the South pursued a strategy of non-compliance. In 1957, President Eisenhower sent troops to the Central High School in Little Rock, Arkansas, so as to ensure that nine black students could attend classes alongside whites. Segregation and the Jim Crow laws only came to an end once Congress agreed to the 1964 Civil Rights Act and the 1965 Voting Rights Act.

2 The Supreme Court has no power of initiative. It is an appeals court, and can therefore only react to cases that are submitted to it. It cannot identify a law or action that it considers unconstitutional and express an opinion. Instead, it must await an appellant who claims to have been unfairly treated by a law or act to bring a case to the courts.

3 Congress has powers over the federal courts. It has the ability to alter the number of judges, both on the Supreme Court and in the lower courts. Although the number of Supreme Court Justices has been stable at nine since 1869, there have been substantial increases in the overall number of federal judges. Congress can also broaden or restrict the jurisdiction of lower courts and create new courts. Furthermore, if Congress feels that the laws have been misinterpreted by the courts, it can amend its own statutes so as to clarify its intentions and wishes. Congress can limit the remedies available to the courts.

   Congress also has the power of impeachment, but this is rare. Only thirteen judges have been impeached, and, of these, only seven were removed from office (Wetterau 1995: 113–14). Furthermore, in almost all of these cases, Congress was responding to accusations of personal misconduct. Its actions were not a challenge to judicial rulings.

4 Although the process is fraught with difficulty, Congress and the states can initiate a constitutional amendment if they oppose a ruling by the Supreme Court. In 1895 the Supreme Court declared a federal income tax unconstitutional. The Sixteenth Amendment was ratified in 1913, specifically authorising such a tax.

5 The Court cannot, in the long run, disregard public opinion. Its legitimacy depends upon its popular credibility. In 1972, in *Furman v. Georgia*, the Court declared all existing death penalty laws unconstitutional. Chief Justice Warren Burger concluded from this that capital punishment had been abolished in the US (McKeever 1997: 145–6). However, there is widespread backing for the death penalty in the US. This led many state legislatures to pass revised death penalty legislation. In *Gregg v. Georgia* (1976), the Court retreated from its original position, and the overwhelming majority of states now include the death penalty in their statutes.

6 In some instances the judges exercise a degree of self-restraint. There are *strict constructionists* who oppose judicial activism. They argue that the judicial

process should rest on the wording of the Constitution and that judges should not make public policy. Furthermore, the Court perceives itself as a legal and not a political body, and it avoids acting in an openly political way. Judicial opinions are expressed in the language of law and not of executive efficiency or popular demands. The courts are reluctant to enter 'the political thicket'.

7 The Courts follow precedent. Decisions are made on the basis of previous rulings or those reached in the lower courts. This is *stare decisis* or, translated literally, 'let the decision stand'. The importance attached to precedent is evident in the Supreme Court's reluctance to overturn *Roe v. Wade*, even though a majority of current judges on the Court would almost certainly not have decided the case in the same way as the Burger Court.

8 Federal courts deal with only a relatively small proportion of cases. They consider about 2 per cent of all the cases brought in the US. Most criminal cases involve breaches of state rather than federal law.

Judicial philosophies

On what basis should judges make their decisions? There are two schools of thought about the principles that should guide the way in which judges reach their rulings. These are known as 'judicial activism' – which is broadly associated with liberalism – and 'judicial restraint', which is tied to conservative thinking.

Judicial activism

One of the most famous judges associated with judicial activism was William O. Douglas (1939–75). A leading contemporary academic advocate is Professor Laurence Tribe. The school is sometimes called non-interpretivist. Supporters talk of a 'living Constitution' that can adapt over time without requiring amendment.

Those committed to judicial activism are not primarily concerned with the text and ideas of the Founding Fathers or subsequent legislators, but with the justice of the decision. When deciding a case, they argue that judges should take three steps. First, the relevant general principles in the Constitution should be identified. Second, those principles should be tied to contemporary philosophies and values. Third, those principles should be applied to the particular case.

The arguments in support of judicial activism are:

1 Justice rather than textual fidelity is the proper basis for determining what is right and wrong. The basic purpose of the courts is 'to do right'.

2 The courts should provide a check on government. The actions of the president and Congress – in, for example, condoning and sometimes endorsing segregation – have at times been both flawed and unjust. This has been because the executive and legislative branches of government have to think

of electoral considerations. It is the responsibility of the Court to compensate for the failures of elected institutions.

3   Judges have a particular responsibility to protect the poor and minorities. Such groups have little political influence, and unless the courts take action, their interests will be neglected.

4   Decisions should be measured in terms of their consequences. The methods by which the decision it reached is less important. The *Brown* ruling should be celebrated because it led to the desegregation of schools.

6   Although some judges and legal scholars argue that rulings should be based on the doctrine of *original intent* and assess the thinking of those who wrote the Constitution and the later amendments that were adopted, supporters of judicial activism assert that intent cannot be identified. The Founders are dead, and furthermore, legislators often have inherently contradictory aims and purposes.

Judicial restraint

The leading justice associated with the doctrine of judicial restraint is Felix Frankfurter (1882–1965). The most prominent contemporary advocate is Robert Bork, whom the Senate refused to confirm as a member of the Supreme Court bench in 1987.

Advocates of restraint are sometimes known as strict constructionists, interpretivists or originalists. In their opinion, the role of the Court is, where the text of the Constitution is unclear, to identify the original intent of the founders of the Constitution or the legislators who introduced later amendments.

Those who believe in restraint argue that decisions should follow three steps, based on text, intention and inference (McKeever 1995: 30). First, the judge should examine the literal meaning of the words as written and understood at the time. Second, the intentions of the authors of the Constitution or the amendments should be studied. One source would, for example, be the speeches of the founders at the Philadelphia Convention. Third, inferences can be made from the principles and the structure of the Constitution. For example, they assert that the Founders intended that the Supreme Court should have the power of judicial review, even though it was never explicitly identified in the Constitution. Supporters of restraint put forward six arguments:

1   The federal judiciary is unelected. Activism assigns power to an elite institution which is not democratically accountable to the people. It thereby takes power from democratically elected institutions. Critics of activism talk of an 'Imperial Judiciary'.

2   Justices who base their rulings on judicial activism are inevitably imposing their own values. However, in many cases, their values and preferences are unrepresentative of American opinion. For example, the Court ruled against capital punishment. However, opinion polls indicated that over 80 per cent

of Americans supported the death penalty. Critics of *Roe v. Wade* note that it was based on a 'right to privacy' which, they assert, has no basis in the Constitution and was based instead on the personal wishes of those serving on the Supreme Court at the time.

3 The law deals in absolutes of right and wrong, while politics involves a balance of interests. Costs and benefits are weighed up. For example, attitudes towards abortion vary greatly between the states. Some are strongly pro-life and others are pro-choice. By imposing absolute rulings that apply across the US, the Supreme Court does not allow for regional and local diversity.

4 The courts lack the specialised knowledge or experience to make decisions. Judges have to rule on very complex cases, such as school administration or environmental protection, involving subjects about which they have no knowledge. They are therefore making judgements with very little understanding of the consequences.

5 Activism reduces the credibility of the federal courts in the eyes of the public. The legitimacy of the courts depends on the acceptance of their rulings by the people. When decisions are made that the public does not accept, it undermines public respect for the institutions of government.

6 Legal systems depend upon reliability and continuity. When judges overturn earlier decisions or precedents that have been established, they undermine confidence in the law. The Supreme Court has reversed its own judgements on at least 150 occasions (Wetterau 1995: 200).

Judicial activism and restraint are frequently described as liberal and conservative theories. This is, however, misleading. In the 1930s it was liberals rather than conservatives who favoured restraint. Liberals claimed that Franklin Roosevelt had a popular mandate for the New Deal economic polices, and the Court should not seek to abrogate the people's verdict. In the 1980s and 1990s, it has generally been conservatives who protest against judges imposing their own values. They often cite abortion as an example.

The Supreme Court and the Internet

The texts of US Supreme Court rulings and opinions can be found at:

http://www.law.cornell.edu/supct/

More general information about all the US federal courts – including the US Supreme Court – can be found at:

http://www.uscourts.gov/

The website answers frequently asked questions (FAQs), provides a news service, links to related websites, and a list of publications for further research.

Politicial or judicial?

Should the Supreme Court be regarded as a judicial body with significant impact on politics, or a political institution that has a judicial edge to its deliberations? In other words, are the judges merely 'politicians in robes'?

Robert McKeever argues that the Court is a 'political institution whose legal characteristics make it different from other political institutions' (1995: viii). The political character of the Court is evident in five ways. First, the Court decides 'who gets what, when and how'. This is a traditional definition of politics. Second, the appointments process itself, as has been seen, is highly political. It involves the president and the Senate, as well as interest groups and public opinion. Third, judicial decision making has become a major focus for interest-group activity. Interest groups play a role in setting the court agenda through the sponsoring of cases and in the presentation of *amicus curiae* briefs. Fourth, the courts are viewed through the prism of competing conservative and liberal philosophies. In other words, they are assessed politically. Fifth, judgements are examined in terms of their political outcomes. Rulings are judged primarily by their consequences for different groupings (Hodder-Williams 1980).

However, Richard Maidment emphasises the judicial and legal characteristics of the Court: 'it cannot avoid a political role. But that does not mean that judges are politicians' (Maidment and Tappin 1990: 40). It is a court insofar as it can only act through litigation. Second, decisions are often determined by technical and legal factors. Third, precedence constrains the rulings that are made. Fourth, the spirit or ethos of the court is non-political. Fifth, the judges do not act or perceive themselves as politicians. Nor do they follow popular opinion. Because they are appointed for life, they are largely 'insulated' from the other branches of government and public pressures. Sixth, judges have to distinguish between their personal preferences and the requirements of the legal process. In June 1989, for example, the Supreme Court ruled that the burning of the US flag as a form of political protest was a constitutional right under the First Amendment. Laws in forty-eight states prohibiting flag-burning were thus judged unconstitutional. The majority in *Texas v. Johnson* included two conservatives, Antonin Scalia and Anthony Kennedy. They undoubtedly regarded the burning of the flag as an act of wanton disloyalty. However, they felt that, given the wording of the Constitution, they had little choice but to allow such actions.

Conclusion

Chapter 3 noted that the US Constitution had weathered all the upheavals and transformations of the past two centuries in a basically unaltered form. The Supreme Court provides a reason why it could do this. The Court's ability to reinterpret concepts such as equality ensured that although many of the words in the Constitution remained unchanged, they were understood and applied very differently. In the 1890s, the Court granted constitutional legitimacy to segregation and, sixty years later, to desegration. Although the legal methodology underlying this shift in thinking has continued to attract criticism from strict constructionists, the Court thereby gave the Constitution an adaptability that enabled it to survive social, political and economic change.

References and further reading

Berger, R. (1997), *Government by Judiciary: The Transformation of the Fourteenth Amendment*, Indianapolis, Liberty Fund.

Bickel, A. M. (1962), *The Least Dangerous Branch: The Supreme Court at the Bar of Politics*, Indianapolis, Bobbs-Merrill.

Hinkson Craig, B. and D. M. O'Brien (1993), *Abortion and American Politics*, Chatham, Chatham House.

Hodder-Williams, R. (1980), *The Politics of the Supreme Court*, London, Allen & Unwin.

Maidment, R. and M. Tappin (1990), *American Politics Today*, Manchester, Manchester University Press.

McKeever, R. (1995), *Raw Judicial Power? The Supreme Court and American Society*, Manchester, Manchester University Press.

McKeever, R. (1997), *The United States Supreme Court: A Political and Legal Analysis*, Manchester, Manchester University Press.

Ragsdale, L. (1996), *Vital Statistics on the Presidency: Washington to Clinton*, Washington, DC, Congressional Quarterly.

Roberts, R. S. (1995), *Clarence Thomas and the Tough Love Crowd: Counterfeit Heroes and Unhappy Truths*, New York, New York University Press.

Thernstrom, S. and A. Thernstrom (1997), *America in Black and White: One Nation Indivisible*, New York, Simon & Schuster.

Tindall, G. B. and D. E. Shi (1989), *America: A Narrative History*, New York, W. W. Norton.

Wetterau, B. (1995), *Desk Reference on American Government*, Washington, DC, Congressional Quarterly.

5

Congress

The US Congress is widely recognised as the most powerful legislature in the world. It is, according to the Constitution, the first branch of government. Its powers include the passage of legislation, declarations of war, the ratification of treaties, the formulation of the annual budget, consent to major political appointments, and the oversight of executive departments and agencies. Although the president has a major influence upon congressional decisions, it is far from certain that his policies will be accepted.

During the nineteenth century, Congress was even more powerful than today. However, as America's role in the world grew, and the federal government assumed more of a role in shaping domestic affairs, the authority of the executive branch grew also. The powers of Congress have correspondingly diminished. Nevertheless, it is still an important institution, and there are those who suggest that it is now in a period of growing strength and revival (Sundquist 1981).

This chapter will consider a number of questions. What are the powers of Congress? What are the differences between the House of Representatives and the Senate? How are laws made? What determines congressional voting behaviour? How important is party leadership? Should we think, as some argue, in terms of 'two congresses'? Does Congress need to be reformed?

Congress and the Constitution

Congressional powers are laid down in Article I, Section I of the Constitution. They shape the relationship between Congress and the president and are also considered in Chapter 6.

1 All legislative power is located in Congress, and federal law must be passed by both houses of Congress in an identical form. The legislative role of Congress stems from the powers assigned to the federal government in the

Constitution. There are enumerated powers such as the control of trade 'among the several States', the regulation of foreign trade, and the raising of an army. However, as well as these, successive Supreme Court rulings led to an expansion of the federal government's role, and Congress progressively acquired *implied* powers.

During the 105th Congress (1997–99), the legislative measures that were agreed included plans to give families a $500 per child tax credit, a $2.3 million rescue plan for Amtrak (the railway network), and the decision to ratify the worldwide Chemical Weapons Convention. Congress can also reject proposals, even if they are backed by the president. In November 1997, the Clinton administration had to withdraw plans to grant the president *fast-track authority*, once it became clear that there would not be a Congressional majority in support of the measure. This made it much more difficult for the president to negotiate trade agreements and the reduction of tariffs with other nations (Bennett 1998: 32–3).

Congress also has the ability to pass resolutions. Concurrent resolutions are used to make or amend rules or express Congressional sentiments. A joint resolution, passed by both houses, and signed by the president – such as the 1964 Gulf of Tonkin resolution that provided the pretext for large-scale US intervention in Vietnam – has the force of law. Congress can, furthermore, propose constitutional amendments, although, to be adopted, they require a two-thirds majority in both houses and the assent of at least three-quarters of the states. In March 1997, an amendment requiring a balanced federal budget – in which expenditure matches revenue – was killed in the Senate by one vote.

2 Congress has the *power of the purse*. Although the president submits a proposed budget annually – drawn up by the Office of Management and Budget (OMB) – Congress decides on taxation, government borrowing, and spending. Money bills originate in the House, but must be passed by the Senate as well.

The standing committees in the House and their counterparts in the Senate that are responsible for the budget process have legitimately been called 'supercommittees'. They are very powerful indeed. The House Ways and Means Committee and the Senate Finance Committee are responsible for the raising of revenue through taxation or borrowing. The Budget Committees set financial guidelines for overall spending. The House and Senate Appropriations Committees are responsible for the allocation of expenditure within the overall budget process. As Peter Woll puts it, the House Appropriations Committee:

> determines the amounts of money that *will* be spent on government programs. The committee and subcommittees do not legislate per se, nor do they determine how much money may be authorized, but in deciding appropriations they profoundly affect a wide range of public policy. The chairman and subcommittee chairmen of Appropriations know that government programs cannot be sustained without their cooperation. (Woll 1985: 122)

The institutionalised separation of revenue raising and expenditure has, at times, created significant administrative difficulties, encouraged the growth of spending commitments, and hindered the development of a coherent economic strategy.

The budgetary process

President's draft budget (one tax bill and thirteen spending bills of 2,000–3,000 pages).

Budget resolution passes through Senate and House Budget Committees and establishes the guidelines.

Taxation Bill by Ways and Means and Senate Finance Committees.

Authorisation by Standing Committees make recommendations on how much should be spent on what.

Appropriations Committees make the final budget proposal designed to match revenue and expenditure.

Budget Conference Committee to reconcile House and Senate versions.

Presidential signature or veto.

Veto overridden by two-thirds in both houses, or negotiations on a new budget between Congress and the administration.

---

3   As the 1946 Legislative Reorganization Act confirmed, Congress has *oversight* powers. It reviews and monitors the executive departments and agencies that constitute the federal bureaucracy. Oversight or 'watchdog' work is undertaken through Congress's committee structure. Many of the standing committees 'shadow' a particular executive department. Others oversee a broader area of policy. The Senate, for example, has an armed services committee, a foreign relations committee, and an agriculture committee. The House has an agriculture committee, but also a small business and science committee. While the standing committees exist on a permanent basis, select committees may also be created by either house or jointly on an *ad hoc* basis, so as to look at matters that fall outside the jurisdiction of the standing committees, or conduct a specific investigation.

   Oversight takes a number of forms. It includes formal and informal communication with administrators, committee hearings, the evaluation of a particular programme by congressional support agencies, or a requirement that an agency issue a report outlining and explaining aspects of its work.

   Observers are divided about the extent to which members of Congress pursue their oversight responsibilities. Peter Woll suggests that scrutiny of the executive branch offers relatively little to the individual members of Congress, the district or state that they represent, and their chances of re-election (1985: 146). In the same vein John Hart concludes that oversight is 'negligible'. Congress, he asserts, 'has neither the will nor the interest nor the incentive to reverse a half century of significant institutional develop-ment in American government' (1995: 237).

However, Joel D. Aberbach argues that oversight work became much more important from the mid-1970s onwards (1990: 19, 72). As public unease about the federal government grew, the political 'payoffs' for over-sight work increased. Some members of Congress sought to eliminate waste. Others attempted to highlight policy failures in response to disquiet among those they represented.

The ability of Congress to oversee and influence the actions of the bureaucracy has been strengthened by the *legislative veto*. From 1932 onwards, legislation often included a provision that particular decisions and actions undertaken by the executive branch should be referred back to Congress. The first legislative veto permitted President Herbert Hoover to reorganise the executive agencies, but established a ninety-day delay before any changes would take effect. During this period, the legislation allowed Congress to veto the organisational changes he had made. The overall effect of the legislative veto was to give Congressional committees authority over day-to-day decisions by sections of the executive branch. In the 1950s, for example, a Congressional committee – the Joint Committee on Atomic Energy -decided where the Atomic Energy Commission should locate power stations and what forms of technology would be adopted.

In June 1983, the US Supreme Court declared that the legislative veto was unconstitutional. In *Immigration and Naturalization Service v. Chadha*, the Court found that by giving Congress a power that was not subject to presi-dential concurrence, this form of veto breached the separation of powers. However, the overall impact of *Chadha* appears to have been limited. The status of laws passed between 1932 and 1983 that included a legislative veto remains uncertain. They have not been repealed. Furthermore, as Louis Fisher argues, more than 140 laws passed since 1983 have included a legis-lative veto (Congressional Quarterly 1997: 18).

4 The Senate has 'advice and consent' powers. It can confirm or reject the appointment of senior federal officers such as Cabinet Secretaries, federal judges, and Ambassadors. The Senate's 'advice and consent' powers also extend to the ratification of treaties signed by the president with foreign powers. Under the Constitution, these require a two-thirds majority. Although the president generally gains the assent of the Senate to his appointments and proposed treaties, there have been important exceptions. These are recorded in Chapter 6.

5 Congress has the power to remove leading officials of the executive, includ-ing the President. However, *impeachment* proceedings have only ever become

a consideration in the most extreme or unusual circumstances. In total, two executive officers and thirteen judges have been impeached.

A president can only be impeached for 'high crimes and misdemeanours'. The process begins with a vote of the House to conduct an inquiry. The results of the inquiry, undertaken by the House Judiciary Committee, are presented to the full House. If the president is indicted, or *impeached*, by the House (and this requires only a majority vote), a trial is then conducted before the Senate. The Chief Justice plays a presiding role, and the Senators constitute a jury. A two-thirds majority (sixty-seven votes) is needed if the president is to be removed from office. The first president to be impeached was Andrew Johnson in 1868. In the aftermath of the Civil War, radical Republicans felt that he was over-sympathetic to the South. They acted when, against this background, Johnson dismissed the Secretary of War. In 1974, impeachment procedings were initiated against Richard Nixon, although he resigned before the matter was considered by the House as a whole. Nixon had been accused of obstructing justice by hiding White House involvement in an illegal break-in at Democratic Party offices. In December 1998, the House voted to impeach President Clinton, following claims that the president had committed acts of perjury and obstructed justice.

6 The Constitution endows Congress with the power to declare war (Article I Section VIII). Congress has declared war only five times, although troops have been sent into action much more often. As a *Congressional Quarterly* study records:

> Presidents have ordered the armed forces to protect settlers from Indians, repel bands of foreign outlaws, punish nations and groups for belligerent or criminal bevior, rescue US citizens abroad, support friendly governments and train their armies, fight pirates and terrorists, warn potential enemies against taking aggressive action, deliver humanitarian aid, and secure disputed lands.
> (Congressional Quarterly 1997: 204)

Congress sought to constrain the president with the War Powers Resolution of 1973. This stipulated that Congressional approval must be given for medium, and long-term military actions overseas.

Comparing chambers

The US legislature is *bicameral*. In other words, it has two chambers. There are similarities. All legislation must be passed by both the House and the Senate. Both chambers have oversight responsibilities, and they review the work of the executive branch. The working life of both is organised around a committee structure. In 1998, there were nineteen committees and eighty-four subcommittees in the House and sixteen committees and sixty-eight subcommittees in the Senate.

Standing Committees in the 105th Congress (1997–99)

House of Representatives

Agriculture	Judiciary
Appropriations	National Security
Banking and Financial Services	Resources
Budget	Rules
Commerce	Science
Education and the Workforce	Small Business
Government Reform and Oversight	Standards of Official Conduct
House Oversight	Transportation and Infrastructure
International Relations	Veterans' Affairs
	Ways and Means

Senate

Agriculture, Nutrition and Forestry	Finance
Appropriations	Foreign Relations
Armed Services	Governmental Affairs
Banking, Housing and Urban Affairs	Judiciary
Budget	Labor and Human Resources
Commerce, Science and Transportation	Rules and Administration
Energy and Natural Resources	Small Business
Environment and Public Works	Veterans' Affairs

Both houses of Congress can draw upon the support of an extensive number of staff. An average member of the House has a staff of seventeen. A Senator has about forty aides. Most are involved in the everyday work of an office, such as the answering of letters. Others advise on policy matters. Some are also employed in district and state offices. Congress itself employs about 26,000 people. They mainly staff the different committees. There are also specialists working in the Congressional Budget Office (CBO). It monitors and evaluates the annual budget. The Congressional Research Service (CRS) provides an independent assessment of all legislation. The General Audit Office (GAO) investigates the executive branch to ensure honesty and efficiency.

However, although there are similarities, there are also important differences between the chambers. The House of Representatives and the Senate have their own distinct identities. They differ in their terms of office, constituencies, size, minimal qualifications, rules, partisanship and collective identity. There are often differences of opinion and there can be competition for power between them.

The House is directly elected by the people in single-member constituencies drawn up on the basis of population. Those who serve have to be over twenty-five years of age, and have been a US citizen for at least seven years. Since 1910, the House has had 435 members. Today, on average, a congressional district will have a voting population of about 550,000. The House is a large and heterogeneous chamber. Its members face re-election every two years, and they therefore have to be district oriented.

House rules are detailed, formal and comprehensive. House members tend to specialise in a limited number of policy areas and serve on only one or two standing committees. The size of the institution has tended to give more power to party leaders and is thus more centralised. It is a *majoritarian* institution insofar as decision making is based upon decision making by a simple majority rather than a shared consensus or super majority, which would require the agreement of a proportion greater than half.

The leader of the majority party in the House takes the post of Speaker. Although the Speaker will often preside, particularly on important occasions, the Speakership is not, in contrast with its British counterpart, a ceremonial role. Instead, the Speaker of the House is an active and influential partisan. He controls the legislative agenda, and influences decisions about the committee to which a bill is assigned. He also has considerable powers of patronage, shapes the membership of select committees, and since 1975 has nominated majority party members to the all-important Rules Committee.

The Senate has, since 1913, been directly elected by the people of the different states. Every state elects two Senators, regardless of size. California has two Senators representing a population of almost thirty-two million. Wyoming's two Senators speak for only 481,400 people.

There are, in total, 100 Senators. Senators have to be over thirty years of age, and have been citizens for at least nine years. One-third are elected every two years for terms of six years. Change in the Senate is a more gradual and less abrupt process because elections are staggered in this way.

The comparatively small size of the Senate allows for a relatively intimate atmosphere in which friendships and personal relationships develop, many of which stretch across party lines. The Senate see itself as more deliberative and thoughtful than the House. Senators tend to be more concerned with national and international interests and affairs than Congressmen. The numbers do not allow for specialisation and Senate members tend to have a more *generalist* approach. They serve on two or three standing committees. More is discussed on the Senate floor and the chamber is less committee-based than the House. Senators are also more *individualistic*, and although the parties now have more of an organised presence than in past years, less constrained by party pressures. The Senate Majority Leader's powers are much more limited than those of the House Speaker.

The Senate also has fewer formal rules. The customs of the chamber ensure that each Senator has much more influence than the individual House member. In place of the House's majoritarianism, there is a tradition of consent and co-operation. Its deliberations are often slower. A determined

Senator can attempt to block legislation by speaking until a bill is dropped in a process known as a *filibuster*. In 1957 Senator Strom Thurmond, then a committed segregationist, spoke for over twenty-four hours so as to block a civil rights bill. A filibuster can only be ended if there is a three-fifths majority or sixty votes calling for the debate to be ended and the taking of a vote. This is called *cloture*.

The House and the Senate have been described as co-equal institutions. The Constitution shares out responsibilities by assigning the House primacy in considering government finances and the Senate principal responsibility for foreign affairs. However, the Senate has greater prestige. This stems, in part, from the smaller size of the Senate. A Senator usually represents a larger number of people. She or he serves longer terms of office, faces re-election less often, and has a more of a national profile. The Senate can thereby offer a more effective starting point for those considering a presidential bid. It is significant that a member of the House will give up his or her seat so as to capture a Senate seat. A Senator would not, however, abandon his or her seat in pursuit of a place in the House.

How are laws made?

The legislative process is long, complex and difficult. The overwhelming majority of bills never become law. In 1996, for example, 6,808 bills were introduced, but only 337 were adopted (Davidson and Oleszek 1998: 278). Many proposals are killed off in committee and are never considered by the chamber as a whole. The bills that survive only emerge in a heavily amended form. A bill has to pass through a seven-stage obstacle course to become law.

1 All bills are initiated or sponsored by members of Congress. Only a minority are inspired by the president. Furthermore, the president does not have the power to propose legislation himself. Instead, he has to find a sympathetic Congressman and Senator to introduce a bill on his behalf.

   All bills must be proposed in both chambers, although the process does not have to begin at the same time. A bill is generally known by the names of its principal sponsors. The 1985 measures to progressively reduce the federal government deficit were, for example, referred to as 'Gramm–Rudman–Hollings' after Representative Phil Gramm of Texas, Senator Warren Rudman of New Hampshire and Senator Ernest Hollings of South Carolina.

2 A bill will then be allocated to a *standing committee* for consideration. Sometimes it will be considered by more than one committee when it involves multiple spheres of jurisdiction. Clinton's health care bill was, for example, considered by two Senate and three House committees.

   Most bills, about 95 per cent, are killed at this stage. There are four steps to committee deliberations. First, the committee chairman decides whether the bill is to be referred to a subcommittee, considered by the committee, or 'pigeonholed'. If it is pigeonholed by the chairman, it cannot progress further. Second, the committee will hold hearings to consider the bill with witnesses and presentations from relevant government departments, experts and interest groups. Third, there will be the consideration of the bill on a line-by-line basis. This is known as the mark-up session. Last, if the committee recommends the bill, it will issue a positive report.

3 Once a bill has been reported out, time must be found to consider it in the chamber. Decisions to provide a place in the calendar and opportunities for debate and amendment are made by the House Rules Committee and, to a lesser extent, the Senate Majority Leader. The Rules Committee has been described as the House's 'traffic manager' (Griffith 1976: 40). It determines the framework within which a bill is handled and the conditions under which amendments can be submitted. Its recommendations can either improve the chances of a bill being adopted – through, for example, the adoption of a 'gag' rule by which amendments are forbidden or restricted – or increase the chances of it being killed off.

4 The bill is then considered and debated by the chamber as a whole. This known as floor action. In the House, debate is usually limited to short speeches of about five minutes. In the Senate, members may speak for as long as they wish, and this can be employed as a tactic so as to block a measure (see above). A bill must obtain a majority in both chambers. Voting may be conducted by voice vote or a recorded *roll-call* vote through an electronic voting system.

5 However similar the bills introduced in the House and the Senate, there will almost certainly be differences between the versions passed in the two chambers. If they are to become law, the bills must pass in an absolutely identical form. A *conference committee*, consisting of between three and nine members from both houses, customarily drawn from the appropriate standing committees, will meet to seek a compromise between the different versions.

6 If a compromise is agreed by a majority of both delegations, the bill must return to both chambers in its revised form for final approval. This is usually forthcoming, although there is a danger that members of either house may feel that too much has been conceded in Conference negotiations.

7 A bill requires the president's signature if it is to pass into law. Under the Constitution, the president can *veto* a bill, and a veto can only be overridden if members of Congress can muster a two-thirds majority in both houses. Faced by a Democratic Congress, President Bush used his veto power forty-six times and was overridden only once. The veto should not, therefore, be underestimated, and the implicit threat of a veto may be sufficient in itself to force Congress to modify its original goals. The role of the veto is discussed further in Chapter Six.

Congress and the Internet

The Senate and the House of Representatives have their own websites. Both incorporate information about individual members, reports on current legislative work, opportunities to search for information on particular topics, voting records, and links to other federal government websites.

http://www.senate.gov/

http://www.house.gov/

The Library of Congress offers THOMAS. Named after Thomas Jefferson, this offers searchable information, the text of bills, Congressional committee reports, and Congressional Record.

http://thomas.loc.gov/home/thomas2.html

Detailed coverage of developments in Congress can also be found at the *Roll Call* website:

http://www.rollcall.com

The role of parties

With one exception, all Congressmen and Senators belong to either the Republican or the Democratic Parties. The party caucuses, or groups, elect leaders. The Speaker, who leads the majority party in the House, is supported by the House Majority Leader and the Majority Whip. For its part, the opposition party is led by the Minority Leader and Minority Whip.

The party leaders in the Senate do not have the same degree of influence. The Senate Majority and Minority Leaders and the party whips organise the work of the chamber, schedule business, structure their party's work, and provide campaign assistance (Davidson and Oleszek 1998: 175–9).

In most legislatures, the party is the most significant feature structuring voting decisions. Members of Parliament (MPs) in the British House of Commons, for example, almost always follow the dictates of the whipping system. Rebellions are rare. Indeed, the backbencher is sometimes dismissed as mere 'lobby fodder'. However, although the parties dominated Congress during the period after the Civil War until 1920, they are now much less influential than in most other national legislatures.

There is little party discipline. Party group meetings, or caucuses, are rare and of relatively little importance. Party leadership plays a significant role in organising the procedures and agenda of the chambers, but the leaders cannot command individual members to act. They can only seek to use their influence. There are therefore only a small number of 'party votes' which pitch the majority of one party against another. It is rare for all of one party to be against all of the other, except in elections for the leadership of the chamber. Even then, there is no certainty. Why are parties so weak in Congress?

1 The federal government – or executive – does not depend on votes in the legislature. In most *parliamentary* systems the chief executive is elected by, accountable to, and dependent upon, votes in the legislature. The defeat of a major bill would, for example, lead to a vote of no confidence in the government. If carried, a general election would almost certainly be called. In the US system, the executive – the president – is elected independently and retains office regardless of his performance or support in Congress. Legislators belonging to the same party can vote against their president without the fear that he may be forced to resign and the other party might gain office.

2 Congress itself offers a career structure. In a parliamentary system, promotion into and within the executive offers a way forward for those with ambition. Advancement, however, generally depends upon loyalty towards the party and its leaders. In Congress, those who are ambitious do not generally look towards the executive branch. Instead, they seek a more powerful position, such as a committee chairmanship or membership of a more important committee, within Congress itself.

3 Congress rests on a committee system. In the words of M. J. C. Vile: 'it is difficult to exaggerate the importance of these committees, for they are the sieve through which all legislation is poured, and what comes through and how it comes through, is largely in their hands' (quoted in Bennett 1991: 17).

   Although the authority and autonomy of committee chairs has fluctuated, power is largely decentralised. Indeed, from the early 1970s onwards, Congress became more fragmented as a plethora of subcommittees assumed greater powers. Although the reforms that followed the 1994 elections partially reversed this by asserting the authority of party structures, shifting the locus of legislative activity to the full committee, and limiting most of the committees to five sub-units, the committees and the associated subcommittees constitute an alternative power network that imposes limits upon the authority of the party leaders (Owens 1998: 51).

4 Committee chairmen are usually appointed on the basis of *seniority*. By tradition, the longest serving majority party member of the committee takes the post. There have been some significant modifications to this. In 1975, three House chairs were replaced, despite their seniority, by their Democratic colleagues. After winning the 1994 elections, the House Republican leadership bypassed the seniority principle in making its appointments to three committee chairs. However, seniority remains the customary method of selection. The most important positions in Congress are therefore not usually dependent on the party apparatus or loyalty to it.

5 The party leadership does not control the selection of candidates. They are chosen in primaries, and the leadership has little control over the outcome. Party leaders cannot threaten to *deselect* candidates who have a record of disloyalty.
6 There are caucuses which are organised independently of the parties and cut across party lines. They include groupings based around the needs and interests of a particular industry, such as the Steel Caucus. There are also state delegations. A Texan member of the House of Representatives has described the work of his delegation thus: 'we have a wide ideological spectrum . . . but we're able to close ranks and work together for any program that benefits any part of the state' (Woll 1985: 183). Weight of numbers can give some delegations significant political leverage. Political cohesion adds further strength. A large, organised state delegation may be able to help an individual Congressman gain committee assignments and leadership positions.

Although the parties have traditionally been weak, and power rested with others – most notably the committee chairs or 'barons' – there have been efforts to increase the role and profile of the parties. In the 1980s, Democratic Speakers such 'Tip' O'Neill and Jim Wright began to play more of a role in deciding which committees considered important bills and the conditions under which legislation was debated on the floor of the House (Owens 1996: 16).

In the wake of Republican election victories in November 1994, former House Speaker Newt Gingrich attempted to increase the power of both the Party and its Congressional leadership. He broke with the seniority rule by selecting the chairs for the Appropriations, Commerce and Judiciary Committees over the heads of more senior colleagues. Those chairing committees were limited to a six-year period of tenure. He placed many of the newly elected members of Congress ('freshmen' and 'freshwomen') – those who were most committed to conservative principles – on the most important committees.

At the same time, Gingrich and other leading Republicans structured the work of the committees around the policies outlined in the *Contract with America*, the platform upon which many House Republican candidates had stood in the elections. The Republican leadership ensured the passage of nearly all the proposals included in the Contract. All were considered within the first hundred days of the new House (Ashford, 1998: 112–13). There was a high level of party unity and voting discipline. In 1995, a majority of Republicans voted against a majority of Democrats on over 73 per cent of votes taken on the floor of the House. Against a background where many members of Congress were relatively inexperienced, but at the same time shared a commitment to radical conservative reforms, the Gingrich leadership could assert itself and the Republican Party as key players in Congressional proceedings.

Although the 'Gingrich revolution' took place in the House, there were echoes in the Senate. Over two-thirds of votes followed party lines, and there were attempts – led by Senator Rick Santorum of Pennsylvania – to remove the long-established chair of the Appropriations Committee. Republican Party discipline was strengthened through the appointment of additional whips, the adoption of measures curtailing the traditional autonomy of committee chairs, and a requirement that they promote legislation supported by the overwhelming majority of Republican senators. John E. Owens concludes that, taken together, 'these changes represent the strongest movement towards party rule and accountability in the Senate in seventy years' (Owens 1998: 61).

However, although there were short-term successes, there was a long-term backlash against the Gingrich leadership. Widely shared resentments nearly resulted in a coup in early 1987. Gingrich was eventually forced to resign in November 1998 after poor mid-term election results. This appeared to signal a return to more traditional forms of Congressional behaviour.

What factors determine Congressional votes?

Although the role of the party fluctuates, it remains the single most important factor in shaping the outcome of Congressional votes, particularly when other factors do not weigh heavily on the individual legislator. Two-thirds of votes are described as party unity votes. A party unity vote is defined as one in which a majority of Republicans vote against a majority of Democrats (Davidson and Oleszek 1998: 260). However, this is a looser definition than that used in European countries, when the existence of a significant minority voting against the party, a frequent feature for Congress, would be considered a sign of party disunity. A more vigorous definition, based on 90 per cent of party members voting on opposite sides, is attained in only 10 per cent of votes.

Although Gingrich's fall appears to suggest that attempts to establish more effective party structures must inevitably founder, the Congressional parties have assumed a more clear-cut identity. There has, for example, been an increase in the proportion of 'party votes' in recent years. At the same time, the parties have become more ideologically coherent. The Republicans have established a more clearly conservative identity. For their part, as they lost conservatives from their ranks, the Democrats have defined themselves in more overtly liberal terms.

Although party is still the single most important determinant of voting behaviour, it is only one factor. Other factors also play a role in determining the outcome of Congressional votes. The district is significant. The votes of Congressmen will be shaped by views and opinions 'back home'. Re-election may depend upon a member's responsiveness to popular opinion in his or her own district or state. As former Democratic Party Speaker Tip O'Neill stressed, 'all politics is local'. Congressmen from farm districts will, for example, be highly sensitive to farm subsidies. Those representing districts where the oil industry is a major presence will concentrate their attention on energy policy. It is not, however, a straightforward process. On some issues there will no doubt where constituency interests and opinions lie. In these cases, the Congressman or Senator's vote is highly predictable. On other issues, however, there is no clear constituency position or interest. In these instances, the Congressman will have more latitude in following his own preferences.

Ideology or political philosophy will influence voting behaviour. Since the 1930s, a conservative coalition of southern Democrats and Republicans has exercised considerable influence. In recent years, however, the parties have become more ideologically homogeneous. There are still, however, significant differences within the parties. Among the Democrats, liberals are organised in the Democratic Study Group and conservatives (sometimes called 'Blue Dogs') in the Conservative Democratic Forum. Among Republicans, conservatives are brought together by the Conservative Action Team and moderates in the Tuesday Lunch Club. When party majorities are small, as in the 1999–2001 Congress, a minority faction within the majority party can exercise considerable influence.

Congressional 'staffers' may, in practice, also influence voting decisions. An average member of the House has a staff of seventeen and a Senator will have about forty working on his or her behalf. They provide a counterbalance to the information and arguments advanced by the executive branch. John Kingdon has noted that 'a high probability exists that a congressman's vote will reflect his or her staff position' (Woll 1985: 189). The influence they exert stems in part from the volume of work and the number of issues facing the individual Congressmen or Senators. They will inevitably be guided by the recommendations of their aides.

The role of lobbyists and interest groups should also be considered. There are an estimated 14,000 lobbyists working in Washington, DC on behalf of companies alone. They utilise a range of techniques. Some organisations will take advantage of the sense of affinity that party members traditionally feel towards a particular group. The trade unions held sway during the long years that the Democrats controlled Congress. Conversely, the Republican victories in 1994 and 1996 brought many business and conservative organisations into the political mainstream. In *Fortune* magazine's ranking of groups in terms of influence, the National Rifle Association was number six and the Christian Coalition was number seven.

Where quiet persuasion fails, interest groups can in some cases mobilise a large constituency. The National Rifle Association – fearing further federal gun control legislation – ensured that Congressmen received three million telegrams in seventy-two hours. Following a call to its supporters by the American Association of Retired Persons (AARP), former House Speaker, Jim Wright, received fifteen million postcards (Cigler and Loomis 1995: 395). In recent years, companies have also sought to organise members of the public in support of their interests. Individuals and groups are encouraged to write to or telephone members of Congress. According to Alison Mitchell, the tobacco companies spent $40 million organising a grassroots campaign against restrictive legislation in the spring of 1998. Companies, she asserts, are now attempting to put a 'public face on private interest'. There are other strategies. Instead of grassroots campaigns, some companies have pursued 'grasstops' initiatives. These are directed towards winning over those 'to whom a member of Congress cannot say no – his chief donor, his campaign manager, a political mentor' (Mitchell 1998).

The president's support for a bill may also influence the individual Senator or Representative. However, the 'chief legislator' will, in practice, only take a formal position on only a small proportion of the bills considered by Congress. In 1996, President Clinton adopted a definite stand on just 19 per cent of legislation. Presidents inevitably have the most success with members of their own parties: 'In 1996 the average House Democrat supported President Clinton seventy four per cent of the time, the average Democrat Senator eighty three per cent of the time. For Republicans the figures were thirty eight per cent for House members and thirty seven per cent for GOP Senators' (Davidson and Oleszek 1998: 267).

As these statistics suggest, party systems are much looser in the US than in Europe, and the president can look beyond those in his own party. He can often also count on a degree of backing from some members of the opposition party. There will be, in particular, a rallying round the president at times of national crisis, although leading Republicans were divided in their responses to the US military attacks against Iraq in December 1998. The president can sometimes also win support from sections of the opposing party through a process of coalition building. In 1993, for example, President Clinton depended on Republican backing to pass the North American Free Trade Agreement (NAFTA).

Conclusion

Congress is portrayed in different ways. It has been depicted as both powerful but also irresponsible. It is praised for representing people, and for the closeness of its relationship with those who elected it, but also accused of being a poor decision maker.

Opinion polls suggest that the American people are critical of Congress as an institution, but – paradoxically – respect their own Congressman (Hibbing and Theiss-Morse 1995). In 1992, 17 per cent of Americans expressed disapproval of Congress, while 54 per cent expressed approval of their own Congressman. The distinction between Congress as an institution and Congress as an aggregate of individual representatives has led some observers to talk in terms of 'the two Congresses' (Davidson and Oleszek 1998).

All national legislatures have to fulfil two functions. They represent diverse interests and constituencies across the nation, but they also collectively decide on issues facing the nation as a whole. The internal culture of the British Parliament – and most national legislatures – is skewed towards the second of these functions. Congress, however, emphasises the representation and promotion of district and statewide concerns.

The tension between the two functions of a legislature was identified by Edmund Burke in a celebrated address to the electors of Bristol in 1774. A parliament, he said, could be:

> a Congress of Ambassadors from different and hostile interests, whose interests each must maintain as an agent and advocate, against other agents or advocates (or) a deliberative assembly of one nation, with one interest, that of the whole, where not local purposes, not local prejudices, ought to guide, but the general good, resulting from the general reason of the whole. (quoted in Davidson and Oleszek 1998: 8)

Burke favoured the latter approach, and was, as a consequence, quite prepared to defy the wishes of those in his constituency.

Assessments and evaluations of Congress depend on which of the 'two Congresses' is under consideration. Congress can be judged as a mouthpiece of the districts and states. Seen this way, its performance is measured by its responsiveness to constituency pressures, its efficiency in assisting individual constituents with problems – such as claims for a higher level of veteran benefits – and the ability of members to attract government projects and businesses to their district or state. From this perspective, Congress will inevitably be decentralised and individualistic. It will be characterised by both short-term thinking and weak party cohesion. If, however, Congress is seen as a collective institution, it is measured by its ability to deliberate and make decisions on a long-term basis. It will also be judged on the nature of legislative–executive relations and the character of legislation that is passed. Such a Congress requires centralisation, a strong party system, and a sense of collective identity.

In practice, Congress is torn between the two forms of thinking, and its members perceive their principal functions in different ways. Some emphasise their role as legislators. They emphasise the need to ensure the smooth running of the institution. Others, however, see themselves as constituency servants (Fenno 1978). Empirical studies suggest that rather more time is devoted to representation than law-making. Research indicates that most members would prefer to give more attention to their role as legislators. David Mayhew has argued in *Congress: The Electoral Connection* (1974) that re-election is the primary motive behind congressional behaviour. He identifies three strategies that they pursue:

1 They attempt to develop a positive image through the use of television, the press, meetings and mailings.

2 They are drawn towards *pork-barrel* politics. They seek legislation that allocates funding, resources and the provision of employment to their own constituency.
3 Members of Congress associate themselves with positions that will prove
   popular in their district or state. Those whose constituency includes
   significant numbers working in the arms industry are likely to back assertive
   defence policies and seek a commitment to high levels of defence expenditure.

Critics argue that a political system oriented towards re-election has flaws
(King 1997). It encourages particularism. The making of public policy is biased
towards local and special interests at the expense of the national interest. It
places constituency service and campaigning before attention to legislation. It
encourages symbolic acts, such as the proposing of bills that have no chance of
success so as to gain publicity. Legislation will often not receive the attention
that is required. As each legislator struggles to promote his or her own constituency, deliberations end in gridlock, fragmentation and incoherence. Elections
become less competitive and are skewed towards the incumbent. Over 90 per
cent of Representatives and Senators are re-elected. There are fewer and fewer
marginal seats.

Some observers want to see Congress reformed to make it more of a deliberative assembly. It could then concentrate on its law-making function. Former
House Speaker Newt Gingrich wanted to strengthen the House's policy making
role and the *Contract with America* brought in reforms. They included independent audits for fraud and abuse, a reduction in the number of committees and
committee staff, a six-year limit on the period that committee chairmen would
serve, a ban on proxy voting whereby absent members pass their vote to
another member, a requirement that committee sittings be open to the public,
and a line item veto for the president. Some observers would like to see other
reforms to strengthen the deliberative nature of Congress as an institution.
These rest on a strengthening of the parties.

Others believe that Washington politics are too distant from the voters.
Congress is failing to fulfil its representative function. It was once a 'citizen-leg-
islature'. Today, those who are elected have become professionals who are tied
to a career structure. Within Congress, reforms have assigned too much power
to the leadership. It has become too partisan. Furthermore, the strength of
incumbency has encouraged arrogance and complacency.

From this perspective, *term limits* offer a partial answer. If such a constitutional amendment was adopted, a representative could only serve in a chamber
for a limited period. Reformers have suggested that an individual could be a
member of the House for only three terms or six years, and of the Senate for two
terms or twelve years. They claim that if term limits were introduced, Congress
would attract candidates who were more closely tied to those who elected them.
There would be fewer incumbents and more open, competitive elections.

However, term limits have also been criticised. Opponents argue that they would exclude the most experienced representatives. This would inevitably increase the political leverage of the federal bureaucracy and the aides who staff the Congressional committees.

Congress has been subjected to hostility from both the American voter and the mass media. However, although criticism is widespread, the nature of the reforms that are proposed depends on the way in which the two roles of Congress are perceived. What is an appropriate balance between them? Which of the 'two Congresses' should be strengthened?

References and further reading

Aberbach, J. D. (1990), *Keeping a Watchful Eye: The Politics of Congressional Oversight*, Washington, DC, The Brookings Institution.

Ashford, N. (1998), 'The Republican Party agenda and the conservative movement', in D. McSweeney and J. Owens, *The Republican Takeover of Congress*, London, Macmillan, 96–116.

Bennett, A. (1991), *American Government and Politics 1991*, Godalming.

Bennett, A. (1998), *American Government and Politics 1998*, Godalming.

Cigler, A. J. and B. A. Loomis (1995), 'Contemporary interest group politics: more than "more of the same"', in A. J. Cigler and B. A. Loomis, *Interest Group Politics*, Washington, DC: Congressional Quarterly, 393–406.

Congressional Quarterly (1997), *Powers of the Presidency*, Washington, DC, Congressional Quarterly.

Davidson, R. and W. Oleszek (1998), *Congress and its Members*, Washington, DC, Congressional Quarterly.

Fenno R. (1978), *Home Style: House Members in Their Districts*, Boston, Little, Brown.

Fiorina, M. (1989), *Congress: Keystone of the Washington Establishment*, New Haven, Yale University Press.

Griffith, E. S. (1976), *The American System of Government*, London, Methuen.

Hart, J. (1995), *The Presidential Branch: From Washington to Clinton*, Chatham, Chatham House.

Hibbing, J. R. and E. Theiss-Morse (1995), *Congress as Public Enemy: Public Attitudes toward American Political Institutions*, Cambridge, Cambridge University Press.

Jacobson, G. (1996) *The Politics of Congressional Elections*, New York, Longman.

Jones, C. (1995) *Separate but Equal Branches: Congress and the Presidency*, Chatham, Chatham House.

King, A. (1997), *Running Scared: Why Politicians Spend More Time Campaigning than Governing*, New York, Free Press.

Mayhew, D. R. (1974), *Congress: The Electoral Connection*, New Haven, Yale University Press.

Mayhew, D. R. (1991), *Divided We Govern*, New Haven, Yale University Press.

Mitchell, A. (1998), 'A new form of lobbying puts public face on private interest', *New York Times*, 30 September.

Owens, J. E. (1996), 'A return to party rule in the US Congress?', *Politics Review*, 6:1, September, 15–19.

Owens, J. E. (1998), 'Congress and partisan change', in G. Peele, C. J. Bailey, B. Cain and B. Guy Peters, *Developments in American Politics*, Basingstoke, Macmillan.

Sundquist, J. L. (1981), *The Decline and Resurgence of Congress*, Washington, DC, The Brookings Institution.

Woll, P. (1985), *Congress*, Boston, Little, Brown.

6

The president

The president is the most visible public representative of the American government. His powers are such that in the 1960s, some observers talked about the *imperial* presidency. However, his authority does not go unchallenged, and in practice, he is subject to a considerable number of constraints. Some believe that this has created an *imperilled* presidency that is unable to exercise its responsibilities. This chapter surveys the president's powers and the limitations that the other branches of government impose upon him.

The Constitution and the presidency

The US Constitution assigns relatively few specific powers to the president. He is America's head of state and, as such, undertakes ceremonial duties. He is Commander-in-Chief of the armed forces. He appoints senior government officials, Supreme Court Justices, and those who serve as US ambassadors abroad. As 'Chief Diplomat', he signs treaties with foreign nations on behalf of the US. He can, furthermore, veto proposed laws passed by Congress.

However, many of these powers are matched – or 'balanced' – by those assigned to Congress. Only Congress can declare war. A significant proportion of a president's appointments have to be confirmed by the Senate. Treaties are subject to ratification by a two-thirds majority in the Senate. The making of law and financial control – known as the 'power of the purse' – remain the prerogative of Congress. Furthermore, the president's ability to veto bills passed by Congress can be overridden by a two-thirds majority in both houses. Last, Congress has the power of impeachment. The Constitution states that a president can be tried by the Senate for 'treason, bribery, or other high crimes and misdemeanors'. If convicted, he is removed from office.

Presidential power and foreign policy

Although the Constitution was delicately constructed around a separation of powers and a system of checks and balances, the authority of the president grew during the course of the nineteenth century. In 1803, President Thomas Jefferson (1801–09) authorised the purchase of French Louisiana. Although this more than doubled the size of US territory, he made the decision without consulting Congress. In the Civil War, President Abraham Lincoln (1861–65) ordered the blockade of southern ports and increased the numbers enlisted in the army without Congressional authorisation. In the First World War (1917–18), President Woodrow Wilson played an important role in directing the war effort. He also promoted the presidency as the only nationally elected position in the US. From 1945 onwards, successive presidents had responsibility for the US nuclear arsenal. By the 1960s – when the Vietnam War was fought – the president had undoubted primacy or *hegemony* in the handling of defence policy and national security matters. This was the era of the 'imperial presidency', as Arthur Schlesinger Jr has described it. Congress – although sometimes vocal in its comments – played a subordinate role.

After Vietnam

The US had to face the prospect of defeat in Vietnam, and this led Congress to impose constraints on the president's ability to deploy troops overseas. For a short period, it seemed that there had been a fundamental shift in the balance of power between the executive and legislative branches of government. Nevertheless, by the early 1980s, commentators were talking of a 'resurgent presidency'. Under Ronald Reagan, the White House was again prepared – in at least certain circumstances – to authorise the use of US forces abroad.

Grenada is a small island in the Caribbean. Following a revolution, it aligned itself with Cuba and the Soviet bloc. In October 1983, a power struggle between different factions within the ruling New Jewel movement offered the US – and the Reagan administration – an opportunity to show that it was prepared to act against communism. US marines occupied Grenada, and the New Jewel movement was removed from power. However, Congress played a negligible role in all of this. Rapid military success, and widespread public support for the invasion, enabled the Reagan administration to keep Congressmen relegated to the sidelines.

In April 1986, following a terrorist attack against American servicemen and a clash between US and Libyan forces in the Mediterranean, the Reagan administration ordered American air attacks on Tripoli and other targets in Libya. These led to over 100 civilian deaths. Congressional leaders were invited to the White House only as the US bombers were approaching Libya. President Reagan argued that the action had been self-defence, and fell within his responsibilities as Commander-in-Chief.

Vietnam

The Vietnam War consolidated presidential hegemony and contributed to the emergence of what Arthur Schlesinger Jr termed 'the imperial presidency'. The war began by stealth. Following a war of independence against French colonial rule, the country was divided in 1954 between the North, under Communist rule, and the South, which had a western-leaning, although authoritarian, form of government.

The government of South Vietnam found itself facing guerilla insurgency. It was being attacked by the National Liberation Front (NLF, or 'Vietcong'). The NLF had the support of North Vietnam and its armed forces. US policy makers, who had between 1950 and 1954 backed the French, began to provide large-scale military backing for the South Vietnamese government. They were fearful that if South Vietnam collapsed, other countries in the region would also fall – like a row of dominoes – to the Communists.

During the Kennedy years, US military advisers played an increasingly visible role in supporting South Vietnam. In August 1964, there were reports that US naval ships had been attacked by the North Vietnamese, although it has been subsequently claimed that no such attack took place. Whatever the true circumstances, the US Congress responded by passing – virtually unanimously – the Gulf of Tonkin Resolution. This authorised President Lyndon Johnson to take 'all necessary measures to repel any armed attack against the forces of the US and to prevent further aggression'.

On the basis of the Resolution, the War escalated and large-scale military resources were committed to South-East Asia. For a decade, the US waged what has been described as a 'presidential war'. The increasingly vocal criticisms of the war made by the Senate Foreign Relations Committee had little effect.

American losses totalled 58,000 lives. These losses, and organised opposition to the war in the US, led to a policy of 'Vietnamisation', whereby the fighting was progressively handed over to the South Vietnamese. Negotiations with North Vietnam followed. However, although a peace agreement was signed with the North Vietnamese, it lasted only for a short period. In April 1975, the NLF and the North Vietnamese forces captured Saigon, and South Vietnam surrendered. Vietnam was reunited under Communist rule. The US had been defeated.

In December 1989, President Bush sent US troops into Panama. The attack – *Operation Just Cause* – followed a period of tension between the country's military ruler, General Manuel Noriega, who had been accused of involvement in the international drug trade, and the US. Noriega was arrested by US forces at the beginning of January, and, after a trial in Miami, imprisoned. President Bush ordered the withdrawal of the troops by the end of February 1990. The invasion took place while Congress was out of session.

Treaties and diplomacy

The president also has significant powers in his role as 'Chief Diplomat'. Although treaties with other nations require the 'advice and consent' of the Senate, successive presidents have drawn up *executive agreements* which do not require Senate assent. In 1940, President Franklin Roosevelt used an executive agreement to 'swap' fifty destroyers for air bases in the British Empire. This assisted the British war effort against Germany, and strengthened US strategic might in the Americas. Despite the long-term significance of the agreement for both countries, the Senate played no part in it.

Although Congress passed the Case Act in 1972, requiring that the Senate and House Foreign Relations Committees be notified of all executive agreements, this did nothing to stem their flow. Indeed, between 1985 and 1989, the Reagan White House signed 1,271 international agreements, only forty-seven of which were treaties. Furthermore, as John Dumbrell records, 'even the reporting provisions of the Case Act have been evaded and undermined by persistent executive delay' (1997: 135).

Presidential hegemony

Why does the presidency have primacy in the making of defence and foreign policy, and why, as a corollary, has Congress been relegated to the sidelines? The Constitution put the president in a strong position, but those who endorse the 'presidential hegemony' thesis identify a number of reasons why his authority has grown still further:

1   During the forty years of the Cold War, a succession of crises took place – most notably Berlin, Korea, Hungary and Cuba – and there was a very real prospect of all-out conflict between the superpowers. The US needed the capacity to offer an immediate military response, and only the president had the ability to do this. As Clinton Rossiter has noted in a celebrated phrase: 'secrecy, dispatch, unity, continuity, and access to information – the ingredients of successful diplomacy – are properties of his office, and Congress . . . possesses none of them' (1963: 26). Congress is, furthermore, the critics note, a parochial and inherently short-term institution. Members of the House of Representatives, in particular, have their eyes on the next election, which will always be less than two years away. Their interests and concerns may not extend beyond those of their home district.
       Congress is also a slow and bureaucratic institution. When faced by drought and famine in Africa, Congress took four months to agree upon a $60 million emergency aid package. The Senate discussed thirty-six amendments.
2   It is the executive branch that takes the initiative. Through the military chain of command, the president orders troops into action. Congress can only respond to decisions taken within the executive branch.

3 In practice, Congress has often held back and acquiesced in administration decisions. The reason for this lies in the widely shared consensus about foreign and defence policy goals that lasted throughout the Cold War. For example, against the background of the Korean War, Congress allowed US forces to fight against North Korean and Chinese troops, despite Truman's failure to consult or seek approval. The consensus is still – to a large extent – maintained today, and shared, albeit with different degrees of emphasis, by both liberals and conservatives.

4 The Supreme Court has also played a role in bolstering presidential authority. In 1937, in *US v. Belmont*, the Court ruled that executive agreements had parity with treaties, and should be considered the 'supreme law of the land'. A year earlier, in the case of *US v. Curtiss-Wright Export Corporation*, the Court had confirmed that the president was 'the sole organ of the federal government in the field of international affairs'.

5 'Presidential determinations' allow the commitment of forces, funds and assistance if, in the eyes of the president, it is essential for the security of the US. Congress does not have to give specific authorisation. For example, the president can use 'drawdown' authority to transfer military equipment from one country to another. He can also reallocate funding to another theatre of operations. In 1993, for example, President Clinton provided economic assistance to Mexico and supported peacekeeping forces in Liberia on this basis (Ragsdale 1996: 335).

6 The scale and character of the executive branch of government prevents effective Congressional oversight or scrutiny. The federal bureaucracy has over two million employees. Many of the president's immediate aides in the Executive Office of the President (EOP) are not subject to Senate confirmation. The role of the bureaucracy is surveyed in Chapter 7.

7 In a period preceding military action, members of Congress may well be uncertain about public opinion. A mission may, or may not, gain majority backing. Often, it will depend upon the success or failure of a particular strike or the level of American casualties. In practice, this may lead members of Congress to adopt a 'wait and see' policy. They will hold back from active intervention at the time when crucial decisions are being made.

Presidential power and domestic policy

According to those who talk in terms of relatively unrestrained presidential power, the president is a pivotal figure in the making of domestic as well as foreign policy. New responsibilities were progressively added to those specified in the Constitution. Presidents, from Thomas Jefferson onwards, have acted as party leaders. They have also become the nation's 'Chief Legislator'. Ever since Franklin Roosevelt assumed the presidency in 1933, it has become customary for presidents to initiate and propose a legislative programme, a package of measures that they wish to see enacted into law.

For example, Ronald Reagan offered a conservative 'revolution', and his campaign for the presidency rested on a promise of decentralisation, military rearmament, tax cuts and deregulation. He hoped to liberate business from what he regarded as restrictive government policies, and thereby generate economic growth. On taking office, Bill Clinton also had a specific series of reforms in mind. His plans included tax reductions for the 'middle class', an 'economic stimulus package' that would accelerate recovery from the 1990–91 recession, the balancing of the federal budget and the reform of health care. Although there are always tensions between the White House and Capitol Hill, presidents can generally use the authority of their office and their powers of patronage to ensure that the measures they support are passed by Congress.

The president also has the ability to issue *executive orders*. These are directives or 'instructions' that stem from legislation already passed by Congress or from the president's constitutional powers. They do not therefore require Congressional approval. Until 1933, executive orders were generally confined to administrative matters. However, since then, they have had greater significance. On taking office, in the midst of economic depression, President Franklin Roosevelt ordered a four-day closure of the banks. In 1942, Executive Order 9066 interned Japanese-Americans living in California when it was feared that they might assist Japanese military actions against the US. In 1948, President Truman used an executive order to desegegrate the armed forces. In 1957, President Eisenhower used an executive order to 'federalise' the Arkansas National Guard so as to allow black students to enrol at Little Rock Central High School. On assuming office in 1993, President Clinton cancelled the executive orders issued by his two predecessors that had imposed a 'gag rule' preventing counsellors at federally funded family planning clinics discussing the possibility of an abortion with clients.

The federal budget

The president, aided by the Office of Management and Budget (OMB), also shapes the federal government's annual budget. The executive branch initiates the budget process, and is therefore well placed to ensure that the budget that is eventually passed by Congress corresponds to its political goals. As Plano and Greenberg note, the Budget's 'size and specificity tend to reduce legislative discretion' (1989: 163). Some presidents have had particular success. President Reagan co-ordinated the 1981 budget process with his supporters in Congress. In May of that year – the time when Congress adopts budget resolutions setting overall spending ceilings – Congressional committees were directed to impose large-scale reductions in expenditure. Even in October 1998, when President Clinton's authority was at a very low ebb following the House of Representatives' decision to initiate impeachment hearings, he was able to win significant concessions from the Republican majority in Congress. These included a $1.1-billion plan to employ 100,000 additional teachers. As *The*

New York Times concluded, those who asserted that the president had been 'terminally weakened . . . underestimated the president's resilience and the inherent authority of the office' (1998).

Managing the economy

From 1933 onwards, when President Franklin Roosevelt took office, presidents have been held responsible for the nation's economic progress and prosperity. This coincided with a change in economic thinking. The federal government budget was increasingly regarded as an instrument of macroeconomic policy. Spending and taxation were to be used so as to modify the business cycle and increase overall employment levels. The 1946 Employment Act confirmed the president's role as 'manager of the economy'. He was 'to avoid economic fluctuations (and) . . . maintain employment, production and purchasing power'.

To some extent, the 'Reagan Revolution' of the 1980s modified expectations that an administration could or should direct a nation's economy in this way. Nevertheless – as polls confirm – the president is still held largely responsible for the country's economic fortunes. George Bush's loss of the 1992 presidential election is widely attributed to the recession that preceded it. In 1991, the economy contracted, and national output fell by 0.9 per cent. In the following year, unemployment rose to 7.5 per cent. Conversely, Bill Clinton's re-election victory in 1996 owed much to relative economic prosperity. The *Wall Street Journal* talked in terms of the 'Goldilocks economy', that was neither too 'hot' nor too 'cold', and in which both inflation and unemployment had been reduced to a minimum.

Presidential vetoes, 1945–96

	All bills vetoed	Regular vetoes	Pocket vetoes	Vetoes overridden
Truman	250	180	70	12
Eisenhower	181	73	108	2
Kennedy	21	12	9	0
Johnson	30	16	14	0
Nixon	43	26	17	7
Ford	66	48	18	12
Carter	31	13	18	2
Reagan	78	39	39	9
Bush	44	29	15	1
Clinton*	17	17	0	1

Note: * Clinton – until the end of 1996.
Source: Congressional Quarterly 1997: 87.

The power of veto

The president has the constitutional right to veto legislation passed by Congress. If he wishes to do this, Article I specifies that he must send a statement to Congress within ten days of a bill being passed, setting out his reasons for refusing to sign it. A presidential veto can only be overridden by a two-thirds majority in both houses, which is difficult to muster. President Woodrow Wilson regarded the veto as a very powerful weapon indeed. It 'is, of course, beyond all comparison, his most formidable prerogative' (Ragsdale 1996: 365).

Presidential veto has, at times, been used extensively. For example, President Ford vetoed fifty-three bills. By the summer of 1990 – just eighteen months after taking office – George Bush had vetoed thirteen bills. None of these vetoes were overridden. Indeed, a 1996 estimate suggested that since the founding of the US, only 0.7 per cent of vetoes had been overridden (Ragsdale 1996: 365).

The president can also employ the *pocket veto*. If the president does not sign a bill within a ten-day period, and Congress has, by this time, adjourned, the bill does not pass into law. Since the early 1970s, it has been accepted that the pocket veto can only be used immediately before the end of a two-year Congressional term, rather than during the days preceding a recess. However, despite this, the pocket veto has been used exhaustively. For example, President Reagan (1981–89) issued thirty-nine pocket vetoes as well as thirty-nine regular vetoes.

However, the use of the veto may be an indication of presidential weakness rather than strength. George Bush frequently threatened a veto so as to gain legislative concessions from the governing Democrats in Congress. At first sight, this appears to have been an effective strategy. Congressional leaders held back from committing themselves to legislation unless they felt that they had a two-thirds – or 'veto-proof' – majority in both houses (Mervin 1996: 116). There is, however, another perspective. Bush may have been compelled to adopt

---

The line-item veto

In 1996, Congress added the *line-item veto* to the president's armoury. It enabled a president to delete individual items in 'appropriations' (expenditure) bills. Although the line-item veto could be overridden by a two-thirds majority in both houses of Congress, it undoubtedly could have strengthened the president's hand in his dealings with the legislative branch. He could, for example, eliminate 'pork' – spending items that benefited a particular member of Congress's district and were included so as to win that member's support in Congressional votes – from legislation. In the past, presidents had either had to accept or veto bills in their entirety. However, in June 1998, in *Clinton v. City of New York*, the US Supreme Court declared by a 6–3 majority that the line-item veto was unconstitutional.

a confrontational approach because he lacked other political resources. The veto is, furthermore, a *negative* instrument. It offers a way of blocking legislation, but it cannot be used to create the type of legislation that a president wishes to see.

Emergency powers

The Constitution does not include references to emergencies or crises. However, presidents have assumed certain powers during periods of economic uncertainty and natural disasters, and times of civil unrest. These powers have included limits on individual freedoms, such as travel restrictions, and the imposition of controls over property and communications. The system by which states of emergency are declared was rationalised under the 1976 National Emergencies Act. This requires that the president specifies the basis for a declaration, transmits information about it to Congress, and allows Congress to bring it to a conclusion after six months have elapsed (Congressional Quarterly 1997: 51).

Limits and constraints

There is, however, another perspective on the US presidency. Despite his powers, some observers argue that the president remains subject to a number of severe constraints. Joseph A. Califano Jr, who served in both Lyndon Johnson's and Jimmy Carter's administrations, claimed that Congress had 'become the King Kong of Washington's political jungle, dominating an executive branch that can no longer claim the co-equal status that the Founding Fathers saw as crucial' (1996: 112). In another allusion to a work of fiction, the president has been likened to Gulliver, who was held down by tiny Lilliputian ropes in Jonathan Swift's classic satire. The ability of Congress to impose its will, and curtail presidential ambitions, was starkly illustrated in 1919–20 when President Woodrow Wilson submitted the Treaty of Versailles to the US Senate. Fearful of further entanglements in European affairs, the Senate put forward amendments, and following the rejection of these, refused ratification. In the wake of this, the US followed an *isolationist* course for two decades.

Fifty years after the Treaty of Versailles was defeated, the constraints on a US president were again graphically illustrated. The shock of military defeat in Vietnam was compounded by other blows to the credibility of the presidency. It became clear that the Nixon administration had used federal government agencies, such as the Internal Revenue Service (IRS), to harass its opponents. The Watergate scandal, which involved an attempt by the president and his aides to hide White House involvement in a bid to plant listening devices in a Democratic Party campaign office, finally led to President Nixon's resignation in August 1974. While the Nixon White House sought to save itself, Congress began to reassert its authority. Steps were taken to 'contain' the powers of the presidency. These measures encouraged some observers to talks in terms of the imperilled or *impaired* presidency.

All the President's Men

Director: Alan J. Pakula (1976)
Starring: Robert Redford, Dustin Hoffman

All the President's Men follows the unravelling of the Watergate scandal. It recounts the investigative work of Carl Bernstein and Bob Woodward, two *Washington Post* reporters. The story starts with a simple break-in at Democratic Party campaign offices in the Watergate building in Washington, DC. Working on hunches, tip-offs and leads, Bernstein and Woodward begin to appreciate that individuals working at the highest levels in the White House are involved. The film is long (138 minutes) and sometimes difficult to follow, but is a classic of political cinema.

The War Powers Resolution

The War Powers Resolution of 1973 – and the War Powers Act which confirmed it in the following year – stated that a president can only commit US troops in 'hostilities' abroad if there is a declaration of war, specific Congressional authorisation, or a national emergency. Unless war is declared, or some other form of authorisation granted by Congress, the troops must withdraw after sixty days. A further thirty-day period is permitted for the withdrawal process, should this prove necessary. The president was also required to consult with Congress 'in every possible instance'.

For President Richard Nixon, the War Powers Act removed 'authorities which the president had properly exercised under the Constitution for almost 200 years'. He, and subsequent presidents, denied its constitutionality. Henry Kissinger, President Nixon's National Security Adviser, also saw the Resolution, and the other measures adopted by Congress, as a fundamental shift in the character of relations between the legislative and executive branches: 'The decade-long struggle in this country over executive dominance in foreign affairs is over. The recognition that the Congress is a co-equal branch is the dominant fact of national politics today' (quoted in Foley and Owens 1996: 372).

The War Powers Act was applied, albeit in a loose form. In 1983, President Reagan sent US forces to the Lebanon. Congress responded by 'starting the clock' established under the Act, although the President was given eighteen months rather than the ninety days specified by the Resolution. However, in the aftermath of a brutally effective terrorist attack, when a suicide bombing led to the deaths of 219 Americans, the President withdrew the troops.

Congress took other steps – aside from the War Powers Act – to rein in the president in his handling of foreign and defence policy:

1 The 1974 Jackson–Vanik Amendment inserted clauses into a trade bill insisting upon the right of Jews to emigrate from the Soviet Union.
2 In 1976, Cuban military forces were deployed in Angola so as to support the Soviet-aligned government against Western-oriented guerilla armies. Although the US is traditionally fearful of Cuban operations, Congress was haunted by the prospect of another Vietnam, and specifically denied funding for military activities in the country.
3 In 1980, President Jimmy Carter withdrew SALT-II – the Strategic Arms Limitation Treaty – that he had concluded with the USSR, once it had become clear that, in the aftermath of the Soviet invasion of Afghanistan, the Treaty would be rejected by the Senate.
4 In 1986, Congress imposed trade sanctions against South Africa, as a protest against the country's system of racial *apartheid*, despite a presidential veto.

Three foreign policy dilemmas in the early and mid-1990s illustrate the way in which foreign policy making has changed since Vietnam. Rather than acting unilaterally, President Bush sought Congressional backing just before hostilities began in the Gulf War of 1991. The Senate agreed by fifty-two to forty-seven votes. The House backed military action against the Iraqi forces by 250 to 183.

Almost two years later, just before his presidency came to an end, President Bush launched *Operation Restore Hope*. This was a response to events in Somalia, where the people faced mass famine, and the country was being torn apart by gangs and rival warlords. The mission was an attempt to secure an environment in which humanitarian relief could be distributed to those in need. The US sent 28,000 troops and other nations sent 2,000. However, the difficulties were underestimated, and within months, eighteen US servicemen had been killed. Five months later, President Clinton yielded to Congressional pressure (from both Democrats and Republicans), and the troops were withdrawn at the end of March 1994.

At the end of 1995, President Clinton committed 20,000 US troops as part of a NATO-led force responsible for policing the peace agreement in Bosnia. There were serious doubts about the deployment in both the House of Representatives and the Senate. As New Hampshire Republican Senator Robert C. Smith put it, 'we've earned the right . . . to sit this one out' (Towell and Cassata 1995: 3818). Although Robert Dole, as Senate Majority Leader, engineered a compromise in the Senate, the House almost invoked 'the power of the purse'. A proposal to withdraw funding for the US military presence in Bosnia was only defeated by 210 to 218 votes.

Loss of primacy

Why, from this perspective, has the president lost much of his authority in the making of foreign and defence policy? First, there was a shift in attitude towards government, and the White House in particular, in the wake of the Watergate crisis and the Vietnam debacle. They were discredited. Furthermore, the communications revolution of the 1980s contributed to changes in the political atmosphere. Earlier, instinctive loyalties towards the president were undermined. Policy units (or 'think-tanks') emerged, and the proliferation of news channels such as CNN broke down White House hegemony over information and analysis. As Michael Foley and John Owens note:

> Instead of a near monopoly of foreign policy information and reflexive Cold War deference to presidential judgement, presidents are now besieged by a multiplicity of groups and organisations not only with information sources and evaluation techniques of their own but with the means and willingness to challenge a president's foreign policy decisions on tactical, strategic, and ethical grounds. (1996: 380)

Furthermore, in the 1990s, the ending of the Cold War placed the foreign and defence policy consensus under considerable strain. Whereas some have called for a return to isolationism, others argue that the US should – given its position as a superpower – promote democracy across the globe, 'police' troublespots, and play a leading role in international organisations such as the United Nations (UN). The removal of the Soviet threat has allowed these different opinions and strategies to flourish.

Trade policy

If foreign trade policy is brought into the picture, the president faces further obstacles. The North American Free Trade Agreement (NAFTA) phases out trade restrictions between the US, Canada and Mexico. Under its provisions, all tariff barriers between the three countries are to be eliminated by 2000. When NAFTA came to a vote in November 1994, it passed in the House by a majority of 234 to 200, and gained a 61–38 majority in the Senate.

However, it was only passed after protracted discussions had taken place and President Clinton had assembled a coalition of support within each house. Trade policy is subject to political bartering and negotiation because:

1 In other areas of defence and foreign policy, there are feelings of national loyalty towards the president in his role as Commander-in-Chief or as a statesman on the world stage. Such considerations are much less of a factor in the formulation of trade policy.
2 Some of the most effective pressure groups – including large-scale corporations and the labour unions – have much at stake in the future of trade policy. They are involved in lobbying activities. Whereas most business organisations endorse the principle of free trade, and believe that it will increase company profitability, many in the unions – and some businessmen

in 'exposed' industries – fear that unrestricted trade with low-wage countries will destroy US jobs.

3 These lobbies are represented within both the major political parties. Sections of the Democratic Party – represented by, for example, House Minority Leader Dick Gephardt – are closely tied to the trade unions, and are suspicious of free trade. There is also a protectionist strand of opinion within the Republican Party which is personified by Patrick Buchanan. However, although Buchanan has won some support from Republican voters in a number of primaries, his calls for the imposition of restrictions on imports have won less backing from Republicans on Capitol Hill.

Although the NAFTA was a success for the presidency, there have been setbacks. The freeing up of trade – and the progressive elimination of tariff barriers – is dependent upon the ability of presidents to gain 'fast-track authority' from Congress. The process was first established in 1974. It rests on an undertaking from Congress that they will consider trade agreements concluded by the administration with other nations as a matter of priority, and that amendments will not be submitted. Armed with fast-track authority, presidents can negotiate with other governments from a position of mutual confidence. The NAFTA was considered on this basis. Without fast-track authority, any discussions with other countries have limited credibility.

In November 1997, President Clinton sought fast-track authority for further international trade deals. He had hoped to expand NAFTA to include Chile, and to create a Free Trade Area of the Americas by 2005. His longer-term vision rested on the construction of a free-trade area stretching across the Pacific Ocean by about 2020.

Clinton was, however, unable to win fast-track authority from Congress. Only about 40 of the 205 Democrats in the House of Representatives endorsed the proposal. The degree of opposition within the Democratic Party reflected the continuing fears of the labour unions about free trade. The President might have been able to construct a majority based around the votes of Republican Congressmen. However, the predictions suggested that he would still have been about thirty votes short of an overall majority, and, in the face of this, the administration decided to withdraw the proposal.

Monetary and fiscal policy

The president's domestic policy powers are also limited. Although the president is 'manager of the economy', his administration has only limited authority over the country's monetary policy. The setting of interest rates is the prerogative of the Federal Reserve Board. Furthermore, although the federal government's annual budget is initially proposed by the president, and he is the key figure in shaping its character, it must be agreed by Congress. A budget is the product of prolonged negotiation and compromise. As David Mervin notes, the eventual outcome 'may be quite at odds with the president's original intention' (1990: 104).

George Bush learned this lesson in an episode that contributed to his loss of the presidency. His 1988 election victory owed much to the soundbite: 'Read my lips. No new taxes.' Faced, however, with spending commitments and an entrenched budget deficit, the 1990 Budget included both tax increases and expenditure cuts. Opposed by both conservative Republicans – who opposed the tax increases – and Democrats – who rejected cuts in welfare provision – the initial budget was defeated in the House of Representatives. The White House and Congress agreed to a revised version, increasing tax revenues by $140 billion over a five-year period, which was passed at the end of October 1990. Bush's opponents repeatedly cited this 'betrayal' in the 1992 presidential election.

There are other constraints upon the president's fiscal – or budgetary – powers. The 1974 Budget and Impoundment Control Act prevented a president withholding funds that had been allocated for a particular purpose by Congress. (President Nixon had, for example, cut about $9 billion from funds appropriated for the Environmental Protection Agency.) The Act specified that funds cannot be 'impounded' by the Administration unless both houses of Congress approve of the action within forty-five days. The Act also created the Congressional Budget Office (CBO). The CBO provides specialist economic analysis, and therefore enables members of Congress to take an independent look at the economic projections drawn up by the executive branch.

Films and the US president

Early representations of presidents were simple hagiographies. They told the life histories of celebrated figures such as Abraham Lincoln and offered them up as national icons.

In some ways, Oliver Stone's film, *JFK* (1991) echoes this by portraying President Kennedy in uncritical terms. He was, the film suggests, assassinated by conspirators acting on behalf of powerful businessmen and military leaders. Although an utterly different film, Rob Reiner's *The American President* (1995) also offers a sympathetic portrait of the president. It is both a romantic tale and a plea for more assertively liberal politics.

However, these are exceptions. Most recent films reflect the growing public disillusionment with Washington politicians. They depict the president in profoundly critical terms. Stone's *Nixon* (1995) suggests that its subject (played by Anthony Hopkins) sold his soul to elite political forces. *Dave* (1993) tells of an ordinary, decent citizen (Kevin Kline) who takes the place of an unpleasant and corrupt president. In *Wag the Dog* (1998), a war is faked by presidential aides so as to divert attention from a sex scandal. In both, as Mark Lawson has noted, ' the leader of the free world is at best a scumbag and at worst a psychopath' (*Guardian*, 23 September 1998).

Federalism

The president faces a further set of constraints. In contrast with those who lead nations that have a *unitary* structure – where political power is concentrated in the hands of the central government – the US has a *federal* structure. Power is distributed between Washington, DC and the individual states. In a number of policy spheres, therefore, decision-making has to be a negotiated process between the president, Congress, state governors and state legislatures. This is explored in Chapter 8.

Appointments

Although he has the power to nominate ambassadors, Cabinet members, other senior officials in the federal bureaucracy (see Chapter 7) and federal judges, his power of appointment is subject to Senate confirmation. This is not necessarily a straightforward process. In 1987, President Reagan nominated a well-known conservative jurist, Robert Bork, to the Supreme Court bench. The Senate Judiciary Committee – guided by prominent Democrats such as Edward Kennedy and Joseph Biden – asserted that Bork's views disqualified him from serving on the Court. He was rejected. Subsequently, in 1989, President Bush nominated a former Senator, John Tower, as Secretary of Defense. However, in March 1989, allegations about Tower's personal life and his relationships with companies seeking military contracts led Senators to reject the nomination by fifty-three votes to forty-seven (Parmet 1997: 379).

Investigations

Recent presidents and their senior staff have been subject to investigation by independent counsels. Under the 1978 Ethics in Government Act – adopted in the aftermath of Watergate – these special prosecutors are appointed, if the

---

The president and the Internet

The US president has a website at:

http://www.whitehouse.gov/

This provides biographical information about the president, the vice-president and their families, a virtual tour of the building, an audio-visual library of speeches, reports on recent initiatives, and the *Interactive Citizens' Handbook*. This gives access to federal government agencies and commissions. The president can also be e-mailed at:

president@whitehouse.gov

Attorney-General considers it warranted, to investigate allegations of law-breaking at the highest levels of government. They report to Congress. Between 1979 and 1998, there have been twenty independent counsel investigations, the most well known of which was Kenneth Starr's inquiry into President Clinton's financial affairs, personal behaviour and legal testimony. His report provided the basis for impeachment proceedings against Clinton.

The powers of the Supreme Court

Although the Supreme Court played a role in strengthening the powers of the presidency, some rulings have curtailed the president's freedom of action. Significant components of the New Deal were struck down in rulings such as *Schechter Poultry Corporation v. US* (1935) and *US v. Butler* (1936). The Court regarded the government interventionism upon which the New Deal rested as a threat to individual liberties and rights.

President Truman's administration took control of steel mills when they were threatened by strike action. There were fears that industrial action would interrupt supplies destined for the Korean War effort. The Court ruled in *Youngstown Sheet and Tube Company v. Sawyer* (1952) that the president's action had been unconstitutional. He had exceeded his powers.

In 1974, the Supreme Court played a role in the Watergate crisis. Its judgement in *US v. Richard M. Nixon* circumscribed the concept of 'executive privilege' by ruling that the president must release transcripts of the tape recordings that had been made of his conversations with aides. In the 1990s, the president's sphere of privacy was narrowed down still further. In a succession of court battles, arising from an allegation of sexual harassment against President Clinton and Kenneth Starr's investigations, it was established that civil proceedings could be brought against a sitting president, and White House political and legal advisers could be questioned and compelled to answer under oath.

Public and press attitudes

The Vietnam War and the Watergate scandal changed attitudes towards the presidency. Up until then, the mass media had been largely deferential. The Washington press corps was, for example, familiar with much of President Kennedy's private life, yet felt that such matters should not be reported.

From the early 1970s onwards – when the involvement of White House personnel in the Watergate scandal became known through the efforts of *Washington Post* reporters – it has been considered legitimate to investigate and expose the private lives of the president and other politicians. In the 1990s, the Internet allowed news to spread beyond the ranks of Washington insiders, and encouraged reports to become more speculative and less dependent on hard evidence. The White House has thereby become subject to closer and harsher scrutiny than ever before.

Measuring presidential success: CQ ratings

Congressional Quarterly is a respected Washington journal. In 1953, it established a system of measurement by which presidential success and failure could be assessed.

The *CQ rating* – as it has become known – is based on formal, 'roll-call' votes in Congress. The rating measures the proportion of these where the president 'took a clear position', and his position was subsequently endorsed in a roll-call vote by Congressmen. It is expressed as a percentage.

Presidents Eisenhower and Johnson come out particularly well. In some years, they attracted CQ ratings of over 80 per cent. Others, however, have fared much less well. President Bush sank to 43 per cent in 1992. In 1973, Richard Nixon gained a rating of only just over 50 per cent. President Bill Clinton's 36.2 per cent score in 1995 represented an all-time low. However, Clinton recovered from this and there was a dramatic improvement during the course of 1996. His rating reached 55.1 per cent, an increase of 18.9 per cent. This was the biggest one-year jump since *Congressional Quarterly* began its system of ratings.

CQ ratings have, however, been criticised. Some observers claim that they are misleading:

1 They treat all votes and legislative proposals equally. There is no attempt to include an assessment of the relative importance or unimportance of a particular measure.
2 Many important issues do not come to a roll-call vote. This is sometimes because a voice vote is taken. It may also be that opposition to the president's proposals is so overwhelming that they are dropped before being formally considered by Congress. In 1994, the plan to reform health-care provision drawn up by Hillary Rodham Clinton and Ira Magaziner, a key presidential aide, had to be abandoned once it became clear it had very little support. It was never submitted to any form of vote.
3 The legislation that the CQ rating measures is not necessarily representative. Since the 1960s, presidents have only taken a position on about a quarter of the legislation put to a roll-call vote in Congress. Arguably, they have been reluctant to adopt a formal position where defeat is likely (Ragsdale 1996: 360).
4 CQ ratings make no attempt to distinguish between presidents who face a Congress dominated by the other party and those who do not. As David Mervin notes, this 'makes a mockery of simple comparisons between, say, Johnson and Nixon, or even Carter and Bush' (Mervin 1996: 112).

Further reading

Congressional Quarterly Weekly Report, 21 December 1996, 3428.

Appraising the arguments

Although both perspectives have their proponents, there are grounds for concluding that the presidency is neither 'imperial' nor 'impaired'. Both terms are inappropriate. There are significant differences between a president's powers in the formulation of defence, foreign and domestic policy. Indeed, some have talked in terms of 'two presidencies'. As Commander-in-Chief the president has, despite the periodic attempts to rein in his authority, had a relatively free hand in deploying US troops. Once a formal request had been made, Congress took only four days to agree to the use of US troops just before hostilities began in the Gulf War. The War Powers Act has not, in practice, tied his hands. Even where Congress has been unenthusiastic, as it was towards the peacekeeping missions in the former Yugoslavia, the president was able to ensure that his view prevailed. As events in the Lebanon and Somalia confirm, Congress has only been able to impose small policy modifications or speed up processes that were already under way.

However, a president's powers are much more restricted in other areas of policy making. Domestic policy always involves bargaining and compromise. He is also limited in his capacity to shape foreign policy where defence or national security considerations are not a factor.

Fluctuations

As well as drawing a distinction between different areas of policy making, there is a further reason why the concepts of an 'imperial' or 'impaired' presidency should be treated cautiously. The relationship between the president and the other branches of government is subject to fluctuations. It is never static. In practice, a number of factors shape its character at any point in time. These include:

Partisanship

Some argue that the president faces particular difficulty during periods of 'divided government'. This is when one party holds a majority on Capitol Hill and the other party occupies the White House. The Democrats controlled Congress for almost all of the period between 1933 and 1995, and Republican presidents faced hostile Congressional majorities. The US again had divided government after the November 1994 elections, when the Republicans won a majority in both houses of Congress while President Clinton, a Democrat, occupied the White House. There were particular tensions because the House Republicans were committed to the *Contract with America*, a platform of reforming measures that included welfare reform and a pledge to take action against crime. At the time, it was seen by observers as an attempt by former House Speaker Newt Gingrich to usurp the president's role as 'Chief Legislator'.

There have been claims that gridlock – when the process of decision making comes to a halt because the White House and Capitol Hill have conflicting goals and priorities – is the inevitable outcome of divided government. However, the 1994 Republican victories led President Clinton to seek a policy of co-operation. Furthermore, even when both the executive and legislative branches are controlled by the same party, there are no assurances of success. For example, in 1979, President Jimmy Carter's plan for energy conservation was rejected, despite a Democratic majority in both houses of Congress. Similarly, President Clinton had to abandon his 1993 plans for health-care reform because of Congressional opposition. David Mayhew has concluded, in a study of Congress's legislative and oversight record between 1945 and 1960, that 'it does not seem to make all that much difference whether party control of American government happens to be unified or divided' (1991: 198). The desire of both branches of government to claim legislative accomplishments encourages compromise and accommodation.

Public opinion

Public opinion can either strengthen or weaken a president. Congress is, as James Q. Wilson has recorded, reluctant to oppose a popular president: 'Other things being equal, the more popular the president, the higher the proportion of his bills that Congress will pass' (1992: 344). Although President Eisenhower (1953–61) was able to maintain relatively high approval ratings throughout his period of office, presidents generally enjoy a fairly brief 'honeymoon' with the US public. After a year or so, their popularity usually begins to slip.

Congressional structures

Changes in the structure and organisation of Congress have had an impact on presidential–Congressional relations. From the 1970s onwards, the structures of Congress became much more decentralised and fragmented. Traditionally, power within Congress lay in the hands of the committee chairmen. Although the 'barons' still hold considerable authority, their position has been weakened by measures such as the Legislative Reorganisation Act of 1970, which required committees to abide by formal rules of procedure rather than follow the, often arbitrary, rulings of the chairman. The devolution of power to sub-committees and the growth of a more independent spirit within Congress also made it more difficult for presidents to construct coalitions that would enable the legislation they favoured to pass into law.

The craft of persuasion

For Richard Neustadt (1967), the power of the president rests upon his 'power to persuade'. Because of the constraints imposed upon him, a president can only achieve his policy goals through a crafted strategy of negotiation and bartering.

Clinton as 'persuader'

In the aftermath of the Republican victories in the 1994 Congressional elections, the Clinton White House pursued a strategy of *triangulation*. The President repositioned himself politically. He had always been on the right of the Democratic Party, but from 1994 onwards, he sought to distance himself further from the 'tax and spend' Democrats in Congress and make a partial shift towards the Republicans.

Why did he adopt this strategy? In part, Clinton had his eye on the 1996 presidential election. The 1994 Republican victories showed that more conservative policies were required if he was to win back public opinion. He also needed the consent and co-operation of Congress if legislation was to be passed. As Richard Neustadt observed in his classic discussion of relations between the executive and legislative branches: 'their formal powers are so intertwined that neither will accomplish very much, for very long, without the acquiescence of the other' (1967: 37). For both these reasons, Clinton began to adopt more overtly conservative thinking:

1 He promised 100,000 more police on the streets and the extension of the death penalty.
2 In July 1995, he issued a five-year programme to ensure that the federal government budget would be in surplus rather than deficit by the year 2000.
3 He endorsed calls for a return to more traditional moral and social values through the introduction of curfews for teenagers, school uniform, and the V-chip which would allow parental control over their children's television viewing. He readily signed a bill denying federal recognition of same-sex marriages.

Particular skills are required. As Nigel Bowles has noted: 'Congress will not be bludgeoned into submission, as Nixon learned to his cost; it must be courted into partnership, as Carter learned to his' (1987: 3). Although both houses had a Democratic majority, President Jimmy Carter had a particularly difficult relationship with Congress. As a former governor of Georgia, he was regarded as a Washington outsider. His staff lacked experience of Congress. He had only a limited strategic agenda and there were difficulties establishing a sense of political direction. The House leadership was sidelined. The president's powers of appointment, which can be used to win allies within Congress, were largely squandered.

Other presidents have been more successful. Lyndon Johnson was a former Senate Majority Leader, and used his persuasive skills to build coalitions of support for his civil rights legislation and the 'war on poverty'. President Reagan adopted a strategy based on the setting of inflated goals. As Martin Anderson, the President's chief adviser on domestic and economic policy issues, notes, Reagan 'almost always got more than he would have been willing

4 He announced in his January 1996 State of the Union Address that 'the age of big government is over'.
5 He modified the welfare reform bill, proposed by the Republicans in the *Contract with America*, but at the same time accepted all its defining features.

However, there were limits to his accommodation with Republicanism. Although he adopted some aspects of their thinking, Clinton also criticised some of the more unpopular issues that they had pursued. He thereby established a distinct political identity. For example, he accepted the need for fiscal restraint, but at the same time, opposed many of the spending cuts proposed by the Republicans. He took a vigorous stand against tobacco smoking, whereas most Republicans talked in terms of individual choice. He defended Medicare – the system of health provision for the elderly – against what he successfully but inaccurately portrayed as Republican determination to bring it to an end. He remained committed to government action to protect and preserve the environment. He was able to depict the conservative Right – particularly House Speaker Newt Gingrich – as 'extreme' in contrast with his own 'moderation'.

Clinton's approach paid off. There was talk of a 'partnership' between the president and Congress. He also immunised himself from many of the criticisms made by Republican opponents in the months preceding the November 1996 presidential election.

Further reading

Drew, E. (1996), *Showdown: The Struggle Between the Gingrich Congress and the Clinton White House*, New York, Touchstone.

to settle for, because in the beginning he instinctively asked for far more than he could reasonably expect to get' (1988: 241).

There are different assessments of President Clinton during the early phases of his period in office. John Owens sees the President's approach during his first year in office as 'skilful', and cites his 'hands-on' style (1994: 8). Clinton was, Owens argues, an effective communicator who employed experienced staff in the all-important Office of Legislative Affairs – the Congressional liaison office located in the west wing of the White House. His skills ensured a number of important legislative successes such as the passage of the 1993 budget, and the 'motor voter' bill that enables citizens to register as voters rather more easily. Clinton's skills in ensuring that Congress passed NAFTA have attracted particular praise. He not only constructed a bipartisan coalition in both houses, but 'defined the issue, took the propaganda initiative, demonstrated considerable legislative finesse and made the necessary compromises and bargains to overcome opposition within his own party to win the vote' (Foley and Owens 1996: 305–6).

The role of the vice-president

Few vice-presidents have considered that the post they occupied had much overall significance. John Adams (1789–97), the first vice-president, noted that 'my country has in its wisdom contrived for me the most insignificant office that ever the invention of man contrived or his imagination conceived'. In another celebrated comment, John Nance Garner, one of Franklin Roosevelt's vice-presidents (1933–41), described the role as worth only 'a garner of warm spit' (quoted in Turner 1982: xiii).

The vice-president's principal role is to assume the presidency if the president dies or resigns from office. In November 1963, Lyndon Johnson became the thirty-sixth president in the wake of the Kennedy assassination. Gerald R. Ford became president in August 1974 when Richard Nixon resigned the presidency. However, under the twenty-fifth Amendment, added in 1967, the vice-president also serves as 'Acting President' when the president is undergoing surgery or is otherwise incapable of fulfilling his role. In 1985, President Reagan transferred his powers to Vice-President Bush for an eight-hour period while he was in the operating theatre.

Beyond that, the role involves few formal responsibilities. The Constitution states that the vice-president should serve as president of the Senate. He takes the chair in the Senate on occasions of particular importance, and has a casting vote in the event of a tie. However, the Senate is chaired on a day-to-day basis by the *President Pro Tempore*, a senior member of the majority party.

The vice-president's other duties are a matter for the president's discretion. He will often take on some of the president's ceremonial tasks such as attendance at the funerals of foreign dignitaries. There is, however, always the problem that Dan Quayle (Vice-President 1989–93), identified: 'anything you do, you are going to be getting into somebody else's domain' (Woodward and Broder 1992: 91). Moreover, the vice-president and president have often had a distant relationship. The vice-president has traditionally been nominated

Anthony Bennett adopts a very different perspective. He talks in terms of 'utter confusion' and failure (1994: 33). There were repeated setbacks. The fate of Clinton's health-care proposals has already been noted. Congress emasculated his economic stimulus package. Clinton was also committed to the early implementation of a campaign pledge to end the ban on homosexuals serving in the armed forces. However, after facing opposition from within Congress and the armed forces, he had eventually to settle for a uneasy compromise structured around a 'don't ask, don't tell' policy.

Conclusion

The relationship between the presidency and other political actors has been interpreted in different ways. Some observers emphasise the growth of the pres-

because he *balances the ticket*. His background, politics and personality are therefore likely to be different to those of the president and his inner circle of aides.

The post of vice-president should not, however, be dismissed too lightly. Some recent vice-presidents have, from Richard Nixon onwards, been able to make more of the role. Although elected on the Republican ticket, President Eisenhower (1953–61) regarded himself as 'above politics'. Nixon, his vice-president, therefore acted as *de facto* party leader. He also made highly publicised visits to the Soviet Union at the height of the Cold War.

George Bush (Vice-President 1981–89) was also assigned specific responsibilities. He chaired a number of inquiries, including the President's Task Force on regulatory reform, a study of responses to terrorism, and a South Florida Task Force on drug smuggling. Dan Quayle had agreed and specified functions as vice-president. These included liaison with Congress, organising the Party, and some foreign relations responsibilities. Quayle also chaired the White House Council on Competitiveness and the National Space Council.

In contrast with his predecessors, Al Gore (Vice-President from 1993) was elected on an *unbalanced* ticket. He and Bill Clinton share a similar background, and Gore appears to be part of the President's decision making circle. Gore has made his mark in different ways. He has had responsibility for the National Performance Review. This was directed towards the reduction of federal government bureaucracy and waste. He has also been involved in advising on environmental initiatives, promoting the 'information superhighway', and assessing airline safety. He has acted as a Democratic Party leader, standing in for the President at the Democratic National Committee and directing, amid controversy, some fund-raising activities. Gore was also able to use his casting vote in the Senate to some effect. In June 1993, there was a tied vote on the Budget Reconciliation Bill (as the final version of the annual Budget is known), and Gore used his casting vote to allow the Budget, in a form endorsed by President Clinton, to pass.

ident's powers. Others argue that the Vietnam War and the Watergate crisis led to a fundamental shift in the nature of the relationship. The president is, they suggest, constrained by the other branches of government. His weaknesses are particularly evident when comparisons are drawn with a British prime minister.

This chapter has argued that the president's powers are not fixed. Instead, they vary between the different areas of policy making, and depend upon a president's political skills. However, there is a further dimension. The president does not only have to contend with the other branches of government. He also has to manage and organise the work of the executive branch. The difficulties that he encounters represent another constraint upon his powers. His role as Chief Executive is considered in Chapter 7.

Impeachment and acquittal

On 19 December 1998, President Bill Clinton was impeached by the House of Representatives on charges of perjury and obstruction of justice. It was only the second time in the US history that a president had undergone such an indignity. As the Constitution requires, he was tried by the Senate and the Chief Justice, William H. Rehnquist, presided. On 12 February 1999, Clinton was acquitted and the protracted melodrama that began when he first met Monica Lewinsky appeared to close.

Where did Clinton's impeachment and trial leave US politics? Despite his acquittal, and proposals to rein in the powers of independent prosecutors such as Kenneth Starr, there seemed to be, as the *New York Times* noted, a 'wounded, weakened presidency' (14 February 1999). Some of its standing as an institution was eroded. However, American politics are not a zero-sum game. Congress also lost some of its authority amidst claims that the Republican majority were engaged in a partisan bid to bring down the Clinton administration.

Yet, paradoxically, although the Republicans lost some of the backing and much of the impetus that had accompanied the Party's election victories in November 1994, both the Republicans and Democrats emerged from the trial with a strengthened sense of identity. This was most evident in Congress. Although party discipline in both the House and the Senate has always been loose, the votes cast during the impeachment proceedings closely followed party lines. Such developments add to the arguments of those who talk in terms of 'party renewal' (see Chapter 9).

References and further reading

Anderson, M. (1988), *Revolution*, San Diego, Harcourt Brace Jovanovich.

Bennett, A. (1994), *American Government and Politics 1994*, Godalming.

Bowles, N. (1987), *The White House and Capitol Hill: The Politics of Presidential Persuasion*, Oxford, Clarendon Press.

Califano, J. A. Jr (1996), 'Imperial Congress', in B. Stinebrickner (ed.), *American Government 96/97*, Guilford, Dushkin Publishing Group, 91–3.

Congressional Quarterly (1997), *Powers of the Presidency*, Washington, DC, Congressional Quarterly.

Dumbrell, J. (1997), *The Making of US Foreign Policy*, Manchester, Manchester University Press.

Foley, M. and J. E. Owens (1996), *Congress and the Presidency: Institutional Politics in a Separated System*, Manchester, Manchester University Press.

Mayhew, D. R. (1991), *Divided We Govern: Party Control, Lawmaking and Investigations, 1946–90*, New Haven, Yale University Press.

Mervin, D. (1990), *Ronald Reagan and the American Presidency*, London, Longman.

Mervin, D. (1996), *George Bush and the Guardianship Presidency*, Basingstoke, Macmillan.

Neustadt, R. E. (1967), *Presidential Power: The Politics of Leadership*, New York, John Wiley.

New York Times (1998), 16 October.

Owens, J. E. (1994), 'Clinton and Congress: An early assessment', *Politics Review*, February, 5–10.

Parmet, H. S. (1997), *George Bush: The Life of a Lone Star Yankee*, New York, Scribner.

Plano, J. and M. Greenberg (1989), *The American Political Dictionary*, Fort Worth, Holt, Rinehart & Winston.

Ragsdale, L. (1996), *Vital Statistics on the Presidency: From Washington to Clinton*, Washington, DC, Congressional Quarterly.

Rossiter, C. (1963), *The American Presidency*, London, Harvester.

Towell, P. and D. Cassata (1995), 'Congress takes symbolic stand on troop deployment', *Congressional Quarterly Weekly Report*, 16 December, 3817–18.

Turner, M. (1982), *The Vice President as Policy Maker*, London, Greenwood Press.

Wilson, J. Q. (1992), *American Government: Institutions and Policies*, Lexington, D. C. Heath.

Woodward, B. and D. Broder, *The Man Who Would be President*, London, Hodder & Stoughton.

7

The federal bureaucracy

The US president heads the executive branch of government. In practice, it is a mosaic of departments, bureaux, corporations and agencies. These institutions form the federal bureaucracy.

The classical or 'textbook' model of government suggests that there is a line of authority flowing downwards from the president in his role as 'Chief Executive'. In this ordered hierarchy, subordinates within the federal bureaucracy follow the instructions and guidelines they are given by seniors, and have relatively little discretion in making decisions or applying federal government regulations.

However, many observers argue that the classical model is a misleading description of the executive branch. Successive presidents, they say, have had profound difficulty controlling the work of the bureaucracy and imposing a sense of direction upon it. McGeorge Bundy, who served as National Security Adviser in both the Kennedy and Johnson administrations, noted that the bureaucracy 'more nearly resembles a collection of badly separated principalities than a single instrument of executive action' (Congressional Quarterly 1997: 7).

This chapter surveys these claims and the evidence that sustains them. However, it also considers a competing perspective. This suggests that a president can – despite all the barriers he faces – mould and shape the work of the bureaucracy.

Problems of control

Those observers who stress the resistance of the bureaucracy to presidential authority emphasise its size, structure, and the character of its relationships with both Congress and interest groups.

Size

The scale of the bureaucracy impedes the co-ordination of its work. The numbers employed by the federal government began to build up during the nineteenth century, but then grew rapidly during the New Deal years. In 1921, the federal bureaucracy consisted of 561,142 civilian employees. By 1941, it had almost tripled to 1,437,682.

At this time, American citizens increasingly regarded the federal government as a guarantor of full employment and a provider of social assistance. Government interventionism was displacing laissez-faire. The federal government was expected to play a much bigger part in the everyday lives of American citizens. President Franklin Roosevelt (1933–45) captured the shift in popular expectations:

> Of course we will continue to seek to improve working conditions for the workers of America. . . . Of course we will continue to work for cheaper electricity in the homes and on the farms of America. . . . Of course we will continue our efforts on behalf of the farmers of America. . . . Of course we will continue our efforts for young men and women . . . for the crippled, for the blind, for the mothers. . . . Of course we will continue to protect the consumer. (Weisberger 1997: 49)

The Second World War and President Lyndon Johnson's commitment to construct a 'Great Society' – which sought to end rural poverty in states such as West Virginia and urban deprivation in cities such as Chicago – fuelled a further period of growth. By 1970, the number of civilian federal executive branch employees had reached a peak of 2,961,000. Although there was a modest fall in numbers after this, 2,856,314 people were employed by the executive branch in 1995. This represented about 2.3 per cent of the civilian workforce.

Structure

The problems that arise in co-ordinating the work of the bureaucracy are not a function of numerical size alone. They are compounded by three further difficulties. First, the dividing line between the public and private sector is frequently blurred. There are significant numbers of 'quasi-bureaucrats' who work on government programmes, and are employed in firms and agencies that are supported by federal funding. They are not, however, directly answerable to senior civil servants. Second, although the bureaucracy is widely seen as a distant Washington-based institution, a very large proportion of federal employees work in field-service offices outside the nation's capital.

Third, and most significantly, many departments, agencies and commissions have overlapping spheres of jurisdiction. Anti-poverty programmes, drug control and intelligence gathering are all, for example, the responsibility of different agencies. Their operations are not co-ordinated, and, against a background where each of the different departments and agencies is anxious to promote its own interests, there will be feuding. At the end of the 1960s, Defense Secretary Robert McNamara clashed with Secretary of State Dean

Rusk, about the conduct of the Vietnam War. During the Ford presidency, Secretary of State Henry Kissinger and Defense Secretary James Schlesinger, were, in Hedrick Smith's words, 'seething adversaries' (Smith 1988: 784).

The proliferation of institutions, the structural complexity of the federal bureaucracy, the tensions between individuals, and the day-to-day autonomy that some sections of it have acquired, inevitably limit the ability of a president to impose his will. The bureaucracy can be divided between departments, bureaux and commissions and agencies.

Executive departments

Executive or cabinet-rank departments are responsible for broad areas of policy such as Defense, Commerce and Transportation. By 1993, there were fifteen such departments. The number has progressively grown since the country's early days. The Department of State, which is responsible for foreign relations, and the Treasury were established in 1789. Others – such as Education, Veterans' Affairs, and Environment – are of much more recent origin. They date from 1979, 1989 and 1993 respectively. Each department is headed, and represented in the cabinet, by a Secretary.

Bureaux

Bureaux have more specialised responsibilities. The most well known is the Federal Bureau of Investigation (FBI). The FBI was established in 1908, but it only achieved national recognition during the gangster era. After the Second World War, the FBI concentrated on the hunt for communist agents and spies. Through its efforts, two communist sympathisers, Julius and Ethel Rosenberg, were executed for espionage in June 1953.

The structural complexity of the bureaucracy becomes particularly evident when the position of the bureaux is considered. They are generally located *within* executive departments. The Bureau of Indian Affairs is situated within the Department of the Interior. The Bureau of the Census – which charts population shifts – is placed in the Department of Commerce. Bureaux therefore create particular problems of command and control. The FBI is, for example, part of the Department of Justice. Its Director is therefore answerable to the Attorney-General, the cabinet official who heads the Justice Department, but also, because the FBI plays such a pivotal role in crime-fighting, has a direct relationship with the president.

Commissions and agencies

Independent Regulatory Commissions (IRCs) have quasi-legislative and quasi-judicial functions. They monitor a particular sector of the economy or society, establish regulations, and make judgements about what may, or may not, be permitted. Those who violate IRC rulings are subject to prosecution.

Some IRCs have a particularly high profile. The Interstate Commerce Commission (ICC), created in 1887, has responsibility for business operations and services that cross state lines. When the Constitution was written, this was only a small proportion of the American economy. As industry took on national, and increasingly global, proportions, the role and responsibilities of the ICC have correspondingly grown.

There are also large numbers of executive agencies, including the Central Intelligence Agency (CIA), and the National Aeronautics and Space Administration (NASA) which is responsible for the US space programme. In contrast to the executive departments, executive agencies have a degree of administrative autonomy.

Government corporations are nationalised industries and enterprises. There are relatively few of these. Whereas European governments assumed ownership and control of strategic industries such as the coal and steel industries in the aftermath of the Second World War, laissez-faire traditions have a stronger hold in the US. In general, the federal government relied upon the regulation of industries rather than ownership.

Nevertheless, some industries and services have come under government ownership. The Tennessee Valley Authority is a government corporation responsible for the hydroelectric programmes established in the southern states during the New Deal years. Long-distance railway services have, since 1970, been provided by Amtrak, the National Railroad Passenger Corporation.

The executive branch and the Internet

The Federal Web Locator – provided by the Center for Information Law and Policy – is 'maintained to bring the cyber citizen to the federal government's doorstep'. It offers a search engine and links to all federal government departments, agencies, bureaux, commissions and corporations. The site also provides access to seventeen other search engines.

The Federal Web Locator can be found at:

http://www.law.vill.edu/Fed-Agency/fedwebloc.html

Statutory limits

The defining characteristic of the commissions, agencies and corporations is that they are *autonomous*. This is codified in law. Despite the importance of their responsibilities and work, the president does not have command authority over their activities. For example, the Federal Reserve System has responsibility for the formulation of monetary policy. This has far-reaching significance for the entire economy. A relatively high interest rate will curb inflation, but it will have deflationary implications. Unemployment and bankruptcies are likely to rise. A relatively low interest rate will increase the level of purchasing power in the economy, leading to falling unemployment. It may, however, contribute to circumstances in which inflation can become a problem.

However, despite the centrality of the Federal Reserve's economic role, the president's powers over the 'Fed' are strictly circumscribed. Members of its Board of Governors are appointed by the president, subject to Senate confirmation, but once in office they cannot be instructed to adopt a particular course of action. They jealously guard this independence. Thus when President Reagan became president, Paul Volcker, the chairman of the 'Fed', refused to meet him in either the White House or at the Federal Reserve Board building, for fear of jeopardising his independence (Anderson 1988: 252). When President Clinton was elected, he was under pressure to replace the sitting 'Fed' chairman, Alan Greenspan, with an appointee who would favour economic expansion. However, Greenspan was reappointed because he had the confidence of Wall Street and the international financial community.

Even where the law does not limit the president's ability to direct the work of government agencies, political considerations can play a role. It has been suggested that for many years, the FBI escaped proper scrutiny by either presidents or Congress. It was, under its long-time director, J. Edgar Hoover, administered as a semi-independent empire.

The role of Congress

The president's difficulties are compounded by the bureaucracy's relationship with Congress. In practice, federal bureaucrats serve two masters. The president is the 'Chief Executive', but the departments, commissions and agencies are also dependent upon Congressional authority.

There are several reasons why Congress has a hold over the bureaucracy. First, Congress has to pass the legislation that establishes government programmes or creates agencies. Second, Congress plays a pivotal role in shaping the federal government's annual budget, which allocates funding and authorises expenditure commitments by departments and agencies. Third, as Chapter 5 noted, the work of the bureaucracy is subject to *oversight*.

Iron triangles

The president's ability to co-ordinate the work of the bureaucracy is frustrated in another way. Some interest groups, particularly 'producer' organisations such as companies, trade unions or small business federations, have established a close association with departments and agencies. They will generally be seeking protection from market forces or an advantage in terms of government funding, subsidies, and price guarantee mechanisms. For their part, departments, bureaux and agencies have an interest in either the expansion of federal government programmes or, at the least, their continued survival. Bureaucrats will wish to increase their salary, status, and sphere of responsibility. Members of Congress also have their own interests at stake. They will hope for an endorsement at election time from groups and lobbies, particularly those that are strongly represented in their state or district. The three institutions – the bureaucracy, an interest group and a Congressional committee – are bound together in a symbiotic relationship. They form an 'iron triangle' in which they depend upon each other, and have a shared interest in the continued expansion and development of a particular federal government programme. The net effect is to detach sections of the bureaucracy from the hierarchy. They are pulled in other directions. As B. Guy Peters notes: 'Each functional area tends to be governed as if it existed in splendid isolation from the remainder of government' (1986: 22).

President Jimmy Carter was confronted by an 'iron triangle' when he sought to transfer the educational programmes offered to former servicemen by the Veterans' Administration into the newly created Department of Education. He encountered determined opposition from the Veterans' Administration itself, veterans' organisations, and the Congressional committees associated with those who had served in the US armed forces. In the face of these pressures, the president eventually had to withdraw his proposals.

Presidential resources

There is, however, another side to the argument. Despite these constraints, the president does have some powers and political resources that enable him to influence the character of the federal bureaucracy.

The power of appointment

The president has the power of appointment. He can attempt to co-ordinate and influence the character of the federal bureaucracy by appointing those who will be sympathetic to his policies. His powers of appointment include those who head the departments and serve in the Cabinet, but they also extend far beyond this. In contrast to the UK, where nearly all senior civil servants are permanent employees whose responsibility is to loyally serve the government of the day, whatever its political hue, the president nominates the most senior civil servants. With each incoming president, there is a turnover of personnel. Together with his aides, a president appoints about 5,200 individuals to positions in the executive branch.

President Reagan, in particular, sought to ensure that all his appointees were individuals who shared his conservative policy goals. As Aberbach has noted: 'whereas in past administrations, notables who had good relations with established interest groups or good connections with key people on congressional committees were likely to get the jobs, in the Reagan administration political ideology was the key' (Aberbach 1991: 227–8).

However, the extent to which the power of appointment enables a president to co-ordinate the work of his administration and impose a sense of direction upon the federal bureaucracy should not be exaggerated. There are constraints:

1 Although a president can make over 5,000 appointments, this is, in practice, a relatively small-scale operation. When President Clinton entered the White House in January 1993, he could only appoint about a hundred individuals in the Department of Transportation, constituting less than 1 per cent of the total workforce. In the Department of Commerce, he was limited to 222 appointments from a total of 37,485 – again, less than 1 per cent (Congressional Quarterly 1997: 4, 21).
2 There are time constraints on a president, as many appointments have to be made hurriedly during the two-month transition period between election and Inauguration Day. As a consequence, he will have to delegate a large proportion of sub-cabinet appointments to others.
3 There may be a shortage of appropriate individuals. Significant numbers will be reluctant to abandon lucrative long-term posts in private companies for short-term service in Washington, DC. Others may also be unwilling to disclose detailed information about their personal lives and financial affairs.
4 A president may feel the need to ensure that his appointments are broadly representative of American society. This will again constrain his choices. Although the appointments process will be dominated by White Anglo-Saxon Protestant – or WASP – males, a president will generally seek to ensure that particular groups have a visible presence. Of President Bush's appointments, 19 per cent were women, and 17 per cent were drawn from a racial minority (Parmet 1997: 358). President Clinton was guided by the so-called 'egg' formula whereby appointments were structured, at least in part, around 'ethnicity, gender (and) geography'.
5 Although interim appointments can be made by the president while the Senate is not in session, his senior appointments are subject to Senate confirmation. The Clinton White House had difficulties with its initial appointments. In January 1993, Zoe Baird, President Clinton's nominee to head the Justice Department, had to withdraw when it was revealed that she had employed an illegal immigrant as a nanny in her household. His replacement nomination, Kimba Wood, had to pull out for identical reasons. Three months later, President Clinton felt obliged to withdraw Lani Guinier, his nominee to a post heading the civil rights division in the Justice Department, once it became clear that she had published articles calling for reforms to the voting system so as to guarantee greater minority representation. The views that she expressed were regarded as too radical.

Just as a president's appointments are subject to Senate confirmation, his ability to remove those he has appointed is constrained. Those who serve on the Independent Regulatory Commissions are, in particular, protected from dismissal. Although a 1926 Supreme Court ruling, *Myers v. United States*, gave the president wide powers to remove executive branch employees, his authority was circumscribed by later judgements. In *Wiener v. United States* (1958), the Court ruled that if an official's sphere of responsibility included adjudicative functions [where judgements are made about individual cases or grievances], the president cannot remove the official for political reasons (Congressional Quarterly 1997: 29–30).

The power of reorganisation

The president has the power to reorganise and restructure the federal bureaucracy. This was confirmed in the 1949 Reorganisation Act. For example, in 1978, the Civil Service Reform Act broke some of the ties between senior bureaucrats, the departments and agencies, and influential interest groups. The Act created the Senior Executive Service (SES). Instead of serving one department, commission or agency on a lifetime basis, the SES is a mobile cadre of senior career officials who are shifted from post to post. They are therefore less likely to develop a strong sense of loyalty to a particular interest group or a departmental way of thinking.

There have been other changes. During the Reagan years, there were attempts to eliminate what the administration saw as overstaffing, and rationalise the bureaucracy. The numbers employed in the Social Security Administration were cut from 80,000 to 60,000, and the Office of Research and Statistics was dismantled (Cohn 1995: 361).

However, reorganisation depends upon the president's ability to reach agreement with Congress. President Richard Nixon was concerned, to a greater extent than other modern presidents, that his administration would encounter 'disloyalty and obstruction', particularly from those in the civil service who had been appointed during the Kennedy and Johnson years. Therefore, in 1971, Nixon proposed that eight existing cabinet-rank departments should be merged so as to form four larger 'super-departments': Natural Resources, Community Development, Human Resources and Economic Affairs. He believed that this would facilitate more centralised direction. However, Congress would not accept the proposals, and they had to be abandoned. In the 1990s, proposals for a rationalised departmental structure were periodically resurrected. Members of the Clinton administration and its Republican critics discussed proposals and options. However, they came to little (Drew 1997: 71–2 and 124).

The Cabinet

At first sight, the Cabinet appears to offer a means by which the entire executive branch can be directed and drawn together. Its membership includes those who head the executive departments – such as the Secretary of State and the Secretary of Defense – and other figures such as the UN Ambassador, the National Security Adviser, the Chief of Staff, and the head of the Office of Management and Budget (OMB).

Reinventing government

Apart from questions of control and direction, the bureaucracy is widely regarded – particularly by conservatives – as inefficient, wasteful and unresponsive.

In 1993, Vice-President Al Gore was asked by the President to head the National Performance Review (NPR). The purpose of this was to meet these criticisms, pre-empt Republican attacks, and consider the ways in which executive branch operations could be improved. Gore's report talked in terms of 'reinventing government'. It criticised the federal bureaucracy for being rule-bound and lacking in imagination. There were, he asserted, few attempts to be innovative. All this led to a 'performance deficit'. The solution lay in the cutting of red tape, the *empowerment* of individual employees, and a reduction in the size of the workforce (Lynn 1995: 344). Gore demanded that government 'work better and cost less'.

Most observers believe that the NPR has been reasonably successful. The number of federal employees has fallen by 300,000 since 1992. The Federal Emergency Management Agency was transformed into a highly efficient disaster-relief unit (Glastris 1998: 16). There are also many small-scale success stories.

Nevertheless, the NPR has been subject to criticism. The empowerment of lower-level officials, it has been said, could weaken Congressional influence over their actions. Other sceptics emphasise the limited character of the NPR. Some of the expenditure cutbacks are the consequence of post-Cold War defence reductions, rather than the 'reinvention' of government. Furthermore, other measures may have had greater overall significance than the NPR. The 1993 Government Performance and Results Act – supported by both parties – required every government agency to establish performance measures. Furthermore, the Republican victories in the 1994 and 1996 Congressional elections, and the GOP's commitment to 'small government', also contributed to a political climate in which it was felt that the federal bureaucracy had to be rationalised. Republican pressure led to cuts in the Department of Energy, a more laissez-faire approach by the Food and Drug Administration, and privatisation of some NASA programmes (Weisman 1996: 2516). However, these reforms were also relatively modest, particularly when set against the original goals of Republican reformers. Many in the Republican Party had hoped to abolish or dismantle departments such as Energy and HUD (Housing and Urban Development). However, writing in 1996, Jonathan Weisman drew the conclusion that the departments and agencies were 'bruised but still standing, [and they] feel they have proven their mettle and beaten the Republicans simply by surviving' (1996: 2520).

It is tempting to draw parallels with the British Cabinet. They both have a membership of just over twenty. However, such comparisons do not extend very far. In the UK, many important decisions are – despite the growth of prime-ministerial power – taken by the Cabinet on a collective basis. Furthermore, a prime minister's authority is derived, at least in part, from the degree to which she or he enjoys Cabinet support. Indeed, a prime minister will be unable to stay in office if Cabinet support is lost. In November 1990, for example, it was the

Cabinet that played a decisive role in persuading Mrs Thatcher that she had no option but to resign.

The US picture is different. Some presidents – most notably Dwight Eisenhower – attempted to establish a Cabinet that would work on the basis of collective decision making. However, in practice, the Cabinet is only as important or unimportant as a president chooses to make it. The great majority of presidents have begun their periods of office by declaring that the Cabinet would become a principal forum for decision-making. However, almost all have within a short period relegated their Cabinets to the political sidelines. In a classic phrase, uttered at the end of a Cabinet discussion, Abraham Lincoln declared: 'Seven noes, one aye – the ayes have it.' In other words, the Cabinet could at any time be overruled by the president. There are other limits on Cabinet members. During the Nixon presidency, most of those serving in the Cabinet did not have regular access to the president. Only John Mitchell, the Attorney-General, was able to see the president freely. The others were unable to get beyond the president's aides (Cunliffe 1987: 306). The Cabinet also tends to meet infrequently. Only about six Cabinet meetings were held in the first year of the Clinton presidency (Bennett 1996: 213). In their place, Leon Panetta, the White House Chief of Staff, gave 'briefings' to Cabinet members.

Although some Cabinet members have at times played an important role in shaping policy, this was not because they served in the Cabinet. Instead, their influence rested on other considerations. Attorney-General Robert Kennedy played a pivotal role because he was the president's brother. James Baker, Secretary of State between 1989 and 1993, had a close personal relationship with President Bush and this gave him a degree of influence as a policy adviser. As Anthony Bennett concludes: 'they were not important because they were in the Cabinet, but in spite of being in the Cabinet' (1996: 164). The reasons why the Cabinet has so little overall significance can be identified as follows:

1 The president is the sole source of political authority. Whereas the British Cabinet consists largely of MPs, US Cabinet members are not elected representatives. They will rarely hold positions of influence within the president's party. Indeed, they may be *non-partisan* or belong to the opposing party. Their influence and role is therefore entirely dependent upon presidential discretion.
2 Because the Cabinet has no formal or established role, it is not respected or trusted by presidents. As Martin Anderson, Reagan's chief adviser on domestic and economic policy, records, only a small number of issues can usefully be discussed in Cabinet meetings. Many only concern one or two Cabinet members, and others are too confidential to be considered in a large meeting.
3 The officials who head Cabinet-level departments may not have been selected by the president because of their ability to co-operate with him in shaping policy. Instead, they will have been appointed for other reasons. A

president may, for example, wish to ensure that his Cabinet has a geographic spread or that particular interests are represented. The Cabinet can play a role in sending political signals or in acknowledging the significance of a particular grouping. In 1992, President Clinton declared that his Cabinet would 'look like America'. His initial Cabinet choices fell far short of this, but included three African-Americans and two Hispanics.

4 Successive presidents have felt that Cabinet members were drawn too closely towards their departments and the interest groups active in their area of policy. There is often a sense in which the departmental secretaries have seemed almost disloyal to the Chief Executive. As President Lyndon Johnson (1963–69) put it:

> When I looked out at the heads of my departments, I realized that while all of them had been appointed by me, not a single one was really mine. . . . I felt like a football quarterback running against a tough team and having his own center and left guard throwing rocks at him. (Mervin 1993: 103)

In practice, decisions are made by the president meeting with Cabinet members on a *bilateral* (or one-to-one) basis. The Cabinet serves purposes other than collective decision making. As noted above, it has a purpose in emphasising the president's commitment to the interests of particular groupings. It may also be used as a means of rallying and mobilising support for a certain set of policies. President Reagan is said to have used his Cabinet meetings to pull the administration behind particular goals, most especially the cutting of budgets. There was no discussion. Instead, the president or his senior advisers would simply outline developments and strategy (Anderson 1988: 223, 232).

Cabinet councils

President Ronald Reagan was elected to office by promising a conservative revolution, resting on 'small government' and the deregulation of the economy. He wanted to ensure that the entire administration shared these goals, and that in particular, Cabinet members would not be sidetracked or drawn away by the inherent inertia of the federal bureaucracy.

Therefore, instead of leaving the process of policy implementation to Cabinet secretaries who were regarded as potentially fickle, the Reagan team established Cabinet councils. They brought together personnel from the bureaucracy and the White House staff, and had a responsibility to develop, implement and monitor policy. Five were established in April 1981, and two further councils were set up in 1982. The principal council was the Cabinet Council on Economic Affairs. It held fifty-seven meetings in the first year of its existence (Anderson 1988: 231).

President Reagan was the nominal chairman of each, but he did not, in practice, attend every meeting. These were, however, always held in the White House. As Martin Anderson recalls: 'Just the act of having to leave their fiefdoms, get into a car, and be driven to the White House was a powerful reminder to every member of the Cabinet that it was the president's business they were about, not theirs or their department's constituents' (1988: 226).

The policy process was also controlled and co-ordinated in another way. The Cabinet councils were provided with support staff called secretariats. Each secretariat was headed by White House staff, thereby giving senior Reagan aides another form of leverage over policy development.

The system of Cabinet councils was rationalised during President Reagan's second term, and two broader bodies, the Domestic Policy Council and the Economic Policy Council, were created. These brought some of the Cabinet secretaries together with figures from the Executive Office of the President (EOP), such as the Director of the OMB. Although the Councils were maintained after Reagan left office, they were weakened by serious infighting during the Bush presidency, and their effectiveness is open to question.

The Executive Office of the President (EOP)

As the scale and responsibilities of the bureaucracy grew, the president appeared to be an increasingly isolated figure. On coming to office, President Franklin Roosevelt brought in a significant number of personal advisers. Then, in 1936, the Brownlow Committee of Administrative Management was established. It studied the position of the president within the executive branch, and concluded that 'The President needs help.'

From this beginning, the Executive Office of the President (EOP) has grown. Congress and successive presidents added units so that it has, as David Mervin records, assumed pivotal significance: 'Presidents have the gravest difficulties as it is in gaining control of a notoriously fractious political system; without the expertise and assistance of the EOP they would be helpless and the United States would be truly ungovernable' (1993: 78).

Indeed, presidents have almost invariably placed greater trust in the EOP than in those who head the federal bureaucracy. Anthony Bennett identifies four reasons for this:

1. Staffers are more likely to be long-term associates of the president and will therefore have a much closer relationship with him. They are *his* people. In contrast, as has been noted, Cabinet members may be virtual strangers who have been appointed because they bring expertise to the post or simply because they have symbolic significance.
2. Staff members are likely to maintain their personal loyalty to the president. Cabinet members are, however, torn between their loyalty to the president, the attitudes and views of the department they head, and the feelings of interest groups which have a close association with that department.
3. Although the State Department is only about a mile from the White House – in the Foggy Bottom neighbourhood of Washington, DC – the EOP is in

much closer physical proximity to the president. These distances are important when decisions are being made.

4 A Cabinet member will inevitably be preoccupied in managing his or her department. As Bennett puts it: 'He may be closeted in some top-level departmental meeting. He may be on Capitol Hill appearing before a congressional committee. He may be in California or Texas or Michigan giving a speech or attending a conference. He may not even be in the United States at all' (1996: 169).

The organisation of the EOP

Over 1,600 people are currently employed in the EOP. It is divided into a number of different components, including the following.

The National Security Council (NSC)

The NSC was formed in 1947 at the beginning of the Cold War. Its membership includes the president himself, the vice-president, the secretaries of defense and state, the Central Intelligence Agency director, and the chairman of the Joint Chiefs of Staff. The NSC has a staff, headed by the National Security Adviser.

Different presidents have used the NSC, and the National Security Adviser, in different ways. Although the State Department's advice on Northern Ireland was sometimes ignored, President Clinton's National Security Advisers have generally been eclipsed by his Secretaries of State, Warren Christopher and Madeleine Albright. However, earlier National Security Advisers were predominant figures. Dr Henry Kissinger – who served as National Security Adviser during the Nixon years – spearheaded foreign policy initiatives, most notably the American rapprochement with China.

Inevitably, there is a long history of tension between the National Security Adviser and Cabinet officials. There were, for example, frequent battles, during the Carter presidency, between Secretary of State Cyrus Vance, and National Security Adviser Zbigniew Brzezinski.

The Office of Management and Budget (OMB)

The OMB has a staff of over five hundred and a number of important functions. It draws up draft executive orders, screens legislation passed by Congress before it is submitted to the president, and monitors the rules and regulations issued by the federal bureaucracy. The departments and agencies must submit a 'regulatory impact analysis' when proposing changes. Most significantly of all, the OMB draws up the federal government budget on behalf of the president. It assesses the budget requests of the different departments, and ties them together within the overall framework of the president's political and economic strategy. The process can, of course, be used by the president and his aides to reign in particular departments and expand others.

These proposals are then submitted to the lawmakers on Capitol Hill. However, although Congress – aided by those who staff the Congressional

The Iran–Contra Affair

Some of the difficulties associated with the EOP – and the ability of the executive branch to evade the will of Congress – were graphically illustrated by the Iran–Contra affair. In November 1986, it was revealed that President Reagan had secretly authorised the selling of anti-tank missiles and other weaponry to Iran. The shipments were worth about $600 million. There were shocked reactions. Iran was a rigid Islamic state thought to be behind acts of international terrorism and involved in the holding of western hostages in the Lebanon. The White House appears to have hoped that although the covert sales were in breach of the Arms Control Export Act, they might strengthen the position of more moderate elements within the Iranian leadership circles and lead to the release of the hostages.

There were, however, further revelations. The National Security Adviser, Vice-Admiral John Poindexter, and his deputy, Lieutenant-Colonel Oliver North, used about $16 million taken out of the profits obtained from the transactions with Iran to purchase weaponry for the *contras*. The contras were guerrillas engaged in a war against government forces in Nicaragua, a small central American nation. The Nicaraguan government was aligned with Cuba and the Soviet bloc. However, the transfer of funds to the contras broke US law. Congress had, through the 1985 Boland Amendment, prohibited the giving of military aid to the contras. As North and his supporters saw it, Congress had abandoned freedom fighters in the field of battle.

It has never became clear exactly how far President Reagan knew about the diversion of funds to the contras. The Tower Commission, which was appointed to examine the decision-making process within the National Security Council, concluded that the president had not subjected the actions of his staff to sufficiently close scrutiny, thereby allowing NSC personnel to pursue what constituted an independent foreign policy.

Budget Office – will introduce a substantial number of amendments, the political initiative in the budget debates generally remains with the president.

The White House Office (WHO)
The four hundred or so staff in the WHO are those who work most closely with the president. They organise his day-to-day work. Some presidents, such as Franklin Roosevelt and John F. Kennedy, adopted a circular model of organisation in the WHO. A considerable number of senior policy advisers report directly to the president. The Clinton administration followed this pattern in its early days: it had an open, informal, almost casual style, in which large numbers had access to the president.

In contrast, other presidents have established a system based upon a hierarchy of authority. Only a few senior advisers have a close relationship with the president. The White House Chief of Staff generally plays a pivotal role. For example, President Nixon's Chief of staff, H. R. Haldeman, was part of a

'Berlin Wall' of advisers. Nixon was disproportionately dependent upon their advice, and access to the president by others depended upon their willingness to allow it.

However, despite the importance of its role, there are limits to the authority of the EOP.

1 Those who staff the EOP are simply advisers to the president. They do not have executive powers, and cannot give instructions to those who work in the federal bureaucracy. In contrast, Cabinet members are empowered by legal authority and have a legitimacy that the White House staff inevitably lack (Bennett 1996: 179).
2 The EOP can, in practice, constitute a 'mini-bureaucracy', presenting problems of management, direction and control (Foley and Owens 1996: 214–15). Presidents have responded to this by increasing the size of the White House Office. However, as Lyn Ragsdale notes, this did not represent a solution: 'presidents could not control Cabinet departments, so they increased the size of the EOP. Because the EOP was itself too big and too diverse to control, presidents then expanded the WHO' (1996: 255). In practice, there are finite limits to the numbers a single individual can manage.

Conclusion

The federal bureaucracy poses questions of control and co-ordination. Aside from the problems that stem from its size and structure, the bureaucracy is torn between loyalty to the president and its obligations to Congress and particular interest groups. There are, however, mechanisms that enable the president to go some way in imposing a sense of direction on the executive branch. The president has the power of appointment to senior posts. The Cabinet and the EOP offer possibilities. However, these are limited by the inherent weaknesses of both institutions. The federal bureaucracy therefore has considerable influence. It can be considered a *political actor* in its own right, and some observers regard it as 'the fourth branch of government'.

References and further reading

Aberbach, J. D. (1990), *Keeping a Watchful Eye: The Politics of Congressional Oversight*, Washington, DC, The Brookings Institution.
Aberbach, J. D. (1991), 'The president and the executive branch', in C. Campbell and B. A. Rockman, *The Bush Presidency: First Appraisals*, Chatham, Chatham House.
Anderson, M. (1988), *Revolution*, San Diego, Harcourt Brace Jovanovich.
Bennett, A. J. (1996), *The American President's Cabinet: From Kennedy to Bush*, Basingstoke, Macmillan.
Cohn, J. S. (1995), 'Damaged goods: before reinventing government, Clinton needs to

repair it', in W. D. Burnham, *The American Prospect Reader in American Politics*, Chatham, Chatham House.

Congressional Quarterly (1997), *Powers of the Presidency*, Washington, DC, Congressional Quarterly.

Cunliffe, M. (1987), *The Presidency*, Boston, Houghton Mifflin.

Drew, E. (1997), *Showdown: The Struggle Between the Gingrich Congress and the Clinton White House*, New York, Touchstone.

Foley, M. and J. E. Owens (1996), *Congress and the Presidency: Institutional Politics in a Separated System*, Manchester, Manchester University Press.

Glastris, P. (1998), 'Undercovered', *The New Republic*, 2 March, 15–18.

Hart, J. (1995), *The Presidential Branch: From Washington to Clinton*, Chatham, Chatham House.

Lynn, L. E. (1995), 'Government lite', in W. D. Burnham (ed.), *The American Prospect Reader in American Politics*, Chatham, Chatham House, 343–53.

Mervin, D. (1993), *The President of the United States*, New York, Harvester Wheatsheaf.

Parmet, H. S. (1997), *George Bush: The Life of a Lone Star Yankee*, New York, Scribner.

Peters, B. G. (1986), *American Public Policy: Promise and Performance*, Basingstoke, Macmillan.

Ragsdale, L. (1996), *Vital Statistics on the Presidency: Washington to Clinton*, Washington, DC, Congressional Quarterly.

Smith, H. (1988), *The Power Game: How Washington Works*, London, Fontana.

Weisberger, B. A. (1997) 'What made the government grow?', *American Heritage*, September, 34–52.

Weisman, J. (1996), 'True impact of GOP Congress reaches well beyond bills', *Congressional Quarterly Weekly Report*, 7 September, 2515–20.

Woll, P. (1985), *Congress*, Boston, Little, Brown.

8

Federalism:
state and local government

The US has a federal system of government. Political power is distributed between the national (or federal) government and the individual states. Each of the fifty states has its own constitution and system of government, structured around a governor, legislature and judiciary. Within the state, there are different forms of local government, such as municipal corporations, counties and townships, as well as school and other forms of administrative districts. The states can, within limits, determine their own policies and laws, but they are also component parts of a single nation.

There are, however, those who argue that there has been a process of *centralisation*, and political power has been progressively transferred from the individual states to the federal government in Washington, DC. However, others dissent from these claims. They suggest that despite centralisation, power is still shared between the federal government and the individual states. This chapter outlines and explains the arguments.

Federalism and the Constitution

The 'Founding Fathers', who drew up the Constitution, were divided among themselves about the precise character that federalism should take. Those around Thomas Jefferson sought to ensure that the rights and freedoms of the individual states would be respected. From their perspective, the federal government should have only limited authority. Jefferson's supporters emphasised that the states existed *before* the federal government and the US came into being. The national government should, therefore, be considered the servant of the states rather than their master. There was, however, determined opposition to the Jeffersonian vision. Alexander Hamilton and his associates emphasised the economic weakness and military vulnerability of a country that lacked national direction. They called for a central government that would have authority and an ability to respond to both domestic and external challenges.

The Constitution sought to bring together and reconcile these different strands of opinion, and it approached federalism in three ways:

1 It emphasised the essential unity of the US in its relationships with other nations. Foreign policy powers are the sole prerogative of the federal government. According to Article I of the Constitution, states may not conclude treaties with other countries, impose taxes on imports and exports, or maintain their own troops in times of peace. These stipulations were intended to ensure that the US came together and remained a single diplomatic, economic and military entity.

   Alongside these limitations, other clauses of the Constitution also restricted the decision-making powers of the states. Article I specifies that the US Congress has the authority to pass laws for the 'general welfare of the United States'. It also, in what became known as the 'interstate commerce' clause, permitted Congress to regulate trade and business between the states. The wording of these phrases – and the *expansive* interpretation that the Supreme Court subsequently put upon them – allowed the federal government to progressively develop its role in American society.

2 The Constitution offers certain specific assurances to the states. These are outlined in Article IV. The states are assured that they will be defended from invasion, that their boundaries will not be changed without their consent, and they will be given equal representation in the US Senate. Article V specifies that the Constitution can only be amended with the assent of three-quarters of the states.

   However, the rights of the states go beyond these guarantees. The Tenth Amendment, which formed part of the Bill of Rights, and was added in 1791, was intended to ensure that these states were not subsumed by the national authorities. It states that 'the powers not delegated to the United States by the Constitution, nor prohibited by it to the States, are reserved to the States respectively, or to the people'. In other words, those decision-making powers not specifically assigned to the federal government are the prerogative of the individual states. The states can make their own laws. There are, as a consequence, significant differences between the states. Regulations regarding marriage and divorce differ. Restrictions on gambling and alcohol depend upon state law. The sales tax paid on retail goods and services varies between the states. Driving is subject to a range of laws and regulations. Legal punishments also differ: the majority of states, for example, have the death penalty on their statute books. Others, such as Vermont, do not. Some, most notably Texas, frequently carry out executions. In other states, they are a very rare occurrence. Euthanasia is also a matter for state policy makers. Following a referendum in 1994, Oregon introduced the Death with Dignity Act, allowing doctors to prescribe drugs so that the terminally ill can end their own lives.

3 The Constitution also established that the states have duties and obligations towards each other. A fugitive who has been charged with an offence in one

Federalism

The system of federalism – on which the US Constitution rests – can be seen as a compromise between a *unitary* form of government and a confederation or *confederacy*. A unitary political system concentrates political power in a central government. The UK is a unitary state in which Parliament is *sovereign*. Although there are other forms of government, such as local authorities (councils), the Scottish Parliament, and the Welsh Assembly, they only hold powers that have been granted to them by Parliament. These powers can be given – as they were in the Labour government's devolution measures – and taken away. The local councils lost some of their powers – most notably their ability to set their own spending levels – during the latter half of the 1970s and 1980s.

In contrast, a confederacy offers an advanced form of *decentralisation*. When the American colonists first established their independence from the British Crown, they agreed upon the Articles of Confederation. These were drawn up in 1776–77 and adopted in 1781. They provided for a loose association of sovereign states. As noted in Chapter 3, the central government had only limited powers. Indeed, it was so weak that it did not have an executive branch. However, the threat to national unity that such a degree of decentralisation represented soon became apparent, and the Confederation only lasted until 1789, when the first president and Congress were elected under the US Constitution.

Seventy years later, another confederation was established on American soil. When, in 1861, the southern states seceded from the US, they formed the Confederate States of America. The Confederacy lasted until the South was defeated in 1865, and had its own president – Jefferson Davis – and Congress.

state, and flees to another, must be extradited and returned to the original state. 'Full faith and credit' has to be given by each individual state to the laws and court rulings made in other states. In other words, one state cannot undermine another by refusing to recognise the validity of its laws and court judgements. This caused concern in some states when the Hawaii Supreme Court considered recognising same-sex marriages.

The growth of the federal government

In the early years of the US, the provisions of the Constitution relating to federalism were generally understood to mean that the federal government and the states had their own separate and distinct spheres of responsibility. The federal government had authority over foreign policy, defence, and some other specifically identified domestic responsibilities such as the regulation of interstate commerce. However, most forms of domestic policy-making remained the prerogative of the states. As James Madison, one of the most prominent of the Founding Fathers put it, the authority of the individual state would 'extend to

Layer-cake and marble-cake federalism

Morton Grodzins devised a metaphor to convey the changing character of American federalism. He described dual federalism – the model of relations between the national government and the states that was accepted from the founding of the US until the early twentieth century – as *layer-cake federalism*. This suggests that the two forms of government each had their own separate spheres of responsibility. The authority of the national government extended to tariff policy, defence, and foreign relations. The state governments had responsibility over matters not specifically cited in the US Constitution such as education, unemployment, law and order, and transportation. In the Grodzins model, the functions provided by the two tiers of government were as distinct as the layers in a layer-cake.

However, the growth of grants-in-aid and the New Deal led to a *reconceptualisation* of federalism. The national government became involved in the provision of education, work-creation projects, transportation, and welfare provision. Increasingly, it was recognised that the efforts and responsibilities of the different governments within the US were intertwined and intermeshed. They no longer had their own separate spheres. Some described it as co-operative federalism. Grodzins talked about *marble-cake federalism*. The two tiers of government were now intermixed.

Further reading

Grodzins, M. (1966), *The American System*, Chicago, Rand McNally.

all objects which, in the ordinary course of affairs, concern the lives, liberties, and properties of the people'. This has been described as *dual federalism* or *layer-cake federalism*, insofar as the federal and state governments were engaged in separate and distinct spheres of activity.

Although there are those who have questioned whether dual federalism ever existed in the pure form that has been depicted, the character of American federalism undoubtedly changed dramatically over the next century and a half. During the nineteenth and twentieth centuries, central government gained in terms of both authority and resources. Four processes and developments made a particular contribution to the shift.

The Civil War

As the nineteenth century progressed, tensions between the North and the southern states grew. Some southerners, such as John C. Calhoun of South Carolina, asserted that the states could, within their territory, *nullify* – or refuse to accept – laws passed by Congress.

In 1861, the argument went a stage further. Southerners argued with growing vehemence that states had the right to secede – or leave – the US. The Civil War (1861–65) began when the southern states created their own independent nation: the Confederate States of America. It was founded in an attempt to ensure the preservation of slavery and resist northern commercialism. The eventual defeat of the Confederacy by northern forces 'saved the Union' and established that the federal government directly represented the American people. It was not simply a compact between states. The individual states belonging to the US did not therefore have the right of secession. The US was a single country.

A significant shift in popular terminology took place at the time. It matched the changing realities of politics. Before the Civil War, the US was a plural concept. People commonly said 'the United States *are* . . .'. After 1865, references to the US took a singular form, ('the US *is* . . .').

Constitutional amendments

The defeat of the South was followed by the passage of amendments to the Constitution. These sought to give some measure of protection to the former slave population. Under the Fourteenth Amendment, every state had to ensure that all those living within its jurisdiction were given 'the equal protection of the laws' and that no person could be deprived of 'life, liberty, or property, without due process of law'. The Fifteenth Amendment required that the right of US citizens to vote could not be denied 'on account of race, color, or previous condition of servitude'.

However, despite these amendments, white rule was re-established in the southern states by the 1880s, and the black population progressively lost the rights that they had won in the aftermath of the Civil War. The system of racial segregation – a form of institutionalised racism under which blacks were consigned to separate and inferior public facilities – and the voting 'tests' that kept the right to vote in white hands, made a mockery of the Fourteenth and Fifteenth Amendments until the 1960s.

However, despite continuing racial injustice, other Constitutional amendments – seeking to establish uniform standards across the nation – did increasingly limit the authority of the individual states. A national system of income-tax collection came into being when the Sixteenth Amendment was ratified by the states in 1913. This gave the federal government an independent and very large-scale source of revenue. Almost sixty years later, the Twenty-Sixth Amendment gave eighteen-year-olds the right to vote in all federal and state elections.

Supreme Court rulings

As Chapter 4 noted, a number of Supreme Court rulings had a profound impact on relations between the federal government and the individual states. In the early years of the US, the Court legitimised the expansion of the federal government's powers. In 1810, in the case of *Fletcher v. Peck*, the Court established that it had the right to declare a state law unconstitutional. Nine years later, the Court bolstered the position of the federal government. In the case of *McCulloch v. Maryland* (1819), the Court asserted that the federal government not only had *enumerated* powers – those specifically identified in the Constitution – but also had *implied* powers. Its prerogatives stemmed, in the words of Chief Justice John Marshall, from both 'the letter and spirit of the Constitution'.

As the nineteenth century progressed, however, the Court became increasingly suspicious of federal government authority, and protective of the states. Its rulings rested on the concept of *dual federalism*. In the closing years of the century, this led the Court to acquiesce as white southerners regained much of the authority that they had held in the years preceding the Civil War, and imposed a system of segregation across the South. The Court accepted the 'separate but equal' doctrine, that underpinned segregation, in the case of *Plessy v. Ferguson* (1896).

By the middle of the twentieth century, judicial attitudes had shifted. The activism of the Warren and Burger Courts (1953–86) represented a sustained attempt to impose uniform standards of justice across the nation. *Brown v. Board of Education (Topeka, Kansas)* (1954) declared segregated schooling to be unconstitutional. Although the southern states initially resisted the ruling, and used 'states' rights' as a rallying call, *Brown* eventually came to be accepted. *Baker v. Carr* (1962) established that the electoral districts for state legislatures had to be drawn on the basis of population. There had to be, the Court argued, periodic reapportionment to reflect population shifts. *Roe v. Wade* (1973) asserted that abortion was a constitutional right. In *Furman v. Georgia* (1972), the Court ruled that existing death-penalty laws were unconstitutional. All these judgements constrained the decision-making powers of the state legislatures.

Economic and social developments

Alongside these other factors, the growing scope and scale of the federal government also contributed to the changing character of the relationship between Washington, DC and the individual states. In particular, the role of the executive branch as 'manager of the economy' added to the relative importance of the federal government. The federal government had begun giving *grants-in-aid* – or financial transfers – to the individual states in 1887. Washington, DC offered financial assistance to help the states develop agricultural research, education, and highway programmes.

President Roosevelt's New Deal brought about a dramatic increase in the number and size of grants-in-aid. In 1925, grants-in-aid amounted to $114 million. By 1937, this had risen to nearly $300 million. Under the 1935 Social Security Act, Washington, DC used grants-in-aid to provide the beginnings of a rudimentary welfare state. There was material assistance for some dependent children, the elderly and the unemployed. However, it was the Tennessee Valley Authority – a large-scale project bringing hydroelectricity to the rural South – that symbolised the role the federal government was now playing. V. O. Key has recorded the consequences of these measures: 'The federal government . . . had been a remote authority with a limited range of activity. . . . Within a brief time, it became an institution that affected intimately the lives and fortunes of most, if not all, citizens' (quoted in Conlan 1988: 5).

The process of centralisation went further during the Great Society years of the 1960s. President Lyndon Johnson committed the federal government to the construction of a 'Great Society'. The most well known of the Great Society programmes was the 'War on Poverty', directed against conditions in both the inner cities and rural areas. The federal government committed large-scale financial resources to this, and its economic and social role expanded dramatically. The growth of 'big government' continued during President Nixon's period of office. In 1970 alone, grants-in-aid to the states rose by 19.3 per cent on the previous year.

Centralisation

In the 1960s – during the Great Society years – observers talked in terms of *creative federalism*. It was a description of the shift in relationships that had accompanied the Great Society programmes. The federal government was constructing a national system of education, social security and housing. Spending grew on a large scale. The federal government was also taking on an increasingly regulatory role.

The scale and character of federal expenditure during this period had three political consequences. First, it created a relationship structured around dependency. Although the share declined from 26.3 per cent in 1980, federal aid still represented 22.2 per cent of all state and local outlays in 1995 (Bureau of the Census 1997: 302). Second, under many of the Great Society programmes, the states were bypassed. Federal government grants were given directly to localities, city authorities and voluntary groups. Third, the financial transfers increasingly took the form of *categorical* rather than block grants. A categorical grant is provided for a narrow, specified purpose. By contrast, a block grant allows the individual state much more discretion in determining the character of its spending plans.

Opponents claimed that *creative federalism* undermined the power and authority of the states. Thomas R. Dye asserts that the US had become 'indistinguishable from a centralized government. State and local governments are viewed as administrative instruments of the national government. If flexibility is permitted at all, it is only better to implement national goals in a local environment' (1990: 8).

The case for decentralisation

Those who favour decentralisation put forward a number of claims. First, they have geographical objections to centralised government. Washington, DC is 2,294 miles from Los Angeles, 991 miles from Baton Rouge and 2,323 miles from Seattle. Whatever the merits of national government, these distances prevent effective governance from the nation's capital.

Second, in contrast to this, state capitals such as Richmond (Virginia) and Atlanta (Georgia) are relatively accessible. Furthermore, the state legislator will generally have fewer constituents than the US Congressman or Senator. For example, in New Hampshire, each state legislator represents only 2,500 people.

Third, decentralised systems of government offer opportunities for policy experimentation and innovation. The states can act as 'laboratories of innovation'. Policies can, in effect, be 'tested' before being adopted on a more widespread basis. For example, Wisconsin first introduced income tax and California pioneered air-pollution laws. These were later adopted at federal level.

Fourth, state governments can balance out the actions of the national government. They can prevent the legislators and bureaucrats in Washington, DC from becoming excessively powerful. Together with the separation of powers dividing out the three branches of the national government, the states provide a check against tyranny.

Last, the different states and regions have their own political and cultural traditions. Only a federal system offers the space that will allow these to flourish. Daniel Elazar (1972) identifies three different *political cultures* within the US. For example, in Upper New England and the upper Midwest, there is a broadly egalitarian culture. Furthermore, citizens are felt to have responsibilities as well as rights. There is a belief that they should contribute towards the community through the 'town meeting'. However, there is a much more individualistic culture in the mid-Atlantic region and the industrial Midwest. This places more of an emphasis on rights and attaches less importance to notions of community. The South rests, to a greater degree, on ordered structures and hierarchies in which each individual has an established place.

New Federalism

From the late 1960s onwards, there was a political and cultural backlash against *creative federalism*. Conservative criticisms of centralisation and large-scale government expenditure gained increasing acceptance. The right was committed to reversing what they saw as the usurpation of state powers by the federal government. They argued that:

1 The federal government had become unresponsive to local and regional needs. Those 'inside the Beltway' (the interstate highway encircling Washington, DC) were not only remote, but were in the grip of lobbyists

and special interests. Legislators, it was said, had become detached from the electorate they were supposed to represent. Instead, they had been 'bought off' by elite groupings. A succession of ethics and corruption cases at the end of the 1980s and in the early 1990s gave such claims added potency.

2 The policies imposed upon the states by the federal government were derived from liberal fallacies. For example, the critics charged, federal administrators were responsible for the introduction of fashionable, 'pupil-centred' learning methods in the nation's schools. As a consequence, educational standards had fallen, discipline was no longer imposed, and essential skills such as literacy and numeracy were no longer being properly taught.

   Observers also claimed that federal government projects were administered by a cumbersome and impersonal bureaucracy. Federal government had killed off the charitable work which had traditionally been undertaken by voluntary and church organisations.

3 The expansion of federal government had economic, as well as political and social consequences. Increasing tax demands and the imposition of bureaucratic regulations stifled individual effort and deterred entrepreneurship. Government borrowing fuelled inflation and 'crowded out' private-sector investment. Deregulation and a low tax regime, would, it was argued, lead to higher levels of economic growth.

Richard Nixon's election as president in November 1968 was an early expression of the conservative backlash. He was committed to a system of *New Federalism*, which he depicted as a means through which the states would regain some of their former authority. His proposals were structured around *revenue sharing*. Tax revenue, collected by the federal government, would simply be handed down – on a 'no strings' basis – to the individual states, and then spent as the states chose. The federal government would insist only upon proper auditing procedures and assurances that there would be no racial discrimination in the allocation of funds.

In 1972, Congress agreed to a limited Revenue Sharing Act. However, revenue sharing did not survive for long. The Reagan administration saw *all* forms of government spending – whether administered by federal, state or local government – as frequently wasteful and inefficient. The administration's scaled-down revenue-sharing programmes in 1980, and they were finally abandoned in the budget of 1986.

However, although he opposed revenue sharing, President Reagan also talked in terms of New Federalism. In his January 1982 State of the Union message, he promised 'a major effort to restore American federalism'. His proposals rested on four principal elements. Firstly, there was to be a 'swap' whereby the states would assume responsibility for welfare (*Aid to Families with Dependent Children* and food stamps), and the federal government would administer *Medicaid*, which provided limited medical assistance for those on low incomes. Second, there would be an overall reduction in the level of federal grants-in-aid. Third, some categorical grant programmes would be merged into *block* grants, thereby giving the states leeway in deciding between different

---

Arguments against decentralisation

The claims of those who talk in terms of 'states' rights' should be set against other arguments. First, centralised forms of government do not necessarily prevent experimentation and the adoption of different forms of policy in particular areas. Even if the decision-making process is centralised, administration can be decentralised.

Second, Americans are citizens of the US and, as such, are entitled to the *nationally set* minimum standards of justice and social provision laid out in the Bill of Rights and federal legislation.

Third, the states should not be presented as a bulwark against tyranny and oppression. Many have a history of deeply undemocratic practices. As William Bennett, a conservative, notes, the devolution of power to the states 'has often meant reducing the Federal Government's capacity to monitor and correct'. Under the banner of 'states' rights', the southern states adopted racially discriminatory policies up until the 1960s. Federal government action – such as the 1964 Civil Rights Act and the 1965 Voting Rights Act – was required to ensure equality and justice. At the same time, a significant proportion of state legislatures were unrepresentative because their electoral boundaries did not reflect population movements. The rural areas were over-represented. This was only resolved by the US Supreme Court in *Baker v. Carr* (1962).

Fourth, although state capitals may be physically closer to the citizen, there is little evidence of widespread public identification with state governments. Indeed, surveys have repeatedly found that few citizens even know the names of their state legislator. It is therefore difficult to sustain the claim that state government is 'closer to the people' than the decision makers in Washington, DC.

Fifth, although 'states' rights' are defended as a check on the power of the national government, Martha Derthick argues that federalism has, in practice, enlarged the role of the federal courts. This is because the division of power between national and state governments has inevitably created uncertainty. Responsibilities and jurisdictions overlapped or were subject to dispute. In such circumstances, the intervention of an an umpire – the federal judiciary – was required.

Further reading

Derthick, M. (1992), 'Up-to-date in Kansas City: reflections on American federalism', *PS: Political Science and Politics*, XXV:4, December, 671–5.

spending options. Last, certain federal regulations that curtailed state discretion would be eliminated.

The Reagan administration had some successes in implementing these goals. Grants-in-aid were reduced. Attempts were made – through executive orders – to reform the maze of federal regulations that circumscribed state and local governments, but these orders had a broad character. In October 1987, Executive Order 12614 instructed federal government agencies to 'recognise the distinction between problems of national scope . . . and problems that are merely common to the states'. The order asserted that the former required action by the federal government, but the latter should be left to the collective or individual efforts of the states. Some new block grants were created through the merging together of separate categorical grants. In the 1981 Omnibus Budget Reconciliation Act (the annual budget as it is finally agreed), seventy-seven were brought together as nine block grants (King 1989: 35–8).

However, the overall significance of these reforms should not be overstated. They fell short of the hopes raised by President Reagan's initial rhetoric. The proposed 'swap' had to be abandoned altogether. The president was unable to win sufficient support within either Congress or among the state governors. David R. Beam has recorded their thinking: 'The impression was created that federalism was nothing more than a code word for stringent expenditure cuts' (quoted in Benda and Levine 1988: 123). New Federalism should be set against the centralising measures that were adopted. For example, in 1984, following lobbying by the Christian Right and groupings such as MADD (Mothers Against Drunk Drivers), the president supported an Act that raised the minimum drinking age to twenty-one. States that failed to implement the measure lost 10 per cent of federal highway funds. All states complied.

The revival of the states

Although many of the specific proposals associated with New Federalism were lost or passed only in a modified form, there was a shift in the character of state–central relations during the 1980s and 1990s. Although it would be fanciful to talk in terms of a return to dual federalism, there was a limited swing of the pendulum and a partial reassertion of 'states' rights'. This can be attributed to four developments.

1 The Supreme Court made a number of significant rulings. These were surveyed in Chapter 4. Although the *Garcia* ruling (1985) enhanced the powers of the federal government, recent Court rulings – covering, for example, the availability of abortion – have bolstered the position of the individual states.
2 The reductions in the size and scale of grants-in-aid, introduced by the

Reagan administration, had consequences. Federal government aid fell as a share of state and local outlays. In 1980, federal aid accounted for 26.3 per cent of state and local outlays. By 1995, such aid represented only 22.2 per cent of the total. At first sight, this might be a reason to conclude that the decision-making abilities of the states were constrained yet further. Certainly, many of Reagan's opponents feared that this would happen. However, the progressive withdrawal of federal funding compelled the states to become more financially self-reliant.

3 In some states, there was a feeling that the federal government had failed to respond to pressing social and economic problems. They have therefore taken action themselves.

4 Following their 1994 election victories, the Republican majority in Congress developed policies that gave the states further decision-making powers. The 1996 Welfare Reform Act represented a particularly important decentralising shift. The essence of the Act was that the individual states would assume responsibility for welfare provision. This brought to an end a federal guarantee – established as part of the New Deal – that eligible mothers with dependent children would receive assistance.

   Under the 1996 Act, federal funding is given in the form of block grants. Although there is a broad national policy framework, intended to ensure that welfare is only a short-term prop, the states themselves have some discretion in determining the level at which, and the conditions under which, assistance is given to individual claimants. States were, for example, given the option of denying welfare to unwed parents under eighteen and to those who had further children while on welfare.

5 Congress also passed the 1995 Unfunded Mandates Reform Act. Unfunded mandates are federal laws and regulations which require the state and local governments to adopt a particular policy that has to be funded by state and local taxes. The Act sought to curb these so as to broaden state discretion or, at least, relieve the financial burden imposed on them. It stated that (with some exemptions) any federal regulation costing $50 million or more had to be funded by Congress. The Congressional Budget Office now assesses every new law so as to judge its impact on the states and localities.

The states responded to the changing political environment by becoming more assertive, imaginative and innovative. They began to promote their own interests more forcefully. They acted as pressure groups within the broader political system through organisations such as the National Governors' Association, the US Conference of Mayors and the National League of Cities. During the 1990s, these bodies had an increasingly visible profile and held frequent meetings with national legislators. The states themselves employed lobbyists to work on their behalf in Washington, DC. The states also experimented with different methods of raising revenue and found ways of administering their responsibilities that reduced or, at least, restrained costs. Others – frustrated by what they saw as federal inaction – attempted to develop policy alternatives. A *culture of innovation* emerged at state level. This can be seen in a number of policy spheres.

First, a number of Republican governors – particularly those influenced by the supply-side theories pursued by some conservative 'think-tanks' – have pursued radical tax-cutting policies. They believe that these will lead to greater investment, stimulate entrepreneurship, and encourage individual effort. New Jersey Republican Governor Christine Todd Whitman has been particularly associated with tax-cutting initiatives. She has combined a relatively liberal approach to issues such as abortion, with 30 per cent reductions in state income taxes.

Second, some states, such as Wisconsin, have adopted new education policies. They have experimented with 'parental choice' or voucher schemes. Instead of being assigned to a public school, parents of school-age children can be given vouchers issued by the state authorities that can be used to pay the fees charged by private schools. Supporters argue that voucher schemes *empower* parents by giving them a degree of choice about the school that their child attends, and can therefore act as an engine of improvement.

Third, some states have been in the forefront of efforts to impose more severe penalties on offenders. New York was one of a tranche of states to reintroduce the death-penalty. Texas implements its death-penalty laws to a greater extent than all the other states added together. It has also established 'boot camps' for juvenile offenders. New Jersey imposes automatic life sentences on those with three convictions involving violence. A number of states, including Illinois, require sex offenders to register with the police.

Fourth, some states, most notably California, have sought to restrict the provision of assistance to illegal immigrants and end affirmative action programmes. Amidst considerable controversy – in November 1994 – the voters of California passed Proposition 187 by a three to two margin. The measure called for an end to the payment of non-essential state benefits, including education and non-urgent health care, to illegal aliens. It also required public officials, including teachers, to report those suspected of being 'undocumented' to the Immigration and Naturalization Service. Two years later, in November 1996, California voted on the California Civil Rights Initiative (Proposition 209). The initiative, which was passed by 54 per cent to 46 per cent, demanded an end to race- and gender-based recruitment programmes in all state institutions.

Other states have adopted different, but equally innovative agendas. Some have developed trade promotion policies designed to bring in foreign investment. Massachusetts and California have taken 'foreign policy' initiatives a stage further. In 1997, they applied sanctions against American companies trading with Burma, a country whose rulers have been guilty of substantial human rights violations.

Local government

Local governments share responsibility for the services they administer – such as education, zoning, transportation and law enforcement – with the state government. In some states, local governments are directly responsible for most of these. In others, the state government is the principal provider.

Local governments take many different forms. There are municipalities, counties, townships and special districts such as those administered by school boards. In some areas, particularly the suburbs, intergovernmental agreements have been made, whereby services are provided across county lines, or a relatively small community pays a city for policing. The internal structure of local governments also differs, particularly in the towns and cities. Some have a weak mayor – with largely ceremonial functions – and a relatively strong council. In others, the position is reversed. In some areas, those who head the different departments are directly elected by the voters. Many smaller cities have a manager, a professional administrator who is responsible for the provision of services, and answers to a relatively small number of council members.

Conclusion

In some respects the US remains a centralised nation. Federal financial aid to the states is still channelled through categorical grants, and the states have very little discretion in deciding how the funding is used. In 1993, there were only 15 block and 578 categorical grants. Criminal law – traditionally a state responsibility – has been increasingly 'federalised' and federal law now includes over three thousand offences (Grant 1998: 4).

However, despite this, there has been a limited and partial reassertion of 'states' rights'. In the 1980s, the US became a more diverse and pluralistic nation than it was in the 1960s and 1970s. Furthermore, both liberals and conservatives are now committed to a steady extension of state decision making. The pattern of incremental change – through which the states gradually gain more discretion in deciding how the services that they provide should be delivered – seems set to continue. These developments may provide a basis for the beginnings of what Thomas R. Dye calls 'competitive federalism', in which federal, state and local governments would compete with each other to provide the services that citizens demand (1990: 175–99).

Federalism and the Internet

The National Conference of State Legislatures can be found at

http://www.ncsl.org/

References and further reading

Benda, P. M. and C. H. Levine (1988), 'Reagan and the bureaucracy: the bequest, the promise, and the legacy', in C. O. Jones, *The Reagan Legacy: Promise and Performance*, Chatham, Chatham House, 102–42.

Bureau of the Census (1997), *Statistical Abstract of the United States 1997*, Washington, DC, US Department of Commerce.

Conlan, T. (1988), *New Federalism: Intergovernmental Reform from Nixon to Reagan*, Washington, DC, The Brookings Institution.

Dye, T. R. (1990), *American Federalism: Competition Among Governments*, Lexington, Lexington Books.

Elazar, D. J. (1972), *American Federalism: A View from the States*, New York, Crowell.

Grant, A. (1998), 'Reshaping American federalism', *Politics Review*, September, 2–6.

King, D. S. (1989), 'US federalism and the Reagan administration', *Contemporary Record*, November, 35–8.

Part III

Parties, elections and interest groups

9

Political parties

Political parties have been defined as organised groups 'sharing common policy preferences' which 'seek, or have, political power' (Robertson 1985: 252). Traditionally, they have eight principal functions:

1 They have a nomination or recruitment function, because they put forward candidates for public office and generally offer the only secure route for individuals seeking political advancement.
2 They have campaigning and fund-raising functions. They direct and organise election campaigns on behalf of candidates. This work, and other party activities, require substantial funding.
3 By providing a conduit between the citizen and the decision-making process, the parties have a communication function. Traditionally, they organised meetings and gatherings enabling the electorate to hear the views of candidates and, in what was a process of dialogue, put forward their own opinions.
4 Parties have a mobilisation function. Activists would traditionally ensure that all the party's grass-roots supporters cast a vote.
5 They bring together diverse political views and fuse them so as to construct an agreed platform. The role of parties in uniting divergent interests and views has been described as an integration or 'brokerage' function.
6 They have a co-ordination function. Without parties, legislatures would be anarchic and unwieldy. Every vote would involve the construction of fresh alliances and voting blocs. Parties offer a degree of leadership and discipline, and they thereby structure the passage of legislation. They can also provide ties between public officials in the different branches and tiers of government.
7 Parties have a policy or issue development function. They are compelled by the process of electoral competition to generate new proposals and policy options within a broad framework set by their core values. As Clinton Rossiter argued, the parties 'are perhaps best fitted of all agencies to convert

formless hopes or frustrations into proposals that can be understood, debated, and, if found appealing, approved by the people' (1960: 50).

8 Parties offer a basis for political identification. The voter can swiftly recognise the political leanings and allegiances of candidates. This simplifies the electoral process and makes it accessible to those who have only limited political knowledge. As Martin Wattenberg notes:

> it would probably take an individual approximately the amount of time required for one or two college-level courses a year in order to cast a completely informed vote for all of these offices in all of these elections. Therefore, voters need shortcuts, or cues, such as partisanship to facilitate their decision-making. (1996: 14)

American parties

Although this typology of functions offers a recognisable picture of the European political parties, the two principal American parties – the Democrats and the Republicans (or GOP, Grand Old Party) – are different. They encompass broad and sometimes irreconcilable spans of opinion. Votes in Congress and state legislatures cannot be predicted with certainty. As Clinton Rossiter put it: 'for many Americans the party is like a church, but on the Unitarian rather than the Catholic model, that is, a church that makes few demands and exercises no discipline' (1960: 57).

Over the past three decades, the US parties have appeared to be growing yet further away from the European model. This has led some observers to assert that they are in long-term decline. The parties, it is said, are being displaced by candidate-based forms of organisation, interest groups and lobbying firms. They have, furthermore, lost the loyalty of the voting public. Others, however, challenge this portrayal. They point to what they see as a process of party renewal. This chapter outlines the history of the parties, surveys their organisational character, and assesses the claims of those who talk of 'party decline'.

The principal parties

Political parties were an established feature of American life by 1840 (Congressional Quarterly 1997b: 162). They had their origins in the small groups and factions created by politicians seeking office at both state and federal level. Those around Thomas Jefferson established the Democratic-Republicans. They put forward a vision of a decentralised nation and sought support from craftsmen and farmers. Alexander Hamilton's supporters, known as the Federalists, were backed by commercial interests and argued for a strong national government.

Mass parties, extending beyond caucuses of elected officials, grew with the broadening out of the right to vote. Andrew Jackson was elected in 1828 through the efforts of the newly formed Democratic Party. Although it drew on the backing of agricultural interests, Jacksonianism also rested on the opportunities that westward expansion offered to the ordinary citizen. Jackson's critics coalesced to form the Whigs. Although they had supporters in every social and economic grouping, they were – like the earlier Federalists before them – a party of business and economic development (McSweeney and Zvesper 1991: 20).

The transformation of the US – through mass immigration – also restructured the political parties. The Democrats became the party of the recently arrived immigrant. In contrast, the Whigs became associated with the interests of White Anglo-Saxon Protestants (WASPs), who increasingly resented the threat to their economic security and culture that the immigrant seemingly posed.

The modern party system, based around Democrats and Republicans, emerged on the eve of the Civil War as slavery came to dominate national political debate. Those who opposed the extension of slavery into the newly created states and territories that westward expansion had created, formed the Republican Party. The Republican candidate, Abraham Lincoln, was elected to the presidency in 1860. Over the century that followed, the white South remained loyal to the Democratic Party.

Although it was sometimes masked by regional and local variations, there was, however, another period of realignment at the end of the nineteenth century. The Democrats added to their support by incorporating the further waves of immigrants who arrived from southern and eastern Europe and small farmers who, feeling abandoned by the federal government and the 'robber barons' of big business, turned to populist politics. For their part, the Republicans were the party of urbanisation and industry. The American industrial revolution and the growth of cities gave them an inherent advantage, and Republicans occupied the White House for twenty-eight of the years between 1897 and 1933.

The Democrats' New Deal coalition

The modern Democratic Party has its origins in the economic depression of the 1930s. Franklin Roosevelt's election victories in 1932, 1936, 1940 and 1944 brought together a broad alliance of economic, racial, religious and regional interests. The 'New Deal coalition' embraced blue-collar industrial workers, Jews, Roman Catholics, African-Americans, and white southerners. It was held together between the 1930s and 1960s by the promise of basic welfare provision, government employment projects, and acquiescence towards the white South's efforts to maintain segregation.

There were, however, inherent strains. As the civil rights movement asserted itself, the Democratic Party had to choose between the political goals of African-Americans and those of the white South. The Party chose, albeit hesitantly, the former, and blacks now represent the Democrats' most loyal constituency. In the 1996 presidential election, Bill Clinton won 84 per cent of black votes. However, white southerners – and those such as Senator Strom Thurmond, who served as their political representatives – responded to the Party's identification with the civil rights movement by defecting to the Republicans. In 1996, Clinton won only 36 per cent of the vote among whites living in the south (*New York Times* 1996).

The New Deal coalition suffered other losses. The party was split apart by the Vietnam War. The rise of new social movements – such as the women's movement and post-civil rights 'black power' organisations – provoked hostility among the Party's more traditional blue-collar supporters. These sentiments were compounded by resentment against 'big government' and the taxation levels required to maintain it. From a blue-collar perspective, the Democratic Party seemed to have been 'captured' by intellectuals and radicals with whom they had little in common. The success of George McGovern, a liberal, anti-war candidate, in winning the Party's presidential nomination in 1972 confirmed their fears.

The Republicans' conservative coalition

The Democratic Party's difficulties were the Republican Party's opportunity. Both Richard Nixon and Ronald Reagan were able to bring disaffected Democratic Party supporters into the Republican camp. The GOP emphasised issues that would solidify the divide between them and the liberalism that held sway among many Democratic Party activists. They held out the promise of tax reductions, small government, traditional cultural values, opposition to race and gender-based policies, and a reassertion of US national interests on the world stage.

Although President Nixon never fully embraced these themes, they increasingly became the political basis of Republicanism. By the 1980s, the GOP had become a conservative party, and the few remaining liberals had been relegated to the sidelines. During President Reagan's period of office (1981–89), there were tax cuts, a sustained attempt to reduce the scope and size of the federal government, and a pull-back from policies structured around gender and race. Cold War hostilities intensified until the USSR began a process of reform.

Although the Bush presidency (1989–93) marked a partial return to a more pragmatic political style, the Republican Party remains tied to conservatism. In the 1996 presidential election, the Party's candidate, Bob Dole, campaigned around solid conservative themes such as tax reductions, welfare reform, and the protection of the family. Support for the GOP is disproportionately drawn from white, southern, rural men in the higher-income groups.

Political parties and the Internet

All the principal political parties (and many minor organisations) have their own websites. Most offer links to related campaigns:

Democratic National Committee – http://www.democrats.org
Republican National Committee – http://www.rnc.org
Reform Party – http://www.reformparty.org
Libertarian Party – http://www.lp.org

The minor parties

The US is a heterogenous nation and there has, as a consequence, always been a plethora of minor parties. James Q. Wilson divides them into four categories (Congressional Quarterly 1997a: 117):

1 There are ideological parties, such as the Socialist Workers' Party. They are generally associated with either the far Left or Right.
2 There are one-issue parties, such as the Prohibition Party, which opposes the manufacture, sale and consumption of alcoholic drink. The Eighteenth Amendment to the US Constitution enforced Prohibition between 1920 and 1933.
3 Economic protest parties have emerged during periods of depression. At the end of the nineteenth century, the Greenback Party and the Populists called for currency reform so as improve economic conditions.
4 Factional parties have generally developed from splits in the principal parties. In 1912, former president Theodore Roosevelt split from the Republicans and established the 'Bull Moose' Party. The issue of segregation led Governor George Wallace of Alabama to form the American Independent Party in 1968.

Today, two of the smaller parties have particular significance. Ross Perot won almost one in five of the votes in the 1992 presidential election. It was the most successful performance for a third-party candidate since Theodore Roosevelt – the former president – gained 27.4 per cent of the vote in the election of 1912. Perot's showing led to the formation of the Reform Party. It is committed to the balancing of the federal government budget and curbs on legislators in Washington, DC. The Party's platform included twelve-year term limits on members of Congress, restrictions on lobbyists, as well as the reform of government health-care programmes such as Medicare and Medicaid. Perot stood again – as the Reform Party's 1996 presidential candidate – but only won 8.5 per cent of the vote. Jesse 'The Body' Ventura, a former professional wrestler and a member of the Reform Party, won the governorship of Minnesota in the November 1998 elections.

The Libertarian Party (LP) was founded in December 1971. It is committed to 'a world of liberty; a world in which all individuals are sovereign over their own lives, and no one is forced to sacrifice his or her values for the benefit of others' (Libertarian Party 1996). The LP puts forward a platform based around free-market economics, the abolition of welfare provision, and minimal government. However, the Party distances itself from others on the Right by calling for the legalisation of all victimless 'crimes' – for example, drug taking – and an end to restrictions on all consensual sexual activity. They support gay rights and the legalisation of prostitution. Since its founding, the LP has put forward large numbers of candidates in presidential, Congressional and state elections. In 1992, there were 700 candidates who together received more than 3,700,000 votes. The twenty-three candidates for the US Senate gained over a million of these votes. In New Hampshire, four candidates were elected to the state legislature. The Party was on the ballot in all fifty states for the presidential elections in 1980, 1992 and 1996.

Others have also talked about the formation of new parties. At the end of the 1960s, there were proposals for a black political party. Twenty years later, some other traditional supporters of the Democrats began to broach the issue. It was considered by the National Organisation for Women (NOW) at its Cincinnati convention in July 1989. Some trade-union activists resurrected the belief that a labour party should be established. Tony Mazzocchi of the Oil, Chemical, and Atomic Workers Union pointed to the degree of disenchantment with the major parties: 'people are angry out there and are rejecting existing electoral choices by staying away' (quoted in Rothschild 1990: 58).

Party structures

Students of British and European parties think in terms of national organisations with a defined membership and formal hierarchical structures. However, although there are positions and structures – precinct chairmen, ward committees, city and county committees, state committees and national committees – the principal US parties are much looser than such a listing suggests. Party membership is almost always an imprecise notion. In practice, it refers to supporters, identifiers and registered voters.

Today, the parties have few committed activists. Participation is often limited to the giving of a financial contribution. Ward and even county committees can often be empty shells. The parties' rules are regulated by state and federal law rather than by activists. The parties are also highly decentralised. As McSweeney and Zvesper note:

> Each unit of the party possesses near autonomy. They are subject to little control or assistance from other levels. Each is responsible for recruiting its own activists, raising funds and conducting election campaigns. . . . Devices for securing hierarchical controls in American parties are few. (1991: 100)

Barriers

Although there are innumerable small parties within the US, none has come close to making an electoral breakthrough. There are eight principal reasons for this.

1 There are ideological obstacles. Many of the attempts to build alternatives to the Republicans and Democrats have been made by groups associated with either the far Left or far Right. The Communist Party of the USA and the Socialist Workers' Party have regularly stood candidates in at least some of the states in both presidential and Congressional elections. However, the American creed that was outlined in Chapter 2 is deeply embedded within the country's political culture. Although institutionalised racism disfigured that culture in the southern states, and gave rise to a number of organisations and small parties, doctrines such as socialism and fascism have, historically, been largely confined to immigrant groups with close European ties.

2 There are administrative and legal obstacles. Many states require that candidates gain a certain number of signatures before their names can be placed on the ballot. The principal parties need only submit a limited number (Davies 1992: 134). The regulations for third parties are, however, much more demanding and they require many more names. If Pennsylvania's 1997 rules for third parties had been adopted in the 1996 presidential election, they would had to have collected 99,000 signatures in fourteen weeks (Bibby and Maisel 1998: 62). There are also 'sore loser' laws in some states that prohibit those who were defeated in the primaries entering the general election contest. In 1996, apart from the Democrats and Republicans, only the Reform Party and the Libertarian Party presidential candidates were able to meet all the requirements and thus gain a place on the ballot in all fifty states.

3 Members of Congress represent a single-member district. There is a 'first-past-the-the-post' electoral system, and few people will vote for a small party that they believe has no realistic prospect of success. Where small parties do win votes, these tend to be dispersed across a number of districts. Presidential elections still rest on the Electoral College (see Chapter 10). This also works on a winner-takes-all basis. In 1992, Ross Perot attracted 19 per cent of the popular vote across the US, yet gained no Electoral College Votes at all.

4 There are also financial difficulties. Under the Federal Election Campaign Act (FECA), candidates contesting the Republican and Democratic presidential

There are, in particular, few connections between the party organisations within a particular state and the national party committee (McSweeney and Zvesper 1991: 106). Indeed, although they have been strengthened since the 1970s, national forms of organisation still remain underdeveloped. The

primaries are awarded matching funds by the federal government. Furthermore, the Democratic and GOP national conventions each attracted a subsidy from the taxpayer. In the November election campaign, the major party candidates have their costs paid in full. Minor parties must be on the ballot in at least ten states and gain at least 5 per cent of the poll to receive tax-payer funding. If they are a new party, these funds are only provided retrospectively rather than when they are most needed.

5 For many individuals and campaigns, interest-group activity offers a more effective avenue of influence than the formation of a party. As Chapter 11 argues, the US political system offers countless access points that enable organised interests to reach decision makers at both a federal and state level.

6 Third-party candidates are often unable to gain media coverage. In contrast, the Democratic and Republican national conventions receive extensive attention. Although Ross Perot participated in 1992, independents are generally excluded from the televised presidential debates that are held shortly before election day.

7 The development of primaries opened up the Democrats and Republicans. Individuals from a broad range of political backgrounds have the opportunity to campaign for support within the two principal parties, and there is therefore less of a likelihood that they will establish alternative party organisations. A strategy of 'burrowing from within' is likely to prove more successful (Bibby and Maisel 1998: 58). David Duke, a former Ku Klux Klan leader, initially attempted to break into politics as the presidential candidate of the Populist Party. He abandoned the Party and contested the 1988 Democratic Parties. In 1989, after success in the primary, he became a Republican nominee for the Louisiana state legislature to which he was elected. In 1992, he entered the Republican Party presidential primaries, winning 11 and 9 per cent of the poll in Mississippi and Louisiana respectively.

8 The principal parties have a loose, heterogeneous and amorphous ideological character. New social movements do not, therefore, form independent parties. They are instead largely absorbed by either the Republicans or Democrats. Black militancy, the women's movement, and green campaigners were drawn into the Democratic camp. The taxpayers' revolt of the 1970s and the Christian Right were incorporated into Republicanism.

Further reading

Bibby, J. F. and L. S. Maisel (1998), *Two Parties – or More? The American Party System*, Boulder, Westview Press.

national committees that bring together representatives from state parties, Congress, and constituent organisations such as Young Democrats and the National Federation of Republican Women, assemble just twice a year. The national headquarters of the parties in Washington, DC are relatively small-scale and modestly equipped. National conventions are only held every four years in the months preceding a presidential election.

Party decline

The party decline thesis suggests that the principal parties no longer perform many of the functions outlined at the beginning of the chapter. The thesis has been succinctly summarised thus:

> the two parties are in full retreat in all the areas that they have traditionally dom- inated. No matter whether it is selecting candidates, fundraising, running cam- paigns, mobilising voters, or co-ordinating government, the argument is that the parties have become less and less relevant. In short, the parties are no longer doing the things which parties are even minimally expected to do. (Bailey 1990: 12)

Nominating candidates

The rise of primaries and caucuses, which enabled ordinary voters to select the parties' candidates, began as an attempt to dislodge the party 'bosses' and 'machine' politicians who had offered rewards (principally jobs) to those who backed them. However, as a long-term consequence, the nomination function was progressively transferred from the parties to the broader public.

The first primary was held in Wisconsin in 1905. By 1912, 32.9 per cent of the delegates attending the Democrats' national convention, which formally chooses the Party's presidential candidate, had been selected in primaries. By 1976, the proportion of delegates selected in the Democratic primaries had risen to 72.6 per cent, although old-style political leaders were able to influence or even dictate the primary results in some states until the 1960s (Hays Lowenstein 1992: 67). Many of the delegates will have been 'pledged' or man- dated to vote for the candidate who won in their state's primary. Those who lost in the primaries generally concede defeat many months before the convention, often in the early stages of the primary season. The outcome of the nominating process is thereby determined in advance of the national convention. The con- vention now simply provides a formal endorsement of the voters' choice and has been reduced from a decision-making forum to a stage-managed media event.

The institutionalisation of the primary in the selection of candidates has had important consequences for the political character of the parties (McSweeney and Zvesper 1991: 129–32):

1 The party may have maverick candidates who do not conform to the overall party image or adhere to its core values imposed upon it. In 1998, Fred Tuttle, a seventy-nine-year-old dairy farmer, stood so as to defeat an out-of-

state candidate, won the primary, and gained the Republican senatorial nomination for Vermont. He declared that he would spend no more than $251 (a dollar for each town in the state) on his entire campaign. During the contest, which Tuttle lost, he emphasised the strengths of his Democratic Party opponent and stated that he would probably vote for him. Open primaries – which allow any voter to participate – are particularly susceptible.

2 The primaries also often lead to disunity within the parties. Disputes are magnified as the candidates establish their own personal profile and distinguish themselves from others in the field. All this inevitably takes place in the public arena. In 1988, as the New Hampshire primary approached, the contest to win the Republican nomination became particularly bitter when Robert Dole accused George Bush of 'lying' about his political record. In 1992, Pat Buchanan's savage attacks on President George Bush during the early primaries contributed to Bush's defeat in the November election.

3 Primaries lessen a party's hold over its elected officials. As noted, they owe their success to the campaign organisations that they established during the primaries rather than to the party apparatus. Indeed, in many elections, the campaign literature issued by candidates does not include references to either a party label or to fellow candidates from the same party.

The overall impact of primaries on party structures was reinforced by the McGovern–Fraser reforms. These were drawn up by the Commission on Party Structure and Delegate Selection established by the Democrats in the wake of the 1968 presidential election. In 1968, the Democratic nominee was former Vice-President Hubert Humphrey, a late entrant into the race, who although backed by party leaders, had not stood in the primaries. It was a 'top-down' selection process and there were allegations from supporters of Senator Eugene McCarthy – who had contested the primaries on a platform opposing America's military intervention in Vietnam – that the system by which national convention delegates were selected had been rigged to deny them proper representation.

The Commission's report – *Mandate for Change*, which was published in 1970 – led to amendments to state law and thereby compelled both parties to make rule changes. Caucuses – meetings which are held to decide on candidate selection – were made more open. In the Democratic Party, the proportionality rules that ensured the delegation's voting at the national convention reflected the votes cast in the primary, were introduced. The Commission also stipulated that delegations should become more socially representative by including women, minorities and young people 'in reasonable relationship to their presence in the population of the state'. The reforms were put into effect at the 1972 national convention. They placed strict limits on the influence of party organisers and made primaries pivotal in delegate selection. A mere 1.1 per cent of the delegates were elected by the state party committees (Congressional Quarterly 1997a: 28).

Campaigning

In the primaries, candidates established their own campaign organisations. Once the nomination is secured, they continue to rely on their own personal apparatus rather than the party. In 1972, for example, President Nixon's successful bid to win a second presidential term was organised around the Committee for the Reelection of the President (CREEP). In 1992, Bill Clinton's election campaign was directed from Little Rock in Arkansas, not from the Democratic National Committee's headquarters in Washington, DC, by his personal appointees, most notably George Stephanopoulos and James Carville.

Fund-raising

Fears that the democratic process was being distorted by the ability of some candidates to spend large sums of money led to the passage of laws regulating election spending. Although Supreme Court rulings have established that their provisions are not compulsory, candidates are only eligible for financial assistance from the taxpayer if they comply with the Federal Election Campaign Act (FECA) of 1971 and the amendments that were subsequently made to it.

   Party contributions to election candidates are only a small proportion of those made by individuals – generally in response to appeals sent by direct mail – and Political Action Committees (PACs). For example, in the 1988 Congressional elections, candidates raised less than 1 per cent of their funds from the parties (McSweeney 1995: 18). PACs can be established by either individuals or interest groups, and under the provisions of the FECA, they represent the only legal channel for the donation of funds to presidential or Congressional candidates by organisations. The number of PACs has mushroomed over the past two decades. In 1974 there were 608; by 1996, the number had risen to 4,079 (Congressional Quarterly 1997a: 51). In 1991–92, they gave a total of over $394 million to presidential and Congressional candidates. The leading donors are PACs established by companies and the trade unions. Dean McSweeney has described the net effect of FECA: 'By circumscribing party capacity to contribute and by promoting alternative sources of finance, FECA amendments immediately reduced candidates' dependence on parties for funds' (1990: 148).

Communication

Modern technology has undermined another traditional function of the parties. Traditionally, they would hold meetings and organise processions in support of their candidates. However, television 'has supplanted the political party as the main conduit between candidate and voter' (Ceasar 1990: 106). Today, television reaches almost 98 per cent of all households in the US. Radio and television offer the opportunity – through paid commercials – to present an unmediated message. In 1992, Bush, Clinton and Perot spent a combined total of $92 million on television advertising (Congressional Quarterly 1997a: 107).

The role played by the mass media has, however, been subject to criticism. Whereas party meetings were a two-way process, TV and radio are a one-way medium. Furthermore, news reporting is a mediated form of communication, and in contrast to the parties, the media cannot be held to account by voters. Newspapers, radio stations and TV channels can treat or depict candidates in a way that they alone wish. Many journalists and broadcasters are said to share broadly liberal aspirations and prejudices and are not representative of American society (McSweeney 1990: 160).

Mobilisation

The role that the parties traditionally played in 'getting out the vote' has been assumed by interest groups. A number of groups have increasingly concentrated their attention on activities intended to maximise turnout levels among those sections of the population most likely to support their aims and objectives. The Christian Coalition canvasses churchgoers through phone calls, direct mail, and the production of voter guides. In 1998, the trade unions – represented by the American Federation of Labor-Congress of Industrial Organizations (AFL-CIO) – spent three times as much on this form of activity as they did on the production of issue-advocacy advertisements (Greenblatt 1998: 2880).

Cohesion and party unity

Studies of British politics draw attention to backbench revolts. The coverage they receive in press reports and academic surveys is testimony to their lack of frequency. For the most part, the House of Commons is a disciplined institution and MPs almost always follow the dictates of party leaders and whips.

Party discipline and consensus has never been a feature of US politics. Indeed, there have always been significant divisions within both parties. The breadth of the coalitions they brought together made this inevitable. From the 1930s until the 1970s, the Democratic Party embraced both northern blacks and white southerners, many of whom were seeking to maintain segregation laws in their own states. Today, although there has been a growth in *partisanship* which is considered below, issues such as abortion, trade protectionism and immigration cut across the party lines and have, at times, led to rifts. Within the Republican Party there are at least three distinct factions:

1 There are supply-siders or economic conservatives such as Jack Kemp, a former Congressman who served as the Party's vice-presidential candidate

in 1996, and Steve Forbes, the magazine publisher, who contested the 1996 primaries. Their influence is evident in the policy statements and proposals put forward by organisations such as Empower America. They stress the importance of removing the barriers that impede the workings of the free market and they regard tax reductions, deregulation and the creation of an environment within which business can thrive as the key to economic recovery. Kemp has appropriated some of the goals historically associated with the Left insofar as he emphasises the ability of the free market to end poverty and disadvantage within the inner cities. On the basis of this, he argues for an 'inclusive' conservatism that reaches out to African-Americans and other minorities. Forbes emphasised the importance of tax cuts. Despite fierce criticism from within the GOP, Whitman has endorsed the 'pro-choice' campaigns of those who support the continued availability of legal abortions.

2 There is also a right-wing populist grouping within the Party. Those associated with it are sometimes described as social conservatives. However, their most visible representative is Patrick J. Buchanan, who draws on both social and economic conservatism and directs his appeal towards the blue-collar communities of 'middle America' to Republicanism. He argues for the imposition of tariffs to prevent cheap imports undermining American industries, and vigorously opposed the North American Free Trade Agreement (NAFTA) which was endorsed by other Republicans such as Newt Gingrich. He opposed the Gulf War and has associated himself with calls for a more isolationist form of foreign policy. He has also proposed a five-year ban on almost all immigration, the prohibition of abortion, and a 'cultural war' against cultural and sexual permissiveness. Buchanan sought the GOP's presidential nomination in both 1992 and 1996, winning 22.8 per cent and 21.2 per cent of the primary vote respectively (Congressional Quarterly 1997b: 218, 227).

3 Others within the Republican Party can be seen as pragmatists. Figures such as President George Bush (1989–93) and former Senate Majority Leader Bob Dole have maintained a distance from the formal ideologies offered by Kemp, Forbes or Buchanan. Although they have had to endorse some of the themes associated with social conservative organisations such as the Christian Coalition, and adopt the calls of the radical tax-cutters, their critics have always felt that they had no genuine commitment to such policies. Bush's abandonment of his 1988 election pledge, 'Read my lips, no new taxes' during the 1990 Budget negotiations with Congress was regarded as testimony to this.

Although the dividing lines are sometimes blurred, there are also divisions among Democrats. Al Gore is, like Bill Clinton, associated with the Democratic Leadership Council (DLC). Formed in the aftermath of the Democratic defeat in the 1984 presidential election, the DLC was formed as an attempt to wean the

Party away from its close association with labour (or trade) unionism and traditional adherence to big government 'tax and spend' policies. Whereas the unions have protectionist sympathies, the DLC called for unrestricted international trade. Government intervention, the DLC asserted, should be confined to certain specific sectors of the economy such as education. Despite the demands of groupings such as the Congressional Black Caucus, the DLC also wanted to modify affirmative action programmes and other race-based policies. In 1997, members of Congress who supported the DLC's approach established the New Democrat Coalition.

However, the New Democrats of the DLC have not gone unchallenged. They have been compared with the 'Boll Weevils' – the white conservative southerners – who, in earlier years, held the balance of power in Congress. According to Jeff Faux of the Economic Policy Institute: 'Their program cannot hold together. It is a tired mixture of conservative intention watered down with liberal tinkering in the hope that it will fill in the crack in the center' (1995: 173). Furthermore, Democratic traditionalism – based around a commitment to what its critics regard as 'big government' and the interests of labour, women and minorities – still has a significant number of adherents. The divisions have become explicit around trade policy. The Democrats associated with the trade unions – including House Minority Leader Dick Gephardt – generally opposed NAFTA and other forms of trade liberalisation. In contrast, New Democrats have pressed for the abolition of trade barriers.

There are also other dividing lines. Members of Congress and contenders for the presidential nomination have sectional and regional interests which lead to policy rifts. As a consequence, votes in Congress are often preceded by a process of coalition building that cuts across partisan lines. This was particularly evident during the years between 1966 and 1975. 'Party votes', in which a majority of Democrats voted against a majority of Republicans, only formed 35.4 per cent of all votes in the House of Representatives. The corresponding figure for the Senate was 39.8 per cent (McSweeney 1990: 152).

Within Congress, the divisions were reinforced during the 1970s and 1980s by the decentralisation and diffusion of power. In the aftermath of Watergate, the traditional power structure which had been structured around committee 'barons' began to crumble, and individual members of Congress began to assert themselves. Rank and file caucuses were formed. Subcommittees gained new powers. Individuals pursued their own agendas (Owens 1996: 15–16). The growth of Congressional individualism was graphically captured by David Broder in 1989:

> In our era of debilitated political parties, Washington is run by 536 individual political entrepreneurs – one president, 100 senators and 435 members of the House – each of whom got here essentially on his own. Each chooses the office he seeks, raises his own money, hires his own pollster and ad-maker and recruits his own volunteers. (quoted in Wattenberg 1991: 165)

Policy development

Policy development is undertaken by interest groups or 'think-tanks' rather than the parties. Conservative 'think-tanks' such as the American Enterprise Institute (AEI), the libertarian Cato Institute, and the more broadly based Heritage Foundation have, for example, been influential in Republican Party circles. Heritage was founded in February 1973. It was established amid concerns that the Republican Party was been pulled towards the pragmatism of centre-ground politics. The Foundation publishes *Policy Review*, a bimonthly journal, offers handbooks for candidates, briefing documents, research papers and conferences, and supports a website which acts as a clearing house for a broad range of conservative organisations and campaigns.

There are, however, liberal counterweights to conservative foundations such as Heritage. The Progressive Policy Institute studies policy options that will 'foster a more inclusive, more democratic capitalism'. The Economic Policy Institute was founded in 1986 and has ties to the trade unions. It 'seeks to broaden the public debate about strategies to achieve a prosperous and fair economy'. The National Center on Education and the Economy is 'dedicated to the development of a comprehensive US system of education, employment and training'.

Party identification

There is evidence to suggest that the parties no longer play a significant role in the voting process. There has been a process of *partisan dealignment*, and the parties have failed to retain the loyalty of voters. As Martin Wattenberg puts it: 'for over four decades the American public has been drifting away from the two major political parties' (1996: ix). The reasons for this are examined in Chapter 10. Some features of dealignment should, however, be considered at this stage. It is not that the American public see the parties in negative terms. Instead, they are largely indifferent or neutral (Wattenberg 1991: 42). These feelings are reflected in the decline in the number of 'strong party identifiers' who are deeply committed to the party of their choice. In 1952, 22 per cent of the electorate regarded themselves as 'strong Democrats'. By 1992, a year in which the Democrats won the White House and maintained their control over both houses of Congress, the figure had fallen to 15 per cent (Bureau of the Census 1997: 287). There was a similar process of detachment among Republicans. In 1952, 14 per cent of the electorate recorded that they were 'strong Republicans'. By 1992, it was 16 per cent. At the same time, the numbers calling themselves 'independents' has grown. It has risen from 22 per cent in 1952 to 35 per cent in 1994 (Flanigan and Zingale 1998: 61).

The progressive erosion of party loyalties can be seen in other ways. Candidates almost always de-emphasise party ties. Although there was a partially renewed sense of partisanship in the 1990s, the proportion of *ticket-*

Table 9.1 *Presidential/Congressional split-ticket voting, 1952–96 (%)*

	1952	1956	1960	1964	1968	1972	1976	1980	1984	1988	1992	1996
Dem. Pres. Rep. Congr.	2	2	4	9	7	5	9	8	6	7	10	13
Rep. Pres. Dem. Congr.	10	13	10	6	11	25	16	20	20	18	12	4

Source: The National Election Studies (NES), Center for Political Studies, University of Michigan. The NES Guide to Public Opinion and Electoral Behavior (http://www.umich.edu/~nes/nesguide/nesguide.htm). Ann Arbor, University of Michigan, Center for Political Studies, 1995–98.

Notes: These materials are based on work supported by the National Science Foundation under Grant Nos: SBR-9707741, SBR-9317631. SES-9209410, SES-9009379, SES-8808361, SES-8341310, SES-8207580 and SOC77–08885.

Any opinions, findings and conclusions or recommendations expressed in these materials are those of the authors and do not necessarily reflect those of the National Science Foundation.

splitters – those who cast their votes for candidates from different parties in the same election – has grown. In the period between 1952 and 1988, the proportion voting for different parties in House and Senate elections increased from 9 per cent to 27 per cent (Davidson and Oleszek 1998: 100–2). It is also evident in voting for the president and Congress.

Survival and renewal

The party decline model has been challenged. It rests, by implication, on the premise that there was a past 'golden age' when parties flourished. The accuracy of this should, however, be doubted. A 1956 study of Detroit revealed that less than one-fifth of local organisations were operating at their full potential. As a Congressman noted, two years later: 'if we depended on the party organization to get elected, none of us would be here' (Wattenberg 1996: 108).

The degree to which the parties are in decline has also been exaggerated. Despite dealignment, almost two-thirds of adult Americans identify with one of the principal parties. Those who endorse the party decline thesis also fail to recognise the extent to which US politics are dominated by the Republicans and Democrats. Of the 535 members of the House of Representatives and Senate, only one Congressman, Bernie Sanders of Burlington in Vermont, does not belong to one of the two principal parties, and he is, in practice, closely aligned with the Democrats. In twenty-one states, parties and party loyalties are strengthened, and split-ticket voting reduced, through the use of single-ticket procedures. Voters can, if they so wish, endorse one party's candidates for every post simply by pulling one lever or casting one ballot. A significant proportion take this option. Furthermore, many state parties retain considerable powers of patronage. They can still influence the appointment of election officials and the award of contracts to firms in the construction and service sectors (Congressional Quarterly 1997a: 105).

The parties have also made sustained attempts to recapture the nomination process. Within the Democratic Party, there was a steady retreat from the McGovern–Fraser reforms which circumscribed the role of party officials and committees. The Commission on Presidential Nomination and Party Structure, chaired by former Michigan Party Chairman Morley Winograd between 1975 and 1980, recommended that party officials should constitute an 'add-on' 10 per cent of uncommitted national convention delegates. They became known as 'superdelegates', and their inclusion reintroduced peer review into the process of nomination. The Winograd proposals were built upon in 1982, when a commission chaired by Governor James B. Hunt of North Carolina recommended a significant increase in their numbers (Congressional Quarterly 1997a: 30–1). By 1992, 'superdelegates' represented 18 per cent of the total numbers in attendance.

For their part, the Republicans established two committees examining their rules for presidential selection. However, although they had to make changes because of amendments to state law, their party structures never lost control to the same degree as the Democratic hierarchy. The GOP had little sympathy with claims that particular groups – such as blacks or women – should be allocated 'quotas'. Republican officials were willing, furthermore, to use the party apparatus to influence the nomination process. Party elites allegedly played a significant role in ensuring that George Bush won the Republican presidential nomination in 1988. They were, it is said, particularly active in the run-up to the New Hampshire, South Carolina and Illinois primaries (Ceasar 1990: 112).

A number of legal rulings have also strengthened the position of parties and party organisers. Following the 1972 Democratic national convention, the US Supreme Court ruled in *Cousins v. Wigoda* (1975) that state courts cannot interfere with the right of national parties to decide who will be seated at their national conventions. This was confirmed in *Democratic Party of the United States v. LaFollette* (1981) (Plano and Greenberg 1989: 64).

Other rulings also gave the parties greater control over their own internal affairs. In 1986, in *Tashjian v. Republican Party of Connecticut*, the Supreme Court established that states could not prevent a party holding an open primary which allowed voters of all political persuasions – rather than simply those who were registered as party supporters – to participate in the election (Plano and Greenberg 1989: 81). Three years later, in *March Fong Eu v. San Francisco County Democratic Central Committee* (1989), the Court declared that the parties had the right to endorse a particular candidate in the primaries (Hays Lowenstein 1992: 81).

National leadership

The parties began to establish more proactive forms of national leadership during the 1970s. Bill Brock, who was Party Chairman between 1977 and 1981, developed a direct-mail programme. By the early 1980s, the Party had attracted contributions from two million people and had raised almost $78 million (Bailey 1990: 13). In 1992 alone, it raised $254.8 million (Congressional Quarterly 1997a: 106). The Republican National Committee (RNC) gained a permanent headquarters a block away from Capitol Hill, and by 1984 the number of staff it employed reached 600, a threefold increase from 1976 (Ceasar 1990: 105). The RNC offers candidate training, a cable TV service (GOP-TV), officials responsible for outreach work among young people and minorities, and fund-raising activities. In 1983–84, $106 million was raised (McSweeney and Zvesper 1991: 117). The RNC played a pivotal role in the 1994 Congressional elections. It spent $20.2 million on campaigns, national advertisements, and financial transfers to state and local parties. As the 104th Congress (1995–97) progressed, the RNC spent a further $200,000 on a campaign to promote the reforms, such as the balanced budget amendment, that were being introduced in Congress.

The work and the role of the Democratic National Committee (DNC) has grown similarly, albeit on a lesser scale. Like the Republicans, the DNC adopted fund-raising strategies and direct-mail techniques. In 1992, for example, it raised $162.2 million (Congressional Quarterly 1997a: 106). Former chairman, Charles T. Manatt, developed ties between the Party and companies. The DNC also acquired a permanent headquarters, owned by the Party itself, in 1984. The number of staff grew. In 1976, it employed only thirty. By 1984, this had risen to 130 (Ceasar 1990: 105). The DNC works closely with Party organisations such as the College Democrats and the Democratic Governors' Association.

Finance

Although the net effect of the Federal Election Campaign Act (FECA) was to weaken their financial role, the Act did in some respects assist the principal parties. Their national conventions receive a subsidy from the FEC. They are allowed to make larger donations to election campaigns than PACs or individuals. Most important of all, despite the limits on spending imposed by the FECA, amendments passed in 1979 allow local and state parties to spend on 'party-building' and 'get-out-the-vote' activities. The distinction between this and campaigning work on behalf of a candidate is, in practice, inevitably blurred.

Furthermore, individuals and organisations can legally contribute to party funds. There is, therefore, a channel through which unlimited funding can be used to add to the efforts allowed under the law. Such funds have become known as 'soft money'. Although 'soft money' is a source of political controversy it has given fresh importance to party structures, particularly bodies such as the Democratic Congressional Campaign Committee and the National Republican Senatorial Committee. In the 1996 elections, party committees spent $210 million in soft money, a threefold increase on the 1992 total (Grant 1997: 57). In 1998, they allocated large sums to both the congressional races and to candidates standing for state legislatures (*New York Times* 1998).

Co-ordination and partisanship

There are other ways in which the parties have assumed a more coherent and organised form. Since the 1960s, white voters in the South shifted in large numbers from the Democrats, the party they had supported since the Civil War, to the Republicans. The changed allegiance of the most conservative element in the Democrats' New Deal coalition had long-term consequences. As Ceasar and Busch have argued, some of the checks and restraints on the Democratic Party's liberalism were removed. Liberals within the Party had to make fewer compromises. At the same time, although some of the Party's supporters and public officials in the Northeast adopt relatively liberal attitudes towards social issues, the GOP's conservatism was reinforced and 'southernised' (1997: 22).

Although there are some GOP moderates in Congress, little is now left of the Republican Party's once-influential liberal wing. Both parties have come to assume increasingly different and polarised ideological identities.

There is other evidence of a resurgent partisanship. In 1981, all but one Republican member of the House of Representatives backed President Reagan's budget plans and proposals for tax cuts (Wattenberg 1996: 136). By 1993, the number of 'party votes' in Congress (where a majority of Republicans opposes a majority of Democrats) had risen significantly to a point where almost two-thirds of votes were party votes (McSweeney 1995: 18). In the November 1994 mid-term elections, the *Contract with America* – a nationally agreed manifesto – was signed by over three hundred of the Republican candidates for the House of Representatives. The *Contract* promised that a Republican-controlled Congress would – within a hundred days – vote on measures such as welfare reform, an anti-crime package, and a balanced budget amendment (Ashford 1998). Although much of the sense of momentum that the *Contract* unleashed was lost, a sense of partisanship remained throughout the remainder of the decade. This was evident in December 1998, when the House voted to impeach the president. The first article of impeachment was opposed by only five Republicans and supported by only five Democrats. It was a party-structured vote.

Party identities asserted themselves in other ways. Newt Gingrich, the former House Speaker, attempted to ensure that despite the decentralised character of Congress, the Republican Party leadership occupied a dominant position. Gingrich himself nominated committee chairs and the seniority tradition, by which the longest-serving member of the majority party takes the chair, was modified. Furthermore, senior committee staff were instructed to liaise with Gingrich's aides. As Philip John Davies concluded a year after the 1994 Republican victory: 'the House now has a command structure more unified than anything seen in Congress for almost a century' (1996: 15).

Dealignment reconsidered

As has been seen, those who talk of 'party decline' emphasise the process of partisan dealignment. They see evidence of this in the decline in the proportion of party identifiers, low turnout levels, the willingness of the electorate to embrace figures such as Ross Perot, and its apparent commitment to forms of government in which the White House and Congress are controlled by different parties.

However, if the electoral statistics are studied closely, it is evident that although there has undoubtedly been a process of dealignment, the extent of it can be exaggerated. First, during the 1990s, voters appear more ready to back a single party. Split-ticket voting between the presidency and the House declined to just 9 per cent in both 1992 and 1996 (Davidson and Oleszek 1998: 100–2). Second, there has been a limited, but perceptible, shift back towards partisanship during the 1990s. Third, much of the dealignment process has been confined to the voting blocs associated with the Democratic Party. Indeed, if those describing themselves as strong and weak Republicans are added together, identification with the Republican Party increased between 1972 and 1996 from 23 per cent to 29 per cent. The concept of dealignment is considered in more depth in Chapter 10.

Table 9.2 *Party identification in the US, 1964–96 (%)*

	1964	1972	1980	1988	1992	1996
Strong/weak Democrat	52	41	41	35	35	39
Strong/weak Republican	24	23	22	28	25	29

Source: Adapted from Flanigan and Zingale (1998): 62.

Conclusion

Should the parties be seen in terms of decline, survival or renewal? There is evidence to back all three claims. A further consideration should, however, be introduced. The US parties cannot necessarily be understood in terms of one all-embracing model. Local, state and national parties have developed in different ways. Local organisations, at ward and precinct level, have been subject to a process of decline. However, the state parties have maintained a presence and the national committees have begun to play an increasingly significant role within the electoral process.

References and further reading

Ashford, N. (1998), 'The Republican Party agenda and the conservative movement', in D. McSweeney and J. Owens, *The Republican Takeover of Congress*, London, Macmillan, 96–116.
Bailey, C. (1990), 'Political parties', *Contemporary Record*, February, 12–15.
Bennett, A. J. (1998), *American Government and Politics 1998*, Godalming.
Broder, D. S. (1971), *The Party's Over: The Failure of Politics in America*, New York, Harper & Row.
Bureau of the Census (1997), *Statistical Abstract of the United States 1997*, Washington, DC, US Department of Commerce.
Ceasar, J. W. (1990), 'Political parties – declining, stabilizing, or resurging', in A. King (ed.), *The New American Political System*, Washington, DC, American Enterprise Institute for Public Policy Research.
Ceasar, J. W. and A. E. Busch (1997), *Losing to Win: The 1996 Elections and American Politics*, Lanham, Rowman & Littlefield.
Congressional Quarterly (1997a), *Selecting the President: From 1789 to 1996*, Washington, DC, CQ Press.

Congressional Quarterly (1997b), *Presidential Elections 1789–1996*, Washington, DC, CQ Press.

Davidson, R. and W. Oleszek (1998), *Congress and its Members*, Washington, DC, CQ Press.

Davies, P. J. (1992), *Elections USA*, Manchester, Manchester University Press.

Davies, P. J. (1996), 'The legislative process in the USA', *Politics Review*, 5:3, 10–15.

Faux, J. (1995), 'The myth of the new Democrat', in W. D. Burnham, *The American Prospect Reader in American Politics*, Chatham, Chatham House, 162–73.

Flanigan, W. H. and N. H. Zingale (1998), *Political Behavior of the American Electorate*, Washington, DC, CQ Press.

Grant, A. (1997), 'The 1996 elections and campaign finance in the United States', *Talking Politics*, 10:1, Autumn, 56–61.

Greenblatt, A. (1998), 'The disengaging voter', *Congressional Quarterly Weekly Report*, 24 October, 2880–1.

Hays Lowenstein, D. (1992),'American political parties', in G. Peele, C. J. Bailey, and B. Cain, *Developments in American Politics*, Basingstoke, Macmillan.

Libertarian Party (1996), *1996 National Platform of the Libertarian Party*, Washington, DC, Libertarian Party.

McSweeney, D. (1990), 'Is the party over? Decline and revival in the American party system', in R. Williams, *Explaining American Politics: Issues and Interpretations*, London, Routledge, 144–66.

McSweeney, D. (1995), 'Unity and disunity in American parties', *Politics Review*, February, 17–20.

McSweeney, D. and J. Zvesper (1991), *American Political Parties*, London, Routledge.

New York Times (1996), 10 November.

New York Times (1998), 3 November.

Owens, J. E. (1996), 'A return to party rule in the US Congress?', *Politics Review*, 6:1, September, 15–19.

Plano J. C. and M. Greenberg (1989), *The American Political Dictionary*, Fort Worth, Holt, Rinehart & Winston.

Robertson, D. (1985), *The Penguin Dictionary of Politics*, Harmondsworth, Penguin.

Rossiter, C. (1960), *Parties and Politics in America*, Ithaca, Signet.

Rothschild, M. (1990), 'Is it time for a third party?', *Utne Reader*, September–October, 56–63.

Wattenberg, M. P. (1991), *The Rise of Candidate-Centered Politics*, Cambridge, Harvard University Press.

Wattenberg, M. P. (1996), *The Decline of American Political Parties 1952–1994*, Cambridge, Harvard University Press.

Wayne, S. J. (1992), *The Road to the White House 1992: The Politics of Presidential Elections*, New York, St Martin's Press.

10

Elections and campaigns

The US electoral system is widely seen as the most democratic in the world. More positions are elected than in any other system. Over one million public offices, mainly local positions such as school board members, sheriffs and judges, are contested. Party candidates are chosen by the voters themselves in what are called primaries, not by party leaders or committed activists. Anyone can run for public office as neither previous party membership nor a record of activity is required. Many state and local issues are decided directly by the voters themselves in referendums.

All this would appear to make the US the most democratic and open regime in the world. However, critics complain that the US elects candidates who are incapable of governing. They observe that the electoral process gives too much influence to the role of money. Its length and complexity discourage people from voting, and, as a consequence, contribute to low levels of turnout.

How is the president elected? How is Congress elected? What is the role of money in elections? Why is turnout so low? What factors determine the way in which the electorate casts its votes? This chapter examines these questions.

Electing the president

The president is elected every four years. Since the Twenty-second Amendment was adopted in 1951, no president can be elected to serve more than two full terms. Candidates for the office face a series of lengthy and complex hurdles. Unless they are running as an independent, as the Texas billionaire Ross Perot did in 1992, they must win both their party's nomination and the general election.

Deciding to run

The American political system allows anyone to run for the presidency, providing they meet the basic requirements stated in the Constitution. An individual must be at least thirty-five years old, a resident for at least fourteen years, and a natural-born US citizen. In practice, however, a credible candidate must be the nominee of either the Democratic or the Republican Party. The initial battle is therefore to establish a profile among party supporters.

In 1992 twelve Democrats ran for the nomination, and in 1996 eight Republican candidates sought to challenge Bill Clinton. Although an incumbent president is sometimes unopposed within his own party, sitting presidents have at times had to face challengers. In 1968, Eugene McCarthy and Bobby Kennedy ran against President Lyndon Johnson in the race to win to become the Democratic Party's nominee. In 1976, Ronald Reagan almost took the Republican nomination from President Gerald Ford. In 1992, George Bush was challenged by Patrick Buchanan, a former host of CNN's *Crossfire* and speechwriter for Presidents Nixon and Reagan.

The War Room

Directors: D. A. Pennebaker and Chris Hegedus (1993)

The War Room is a documentary record of the 1992 Clinton presidential campaign. It follows, in particular, the work of two of Clinton's closest aides and 'spin doctors': James Carville and George Stephanopoulos. The film tracks their tactics in the days and weeks preceding the New Hampshire primary, their orchestration of the Democratic national convention, and the eventual election victory.

Candidates need not have held any form of public office. They do not even need to have been members of the party in question. President Dwight Eisenhower (1953–61), who commanded the victorious allied forces during the Second World War, was courted by both parties before finally standing as a Republican. As the 1996 presidential election approached, there were attempts to persuade General Colin Powell, the black former Chairman of the Joint Chiefs of Staff, to run as the Republican candidate. Steve Forbes was a successful publisher of a business magazine. Jesse Jackson ran for the Democratic nomination in 1984 and 1988 as a civil rights leader. However, in practice, although there are exceptions, most candidates have held elective office. They have either served in Congress, as the governor of a state, or as vice-president.

The process of winning name recognition, attracting campaign workers, building up financial resources, and gaining endorsements from well-known supporters begins almost as soon as the result of the previous election is known. The three- or four-year period preceding an election year has been dubbed the 'invisible primary'. Candidates have to establish themselves in the public opinion polls. They need to be represented in the lists of presidential hopefuls considered by newspaper 'op-ed' columnists and TV commentators. To win credibility, they have to build personal campaign organisations and accumulate financial 'war chests'. By the end of June 1995, over a year before the 1996 presidential election, the leading contenders had already raised substantial sums. Bob Dole had accumulated $13.3 million. Lamar Alexander had attracted $7.5 million. Patrick Buchanan had $2.2 million. Some state parties also organise 'straw polls' so as to gauge opinion among their supporters. In October 1975, Jimmy Carter first began to establish himself as a candidate when he gained 23 per cent of the vote in a straw poll of Democratic Party supporters in Iowa (Congressional Quarterly 1997: 64). In November 1995 – as the 1996 presidential election approached – Senator Robert Dole was increasingly seen as the front-runner after he had topped Florida Republican Party's presidential straw poll.

Individuals often fall away at this stage. They consider the prospect of running, but decide against it because they have not found sufficient support, cannot raise the necessary money to run an effective campaign, or have decided that they are not able to devote such a long period of time to a single, and probably unreachable, goal.

Pre-nomination (February–June)

The presidential candidate is formally chosen by majority vote at a party's national convention. Candidates therefore seek to maximise the number of supporters among the state delegations. Delegates to national party conventions, which decide who will serve as the party's presidential candididate, were traditionally chosen by political 'bosses' and activists at a state party convention. However, although there are significant procedural differences between states, the primary election has become the norm. The primary allows members of the public, who support a particular party, to participate in the nomination process. They can decide who they wish their state party delegates to back as the candidate when the national convention is held.

In 1996, 65.3 per cent of Democratic national convention delegates and 84.6 per cent of Republican convention convention delegates were selected in primaries (Congressional Quarterly 1997: 141). Of these, some were closed primaries that restricted voting to those who are already registered as Democrats or Republicans. Others were open primaries. Members of the public did not have to be registered supporters of a particular party, but could instead simply decide to participate on the day that the primary was held. The states that do not hold primaries organise caucuses. These are meetings, often lasting over several weeks, allowing discussion of the rival candidates' strengths and weaknesses. Participation tends to be limited to the committed party activist. The caucuses either directly elect the national convention delegates or, in Hawaii and Delaware, for example, choose those who will attend a state party convention which, in turn, decides upon the delegation (Congressional Quarterly 1997b: 140).

In the Democratic Party the delegates are elected on a proportional basis. Candidates receiving a minimum of 15 per cent of the vote obtain a share of national convention delegates in that congressional district that is proportional to the vote they received (Polsby and Wildavsky 1996: 120). Among the Republicans, some states adopt proportionality, while others have a 'winner take all' system whereby the candidates with the most votes win all the delegates from that state.

Candidates who perform poorly in the early primaries may decide to withdraw. They are likely to lose much of their financial backing. In the 1992 Democratic primaries, both Senator Tom Harkin of Iowa and Senator Bob Kerrey of Nebraska had pulled out of the race by early March. However, a strong showing at an early stage will create a sense of momentum and attract further support.

Although it is preceded by the Iowa caucuses, the first state to hold a primary is, by tradition, New Hampshire. States appreciate that the early primaries give them more influence over the final nominee and, for their part, candidates want the states where they will gain the greatest support to come early. There is, therefore, constant pressure to front-load the primaries and move them ever earlier. California traditionally held its primary in June. In 1996, it was moved to 26 March, and there are plans to bring it further forward.

Although the Iowa caucus and the New Hampshire primary are the initial tests, the primaries that are held in early March are decisive. 'Super-Tuesday', in particular, plays an important role. A significant number of states, predominantly in the South, hold their primaries on the same day. By winning most or all of these, Bill Clinton and Bob Dole were able to establish a commanding lead in the contest to win their party's nomination in 1992 and 1996 respectively.

The development of primaries opened up the nomination process, shifted power from party leaders to the ordinary voter, increased participation, and tested the stamina of potential candidates. However, they have been subject to criticism.

1 The primary election 'season' is said to be too long. It stretches from January until June, and although the Federal Election Commission offers matching (dollar for dollar) funds to candidates fulfilling a set of conditions, candidates have to withdraw if they cannot gain the finance necessary for such a prolonged campaign.
2 The system is 'front-loaded' insofar as the early caucuses and primaries matter most. Traditionally, Iowa and New Hampshire hold the first caucus and primary respectively. Candidates must, at the very least, achieve a respectable showing in New Hampshire if they are to be considered serious contenders. Both states, however, are unrepresentative of the nation insofar as they are largely rural, white and Protestant. Despite this, they are accorded a pivotal role in deciding the fate of presidential hopefuls.
3 In the early primaries a candidate is judged on his or her electoral performance in relation to the expectations that have been set. In February 1992, Bill Clinton gained only 26 per cent of the vote in the New Hampshire

primary. He was 9 per cent behind Paul Tsongas, the victor. However, Clinton could call his result a victory and dub himself the 'comeback kid' because his vote exceeded expectations. However, such expectations are largely set by media predictions. The newspapers, radio stations and TV channels thereby gain undue influence.

4 As has been seen, some states have open primaries. Critics claim that they encourage wrecking tactics. Supporters of an opposing party can participate and may well deliberately back a weak candidate.

5 The primary system eliminates peer review from the nomination process. Presidential candidates are generally state governors or serve in Congress. They should, it is said, be judged as candidates by their colleagues rather than members of the public, who will inevitably have little detailed knowledge about their record or suitability.

6 The system of primary elections has weakened the American political parties. First, they have removed the parties' ability to nominate their own candidates, thereby making them 'public property'. Second, the primaries have encouraged the creation of personal campaign organisations built around candidates rather than the party (see Chapter 9). Third, the primaries often lead to public disunity. The 1984 Democratic primaries created bitter divisions between supporters of Gary Hart and Walter Mondale, thereby contributing to the Party's defeat later in the year. As Martin Wattenberg notes, even if a popular candidate eventually wins the party nomination, this can be 'insufficient to heal the wounds of the primary season' (1991: 59).

7 The turnout is often relatively low. It also tends to be confined to the stronger party identifiers. The *Committee for the Study of the American Electorate* esti-

---

Reforming the primaries

The criticisms of the primary system have led to calls for reform. Since 1911, there have been proposals for a national primary. States such as New Hampshire would no longer have a disproportionate role. Instead, all votes would count equally. There have also been proposals for regional primaries. These would be held within a few weeks of each other, and the order would be determined in a draw.

However, both systems would end the grass-roots, door-to-door campaign that is a hallmark of the early primaries at the moment. They would be media-dominated events. There would also be few opportunities for little-known candidates to establish themselves.

Further reading

Congressional Quarterly, *Selecting the President: From 1789 to 1996*, Washington DC. Congressional Quarterly.

mates that only 16.86 per cent of those eligible voted in the early 1998 primaries. There has been a process of steady decline since 1970, when turnout reached an all-time high of 32.22 per cent. There is usually a higher level of turnout for Democratic primaries. As a consequence, a Republican candidate could win with less than 5 per cent of the eligible vote (Committee for the Study of the American Electorate 1998a).

National party conventions (July–August)

The presidential candidates are chosen by the Democrat and Republican parties at a national party convention (or conference). Historically there were several candidates at the convention and the nominee was finally chosen only after a succession of ballots, compromises and deals in 'smoke-filled rooms'. Nowadays, however, the candidate is invariably known before the convention even begins because most of the convention delegates are pledged to back the person who won their state primary. Often, the other candidates will have decided to withdraw although, within the Democratic Party, both Jesse Jackson (1988) and Jerry Brown (1992) insisted that a formal convention vote be taken. However, since 1956, every presidential nominee has won on the first ballot. Conventions therefore simply crown an already anointed candidate. The last properly contested or 'brokered' convention was the Democratic national convention in 1952 when, after three ballots, Adlai Stevenson was finally selected.

The convention considers and agrees upon the party's platform (or manifesto), but it is either full of high generalities or largely ignored by the candidate. However, it is an important battleground between the party factions, who seek to adopt positions, or 'planks', closer to their favourite causes. For example, in 1996 there was a fierce debate around the precise character of the Republican Party's strong anti-abortion plank.

The nominee also announces his vice-presidential candidate or 'running mate', although the evidence suggests that vice-presidential candidates make little overall difference to the eventual result. The nominee's choice is often the subject of speculation before the convention. According to traditional wisdom, the ticket should be 'balanced'. In other words, the running mate should from a different part of the country or a different wing of the party. In 1988, the Democratic candidate, Governor Michael Dukakis, picked Senator Lloyd Bentsen as his vice-presidential candidate. Dukakis was from Massachusetts and a relatively liberal figure. In contrast, Bentsen was much more conservative and from the state of Texas. Bob Dole chose Jack Kemp as his 1996 Republican running mate to satisfy sections of the conservative movement and dissipate fears about Dole's age. At first sight, it seems that the Democrats abandoned the balanced ticket in 1992 and 1996. Bill Clinton's nominee, Al Gore, was from neighbouring Tennessee, and he shared Clinton's moderate politics. However, he was closer to organised labour and the environmentalist groupings within the Party who were suspicious of Clinton.

The convention is the only opportunity for party activists to meet as a national party, and it is therefore a major party-building exercise. Party activists are generally organised around local and state elections. At the convention, they can consider the party as a national institution and focus on electing the candidate to the only nationwide office in the US.

The modern national convention is primarily, however, a media event. This is conveyed in a portrait of the 1988 Republican National Convention:

> With a color-coordinated stage; a band playing upbeat, patriotic music; speakers carefully timed, rehearsed, and designed to heighten the campaign themes; balloons set to fall like rain on the nominees and the delegates dressed in all types of garb, the result was pure theater. (Wayne 1992: 161)

The convention is a major opportunity to attract free national media coverage and the attention of voters, many of whom have little interest in national politics. If the party is able to promote its candidate and convey a picture of a united party, it should be able to gain a post-convention 'bounce' in the public opinion polls. Between 1964 and 1992, the average 'bounce' for the Republicans and Democrats was eight and five percentage points respectively. The 1992 Democratic National Convention was very effectively orchestrated by Bill Clinton's campaign strategists and he gained a twelve-point 'bounce' (Bennett 1993: 20). Correspondingly, a divided convention inevitably damages the party's prospects. The 1968 Democratic convention was bitterly divided over the choice of nominee. The televised scenes did much to ensure that the Republican contender, Richard Nixon, won the November election. The 1992 Republican convention organisers awarded Patrick Buchanan, who had been defeated in the primaries, a prime-time slot. His address to delegates – which called for a cultural 'war' – was widely seen as abrasive and divisive. Some observers have attributed the Republican defeat to the image of the convention created by Buchanan's speech.

Post-nomination (September–November)

The Constitution specifies that the election must be held on the first Tuesday after the first Monday in November. The general election campaign usually lasts for two months, beginning after the Labor Day holiday in early September. It has, however, been edging forward. Bill Clinton started a nationwide bus tour immediately after his selection in 1992, thereby giving his campaign a significant boost.

The candidates from the principal parties, who may have been joined in the contest by independents and third-party nominees, now seek to appeal to the broad interests of the nation. They will almost certainly have to adopt different themes to those that won them the party nomination. They tour the entire country, speaking to meetings, dinners and breakfasts. However, in such a large nation, there is no possibility of meeting more than a very small proportion of the American public. Television therefore assumes a critical significance and the campaign is driven by the need to attract coverage and raise the finance required to buy paid advertising.

The televised presidential debates have come to occupy an important place

---

Primary Colors

Director: Mike Nichols (1998)

Starring: John Travolta, Emma Thompson, Adrian Lester, Kathy Bates

Primary Colors first appeared as an anonymously written novel. The book's author eventually emerged as Joe Klein, a political correspondent for *Newsweek*.

The film tracks the political fortunes of Jack Stanton, a southern governor seeking the presidency. The parallels with Bill Clinton are only too evident. Stanton has few political principles, and is instead guided by self-interest, focus groups and polls. He has a long history of casual sexual encounters, and a powerful, ambitious lawyer wife.

The film is a cleverly cynical portrait of the election process. It follows Stanton through the primaries, the national convention, and onwards. However, the film lacks the novel's cutting edge. Some of the later scenes become increasingly surreal. It is also hard to discern *Primary Colors'* overall message. At times, the film seems to suggest that politicians – although self-serving – can bring about important reforms. At other points, there is greater pessimism: the political process is inherently corrupt and those who have scruples are either bought off or destroyed.

Bob Roberts

Director: Tim Robbins

Starring: Tim Robbins, Alan Rickman, Gore Vidal

Bob Roberts is the fictional senatorial candidate for Pennsylvania in 1990. Although his party is never specified, Roberts is a representative of the conservative Right. He is committed to rolling back the politics and culture of the 1960s by utilising some of the themes and techniques associated with the Left. He is a singer, and his music videos are a pastiche of the early Bob Dylan. This time around, however, 'the times they are a-changin' back'.

Roberts's opponent is a survivor from the Kennedy era, played by the novelist, Gore Vidal. His weary pleas for a renewal of liberalism and indictments of the 'military–industrial complex' seem out of place in the modern age. Roberts represents the American future.

Bob Roberts was made in the form of a commentary by an English news reporter. It does not always sustain itself as a film, but is interesting as a leftist critique of contemporary American conservatism.

in the campaign calendar. They were first introduced in 1960 and have been institutionalised from 1976 onwards. They sometimes appear to have played a decisive role. John F. Kennedy's victory in the 1960 presidential election is widely attributed to the perception by television viewers of the debate that his Republican opponent, Richard Nixon, looked evasive. In 1996, however, 92 per cent of those asked in a CBS News poll said that the first debate between Bill Clinton and Bob Dole had done nothing to alter their opinion of the candidates (Bennett 1997: 24).

The Electoral College

The electorate's vote and the result are known on election day – often before polling has finished on the west coast – but, under the terms of the Constitution, the formal election only takes place some weeks later through the Electoral College.

Article II of the Constitution outlines the procedures that must be adopted. Each state is allocated a number of Electors or Electoral College Votes (ECV) based on its Congressional representation. Washington, DC has a further three Electors. In total, there are 538 ECV. Of these, California has – as the most populous state – fifty-four Electors. Other states with large populations are also well represented. New York and Florida have thirty-three and twenty-five ECV respectively. The least populous states, such as Montana, Vermont and Alaska, have three Electors. To allow for shifts in population, there are some changes to state representation in both the House of Representatives, and therefore the Electoral College, every ten years.

In every state, except Maine and Nebraska, the candidate who wins the most votes in that state is allocated all the ECV. The Electors meet in their state capitals and formally elect the president. The successful candidate must obtain an absolute majority in the College – at least 270 ECV. If there is not such a majority, the Constitution specifies that the election should be conducted by the House of Representatives, although each state delegation is only awarded one vote.

The Electoral College was established by the Founding Fathers for two principal reasons. First, it was based on a recognition of 'states' rights'. The College allowed each state to determine for itself who could vote. Second, despite all the restrictions on the franchise (the right to vote) that existed at the time, the framers of the Constitution distrusted mass democracy. An indirect system of election offered a safeguard against the possibility that a radical could be elected to the presidency. The College has, however, been subject to sustained criticism in modern times by those who see it as an undemocratic relic of an earlier age. They observe that:

1 Because the winner in each state is allocated all of that state's ECV – regardless of the margin of victory – the Electoral College distorts the popular vote.

In 1996, Bill Clinton gained 49 per cent of the vote. This, however, enabled him to win 70 per cent (379) of the ECV. However, although Bob Dole won 41 per cent of the vote, he gained only 30 per cent (159) of the ECV.

2 The mathematics of the Electoral College can allow a candidate with fewer ECV than an opponent to win among the Electors. This happened in 1888 when Grover Cleveland (Democrat) won over ninety thousand more votes than Benjamin Harrison (Republican). However, Harrison won in the Electoral College by 233 ECV to 168.

3 The system allows the occasional 'faithless Elector' to vote for a candidate who did not win the popular vote in a particular state. In 1972, a Nixon delegate from Virginia voted for John Hospers, the Libertarian Party candidate. In 1988, a West Virginia Elector cast her vote for Senator Lloyd Bentsen, the running mate, rather than Michael Dukakis, the Democratic presidential candidate who had won the popular vote in the state.

4 Unless their votes are concentrated in particular states or regions – such as the South – independent and third-party candidates fare badly in the Electoral College. In 1992, Ross Perot gained 19 per cent of the popular vote, but because his support was dispersed across the country, received no ECV at all.

5 Under the Constitution, the House of Representatives decides the election if there is no absolute majority in the College. Each state delegation in the House is assigned one vote. Although this only happened in 1800 and 1824, a shift of only thirty thousand popular votes would have thrown both the 1860 and 1960 elections to the House (Congressional Quarterly 1997: 128). Such procedures can, however, be seen as a breach of the separation of powers between the legislative and executive branches of government.

Reforming the Electoral College has, periodically, been the subject of debate. Some call for the direct election of the president. Others propose that each state's ECV should be divided proportionately on the basis of the popular vote. The Maine system by which the state's Electoral Vote is divided up on the basis of results in each electoral district has been proposed as the basis for a more proportional national system (Bennett 1990: 26–38). However, reform is unlikely. There are two reasons for this. First, there is no consensus on alternatives. Second, there is little pressure for change. The Electoral College has not had genuine political significance since Grover Cleveland was defeated in 1888. Unless a future election again produces an outcome in which the winner of the popular vote loses in the College, there will be few calls for reform.

Inauguration

An incoming Prime Minister in Britain takes office the day after a general election is held. In the US, a new president is sworn in – traditionally by the Chief

---

The role of the mass media

TV and newspapers are the principal source of information about both the issues and the candidates.

The media offer candidates the opportunity to convey *unmediated* messages. In contrast with Britain, the candidates can buy TV commercials. In 1992, for example, Bill Clinton, George Bush and Ross Perot spent $92 million on TV advertising. Some of Perot's broadcasts were thirty minutes in length. Many TV commercials are based around an opponent's alleged flaws rather than the strengths of the candidate. The use of negative advertising or 'attack-ads' has a long history. In 1964, the 'Daisy Girl' commercial suggested that Barry Goldwater, the Republican candidate, would be too ready to use America's nuclear arsenal. It portrayed him as an irresponsible extremist.

The media also carry *partially mediated* messages, most notably the debates between the candidates, and *mediated* messages such as news reports. Although controlled by the networks, many of these reports will have been, to some extent, orchestrated by the candidates' campaign aides insofar as they will be structured around 'soundbites' or well-planned backdrops (Congressional Quarterly 1997: 107).

There are suggestions that these 'messages' determine the outcome of elections. The opinions of the electorate, it is said, are open to manipulation by 'spin doctors' who are employed by candidates to present, structure or create news stories that will be to their advantage. In 1992, George Stephanopoulos and James Carville played a pivotal role in 'selling' Bill Clinton. The theme underpinned Barry Levinson's film, *Wag the Dog*. In the film, an incumbent president is embroiled in a sex scandal just days before an election. His spin doctor enlists the assistance of a Hollywood producer to create the appearance of a war with Albania. The war diverts attention from the scandal, and amid a wave of patriotic fervour, the president is re-elected. The media and the American public are, the film suggests, open to manipulation (see also Chapter 6, p. 100).

However, despite this, the overall significance of the mass media should not be exaggerated. They may shape, but they also reflect, mass opinion. Furthermore, the viewer is not a passive consumer of media coverage. Viewers apply 'filters' based on their own experiences and attitudes. Only certain news stories register

---

Justice – at an inaugural ceremony in January. The two-month transition period allows the president-elect to prepare his administration and appoint senior officials. The Inaugural Address, delivered once the oath of office has been taken, offers signs of the style and direction that will be adopted by the new administration. In 1933, Franklin D. Roosevelt asserted, in a call for government action against economic depression, that 'the only thing we have to fear is fear itself' (Maidment and Dawson 1994: 185). In January 1961, John F. Kennedy spelt out the US's commitment to resisting the expansion of communism: 'Let every nation know, whether it wishes us well or ill, that we shall pay any price, bear any burden, meet any hardship, support any friend, oppose any

in the public mind. Research conducted in the 1960s suggests, for example, that although there was extensive news coverage, a much higher proportion of African-Americans than whites registered the murders of Medgar Evers, a civil rights activist, and Malcolm X, a black nationalist leader (Graber 1997: 195). People mentally 'edit' the news in other ways. Evidence indicates that individuals avoid information that is disturbing or material that conflicts with attitudes that are already held.

The mass media do not, therefore, convert or transform individual opinions. Instead, their role is more limited. First, they appear to play a role as a 'gatekeeper' insofar as they determine what is, or is not, 'newsworthy'. Second, although they do not change beliefs, they appear to have a *reinforcement* effect. In 1976, the TV stations helped to establish Jimmy Carter's credibility as a presidential candidate. However, it was his early primary victories that initially made his candidacy viable. The media simply reinforced the voters' judgement. As Leon Sigal has noted: 'Newsmen do not write the score or play an instrument; they amplify the sounds of the music makers' (quoted in Graber 1997: 263).

The American mass media and the Internet

Nearly all newspapers have websites. These offer an Internet edition of the day's paper, news features, and searchable archives (although a charge is sometimes made). Some TV channel sites have interactive features and audio-visual clips.

Newspaper websites

The Boston Globe – http://www.boston.com/globe/
The Chicago Tribune – http://www.chicagotribune.com/
The New York Times – http://www.nytimes.com/
The Washington Post – http://www.washingtonpost.com/
The Washington Times – http://www.washtimes.com/

TV channel websites

CNN – http://www.cnn.com
NBC – http://www.nbc.com/news/index.html

foe to assure the survival and success of liberty' (Maidment and Dawson 1994: 190).

Electing Congress

Congressional elections also rest on the use of primaries. They are closed in forty states and open in eight states. Two states – Alaska and Washington – have blanket primaries, where voters can choose the Democratic candidate for some posts and the Republican for others. Louisiana has an unique open system whereby all candidates contest the same primary and the two leading candidates (who could be from the same party) stand against each other in a run-off election.

Members of the House are elected every two years. The general election is held using the plurality – or first-past-the-post – system. Districts are roughly equal in population and are redrawn every ten years on the basis of shifts in population. The process, known as *redistricting*, is carried out by state legislatures and can be highly partisan. Indeed, some of the 1998 races for state legislatures were fought with a particular intensity, and well funded by the national party committees, because those who were elected would redraw the congressional districts after the 2000 census (*New York Times* 1998). Senators represent the entire state, and therefore do not face the traumas of redistricting.

Two further characteristics of Congressional elections should be noted. First, the threat of a primary challenge, and the competition for money and workers with campaigns for other elective offices, mean that Congressmen retain their own personal campaign organisation. Second, incumbents enjoy considerable advantages. Even in 1994, when the Republicans took control of both houses, incumbency rates were very high indeed. Of those Senators who stood for a further term, 92.3 per cent were re-elected. In the House, the figure was 90.2 per cent (Bureau of the Census 1997: 281). In the 1998 elections, all but six of the House's 401 incumbents were returned. There are reasons why incumbents are so frequently returned. Office-holding, at both state and federal level, provides substantial in-built advantages. These include access to the mass media, name-recognition, the provision of constituency services, and the ability to attract large-scale campaign contributions. Serving legislators and office-holders can also press for, and play a part in allocating, the funding of federal government projects for their own district or state. In recent years, 'pork-barrel politics' have attracted fierce criticism. However, conclusions should only be drawn with caution. Many districts are electorally uncompetitive. In other words, they are 'safe', and a candidate nominated by the rival party cannot mount a serious challenge. Furthermore, weak incumbents often decide not to run, fearing that they will lose the election. The incumbency statistics may therefore exaggerate the ability of incumbents to remain in office.

Financing campaigns

American elections inevitably require large-scale financial resources. Candidates have to fund advertising campaigns, staff salaries, and travel costs. Presidential campaigns must reach a voting public distributed across the country. Coast-to-coast advertising and campaigning is inevitably costly.

By the early 1970s, there were widespread fears about spending levels in presidential elections. Candidates, it was argued, were over-reliant on small numbers of wealthy and often anonymous donors. The winner would inevitably be indebted to those who had contributed. Those without funding were deterred from standing. All too often, it was claimed, election victories depended on a candidate's ability to out-spend opponents. Contests had become profoundly unequal.

In 1971, Congress responded to these arguments by passing the Federal Election Campaign Act (FECA). The Act was strengthened in the wake of the Watergate scandal. It established taxpayer funding for presidential campaigns, limited individual contributions and banned direct contributions by companies and trade unions.

Today, under the provisions of the FECA, Americans can tick a box on their income-tax returns and award three dollars of their taxes to a fund that pays for presidential election campaigns. It is administered by the Federal Election Commission (FEC).

During the pre-nomination stage of presidential elections, when candidates are competing for their party's nomination, they can – if they adhere to specified conditions – obtain matching funds from the FEC. These provide dollar-for-dollar assistance. To qualify, and deter fringe candidates, a candidate must raise a total of at least $100,000 in twenty or more states. $5,000 must be raised in each state and there is a ceiling of $250 on donations from any one individual. The funding is, however, restricted to those who gain at least 10 per cent of the vote in at least one of the two final primaries that they contest. This leads candidates who perform poorly to withdraw at an early stage. They fear that if they stay in the race they will lose their eligibility for matching funds (Congressional Quarterly 1997: 46).

In the post-nomination – or general election – phase, the candidates nominated by the major parties receive all their funding from the FEC. It is awarded equally, and is generally about twice that given during the primaries. The principal parties also receive funding for their national conventions. In 1996, each party received $12.4 million (Wayne 1996: 45). Candidates from the minor parties are given some funding based on a sliding scale if they receive over 5 per cent of the vote.

In accepting financial aid under the FECA, candidates agree to abide by its provisions. They must observe the overall campaign spending limits set by the FEC. In 1996, this was $31.0 million for the pre-nomination phase. The figure for the post-nomination, or general election, phase – all of which was given as a grant by the FEC – was $62.2 million. The law stipulates that candidates must not spend over and above these sums. They must also disclose all campaign expenditure and contributions and the names of individuals giving $200 or more.

There are also constraints on the citizen. Individuals may only contribute a maximum of $1,000 to a candidate in the primary and general election campaigns. An organisation wishing to contribute to a campaign must – by law – establish a political action committee (PAC). PACs have proliferated since 1974; in 1996, there were 4,079 (Congressional Quarterly 1997: 51). Nearly every industry has a PAC which will offer donations to sympathetic candidates. The trade unions have also established PACs. In 1992, seven company PACs gave more than $1 million and eight trade union PACs gave more than $2 million each. Single-issue groups, such as organisations campaigning on the abortion issue, are also active. Under the provisions of FECA, a PAC can only contribute a maximum of $5,000 to a candidate, but there is no total annual ceiling (Grant 1995: 9). The average donation is, however, only $300. PACs accounted for 2 per cent of presidential contributions, and about 25 per cent of contributions to House races in 1996.

Despite the apparently stringent egalitarianism of the FECA, the campaign finance regulations raise significant problems. There are ways in which the limits and restrictions imposed by FECA have been bypassed or evaded:

1 Some individuals are exempt from the spending limits. In 1976, the US Supreme Court ruled in *Buckley v. Valeo* that the FEC could not impose restrictions on candidates who did not accepted public funding. In 1992, Ross Perot funded his campaign for the presidency personally. In 1996, Steve Forbes spent an estimated $38 million of his own money in a bid to win the Republican primaries. Neither sought funding from FEC funds, and both did not therefore have to abide by the limits imposed under the Act.
2 It is possible for individuals and groups to organise well-funded campaigns that may influence the election outcome without being restricted by the provisions of the FECA. *Buckley v. Valeo* also established that 'independent' campaigns by individuals or PACs either in support of, or in opposition to, a particular candidate could not be restricted. Such restrictions would, the Court ruled, be a breach of the First Amendment's guarantee of free speech. Thus, providing there is no formal connection with a candidate's organisation, a campaign can be mounted.
3 In 1979, amendments were made to the FECA, allowing the parties to raise and spend money on registration drives, other party-building activities, and 'get-out-the-vote' efforts (Grant 1995: 10). In practice, such activities cannot be easily distinguished from campaigns to support the parties' candidates. Furthermore, the amounts spent by the parties on this form of campaigning have grown dramatically. In the 1996 elections, the party committees spent a total of $210 million, a threefold increase on the 'soft money' spent in 1992, and eleven times the amount spent in 1980 (Grant 1997: 57).

    The role of the party committees will probably grow even more. In June 1996, in *FEC v. Colorado Republican Campaign Committee*, the Supreme Court extended the scope of *Buckley v. Valeo* by ruling that political parties also have the legal right to fund and organise 'independent' campaigns (Grant 1997: 60).
4 The law forbids donations from foreign sources. However, immigrants with permanent residency status can make donations. During the 1996 elections, it became clear that an official working for the Democratic National

Committee had persuaded Asian residents to act as a conduit for funds donated by Asian sources (Grant 1997: 59). It was seen as an attempt to 'buy' a degree of influence in the making of trade agreements.

5 The law does not allow organisations to fund candidates. As has been noted, they must instead establish PACs which are subject to rigorous spending limits. However, as Alan Grant notes, organisation and parties have directly funded 'issue-advocacy ads'. These are a form of negative advertising that does not identify its intended target by name. It is, however, evident by implication. The trade unions – represented by the American Federation of Labor – Congress of Industrial Organizations (AFL-CIO) – directed an issue-based campaign around issues such as the minimum wage in Republican-held districts (Grant 1997: 60).

6 The FEC has only limited powers if candidates do exceed the spending limits and the penalties cannot be considered a deterrent. In 1984, Walter Mondale's campaign in the New Hampshire primary spent $2.85 million, despite a state ceiling of $404,000. He was later fined $400,000 (Congressional Quarterly 1997: 46).

As a consequence – despite the rigours of the FECA – election expenditure has escalated dramatically within recent years. In 1996, the cost of the presidential election was put at about $563 million (Miroff, Seidelman and Swanstrom 1998: 204). In the Congressional elections, successful candidates spent an average of $700,000 for a seat in the House of Representatives and $4 million for the Senate (Kirksey 1998: 313). Why do candidates need such large sums of money? There are six principal reasons:

1 The voting age population has grown. It expanded by 39 per cent between 1974 and 1998 (Brubaker 1998: 37).

2 Campaigns have become much longer. The emergence of the 'invisible primary' (see above) has – by stretching campaigns back over the three or four years preceding the presidential election – had important consequences for overall costs.

3 Campaign techniques have changed. Party volunteers have been displaced by professionals. In place of door-to-door campaigning, candidates rely on direct mail. Costs have also increased because candidates have to mount extensive TV advertising campaigns.

4 Modern campaigns depend upon the services of polling organisations. They test public opinion through both conventional sampling techniques and the use of focus groups. These are representative gatherings who inform pollsters about their responses and feelings towards the candidate, the opponent, and different campaign strategies.

5 Campaigning often takes the form of negative advertising – or 'attack-ads' – whereby candidates appeal for votes on the basis of their opponent's alleged weaknesses. This leads to a vicious circle whereby candidates seek to defend

themselves against the charges that have been made and also make counter-attacks. The 1998 race in New York for the Senate seat between Charles Schumer and Alphonse D'Amato took this form and cost an estimated $36 million.

The dramatic rise in spending levels has led to signs of public unease. By the end of 1998, four states had adopted plans to regulate overall candidate spending – through the provision of public financing – in state elections. In 1998, Senators Russ Feingold and John McCain put forward plans for curbs on federal election spending. A number of reform proposals have been put forward. Some observers point out that the limits for individual and PAC contributions were set in the 1970s and should be adjusted to allow for inflation. If this were done, it is said, candidates would have less need for 'soft money'. Other proposals that have been put forward include wider restrictions on the level of contributions, limits on campaign expenditures, comprehensive and prompt public disclosure, and fuller taxpayer funding of campaigns. However, reforms to restrict contributions and expenditures that go beyond the existing largely 'voluntary' system may infringe free speech rights under the First Amendment. Furthermore, by restricting the amounts spent by challengers, they might simply reinforce the advantages already held by incumbents.

However, although there is considerable disquiet about the role of finance in the electoral system, and the 1996 elections were undoubtedly conducted in a very different way to that intended by the reformers of the 1970s, the overall role of money in politics should not be exaggerated. First, although the sums are large, they should be seen alongside other forms of spending. As Stanley C. Brubaker observes, total spending in the 1996 elections was less than half that spent by Americans on cologne and perfume during the same period (1998: 38). Furthermore, although the critics claim that money can 'buy' elections, Congressional votes, and presidential decisions, there is little hard evidence to support this. As Congressional election results show, the outcome depends on other factors apart from finance and the TV advertising that can thereby be purchased. In November 1994, Michael Huffington spent $53 million of his own fortune in an attempt to win the Senate seat from California, and lost. The role of finance is limited in other ways. Much money is given to candidates who are already in a strong electoral position or have already adopted a favourable policy position from the perspective of the donor, rather than to those who might change their vote. Many PACs give money to competing candidates on the expectation that they will be given a chance to put forward their case before the congressman takes a position, whoever wins. While incumbents are most successful at raising money, there is little evidence that it increases their likelihood of re-election. Instead, the crucial role of money is for challengers, when a well-funded campaign may make a difference.

Initiatives and propositions

At state level, American voters have the opportunity to vote on issues as well as for candidates. If passed, the proposition becomes law.

In most cases, propositions are put on the ballot by state legislatures. However, many states offer opportunities for individual citizens, who can collect a requisite number of signatures, to put issues before the electorate. In 1994, the voters of California backed Proposition 187 denying non-emergency state benefits to illegal immigrants. Two years later, they supported Proposition 209. This brought state affirmative action programmes to an end. In November 1998, voters in 44 states voted on nearly 240 ballot issues. These included the legalisation of cannabis for medicinal purposes, the opening of birth records to adults who were adopted, and the extension of gambling. On the same day, voters in other states rejected same-sex marriage and banned 'partial-birth' abortions (*USA Today*, 6 November 1998).

Supporters of initiatives argue that they add to democracy by allowing the voice of the people to be heard. They limit the ability of elected officials to ignore the popular will. Others, however, assert that the voters do not have the expertise or knowledge to write the law. In some cases, ambiguous wording has led to laws based on initiatives being overturned as unconstitutional by the courts. Critics also claim that the entire process has become finance-dependent. Initiatives are generally put forward by well-funded groups rather than individual citizens.

Evaluating the electoral system

Other features of the electoral system – apart from the role of money – have also been subject to criticism.

1 The electoral cycle is said to be too long. Campaigning for the House of Representatives is a constant process. The institutionalisation of the 'invisible primary' has extended the presidential contest to almost four years. The primary and caucus season extends over five months. However, although the cycle could be shortened by introducing one national primary, it does test candidates and enable the electorate to become familiar with their strengths and weaknesses.
2 Some observers assert that the process of nomination is controlled by unrepresentative ideologues and single-issue extremists. For example, the religious Right and feminist organisations have established a hold for themselves within the GOP and the Democratic Party respectively. As a consequence, it would be difficult for a 'pro-life' candidate to be chosen as the Democratic presidential nominee or a 'pro-choice' candidate for the Republicans. Some observers suggest that more influence should be given to party officials who will be unconcerned with ideological purity and will instead judge candi-

dates on the basis of their political abilities. In practice, this would increase the role of superdelegates at nominating connections, and give state parties more influence in endorsing and choosing candidates. Defenders of the status quo argue that primaries are open and allow participation. Reform could see a return to the control by party bosses who are unaccountable to either party activists or the voters.

3 Campaigns are conducted on the basis of image rather than policy substance. The mass media have trivialised the political process. In particular, critics argue that paid advertisements either present manipulated images or are negative 'attack-ads'. Particular advertisements are said to have swung elections. In 1988, for example, advertisements placed by Republican supporters suggested that the Democratic candidate, Massachusetts Governor Michael Dukakis, was weak towards criminality. They highlighted the case of Willie Horton, who had attacked a woman while released on weekend leave from a Massachusetts prison. In a brutal phrase employed by the Republican Party Chairman, Horton became Dukakis's 'running mate'.

4 Relatively few Americans vote. The US has one of lowest voting turnouts of any Western democracy. In 1988 barely half the voting-age population (50.1 per cent) cast a vote. The turnout improved slightly in 1992 to 55.2 per cent, but declined again in 1996 to 49 per cent. This was the lowest figure since 1924. The figures for mid-term elections are even lower. The turnout was 36.1 per cent in November 1998 (Committee for the Study of the American Electorate 1998b). By comparison, 71.5 per cent of the electorate voted in the United Kingdom 1997 general election.

There have been many attempts to explain the low level of turnout. First, US citizens must register to vote. In 1994, only 62 per cent of adult Americans had registered. Among some groups, the figure is much lower. For example, only 30 per cent of Hispanics were registered (Bureau of the Census 1997: 288). There are many reasons for this. The registration process is difficult. Although a form is sent to every household in the UK, and officials often follow this up with a personal visit if it is not returned, American voters have to register themselves. The 1993 National Voter Registration Act (the 'motor-voter law') simplified procedures by allowing citizens to register when applying for a driving licence or other forms of documentation from government agencies. However, registration barriers provide only a partial explanation of US turnout levels. Estimates suggest that if they were to be lowered, it would only increase overall turnout by about 8 per cent (Flanigan and Zingale 1998: 45). Second, there is a high level of geographical mobility in the US, particularly among the young. The Committee for the Study of the American Electorate suggests that Americans move home at a rate of about 16 per cent a year. Inevitably, if people settle in a different state, they will know less about the process of registration, local candidates and races. A third explanation points to a decline in the US civic culture. Some of the lowest levels of turnout are to be found in low-income communities. Turnout is less than 40 per cent among the poorest fifth of the population (Kuttner 1996: 164). They feel little sense of involvement in society and have become increasingly alienated from the political process. Fourth, many states have laws limiting the voting rights of those convicted of a felony. These not only apply to prison inmates, but also to those on parole or probation. In some states, the right to vote is permanently forfeited. This has a significant impact on African-American voting patterns. An estimated 15 per cent of black males have either temporarily or permanently lost the right to vote (Flanigan and Zingale 1998: 31). Fifth, some attribute low turnout to weak party organisation. In the US, the political parties are the main instruments for encouraging the electorate to vote. However, the parties are poorly organised and lack activists. This inevitably brings down the turnout. Sixth, some argue that the very large number of elections discourages turnout. Voters, they say, become bored and confused. Seventh, although the evidence is unclear, there are suggestions that many contests can be considered 'low-stimulus elections'. This is either because the outcome is regarded as a foregone conclusion or because the candidates are seen as unattractive. The relatively low turnout for the 1988 presidential election – where voters had a choice between George Bush and Michael Dukakis – has been explained in these terms. Last, there are claims that government plays a much smaller part in everyday lives than in Europe. The contrast in turnout figures between the US and Europe reflects differences in political culture.

Voting behaviour

What determines the way in which Americans vote? A distinction should be drawn between long- and short-term factors.

Long-term factors

Voting behaviour is shaped, to at least some extent, by the primary and secondary social groupings to which individuals belong. As Chapter 1 emphasised, American society has a diverse and heterogeneous character. It is divided by race, ethnicity, region, religion, gender and religion. These divisions provide a basis for party identification and voting decisions.

In the 1930s – during the New Deal era – the Democrats built up a coalition of support drawing together blacks, Jews, blue-collar trade unionists, and those employed in the public sector. At the same time, the Party retained the loyalty of white southerners who had backed the Democrats since the Civil War. These groupings formed a *bloc* that constituted the Party's core vote for three decades.

Subsequent strains led to changes in allegiance and the coalition lost the breadth of support that had formerly characterised it. The civil rights revolution of the 1960s and the subsequent shift by the Democratic Party towards race and gender-based policies swung growing numbers of white southerners towards the Republicans. In the 1950s, as Marjorie Randon Hershey notes: 'The south was the most dependably Democratic region of the country; to be openly Republican was a form of deviance' (1997: 228). Such was the region's loyalty to the Democrats that it had become known as the 'solid south'. In 1952, for example, 85 per cent of southern whites identified with the Democrats. By 1988, however, the proportion had fallen to 46 per cent. (Wayne 1992: 73) After the 1994 Congressional elections, the GOP had a majority of House seats in seven of the thirteen southern states. In 1996, the Republicans' overall gains in the House of Representatives were confined to the South (Hershey 1997: 228).

During the same period, evangelical Christians also moved towards the GOP. Supreme Court rulings establishing abortion rights and outlawing school prayer in public schools, and the Democrats' identification with what appeared as an assault against long-established values, led to a weakening of traditional political affiliations. Although they had initially, in 1976, supported Jimmy Carter's candidature for the presidency, the Republicans were 'seen as more attractive, resisting cultural change and an increasingly intrusive government' (Durham 1996: 26). Evangelical Christians gave decisive support to Ronald Reagan in 1980, and in the 1996 presidential election, 65 per cent of born-again Christians voted for Robert Dole, the Republican candidate. Only 26 per cent supported Clinton (Pomper 1997: 180).

The Republican Party, traditionally the party of business, the farmer and the WASP (White Anglo-Saxon Protestant), gained strength from the Democrats' difficulties. Increasingly, after Reagan had taken office, observers claimed that the Republicans had established a dominant bloc. There had been, it was said, a process of *realignment*.

Suggestions of realignment rest on the assertion that electoral history is divided into distinct and separate eras. The period between 1932 and 1980 is presented in terms of Democratic dominance. Where the Republicans won the presidency, as they did during the Eisenhower and Nixon years, and at least one house of Congress as they did between 1947 and 1949 and again between 1953 and 1955, these were *deviating* elections. They were, in other words, exceptions to the norm. The election of 1980 was, however, a *critical* or *realigning* one. From then onwards, the US entered an era of Republican dominance. The Senate had a Republican majority from 1981 until 1987, and the GOP won a majority in both houses of Congress from 1994 onwards.

The loss of faith in the Democrats and the process of realignment has been attributed to the shift from an industrial to a post-industrial society. The age of large-scale manufacturing industry demanded the forms of 'big government' with which the Democrats are associated. The modern era is, however, characterised by the break-up of monopolies and the growth of smaller enterprises. Public opinion is now marked by a 'new mood of doubt' about the role and purpose of government (Ladd 1996: 171). This has led voters towards the GOP.

However, suggestions that realignment has taken place, leading to long-term Republican hegemony, should be qualified. As Richard Wirthlin has observed, realignment has, at most, been partial. The gap between the two parties in terms of identification narrowed, and Republican notions of 'small government' were widely accepted. However, the Republicans have only made limited headway at state and local level (Ladd 1996: 167). The results of the 1998 Congressional elections suggested that Republican hold over the South was rather less secure than it had once seemed. Furthermore, despite the Democrats' long-term difficulties, the Party has won increased support among two groupings:

1 They have made significant gains among minorities. At the same time, minority turnout has risen. In 1992, 61 per cent of Hispanics voted for the Party. By 1996, this had risen to 72 per cent (Pomper 1997: 180). There were several reasons for this. The introduction of 'motor-voter' registration increased the numbers in lower-income groups who were able to vote. Furthermore, many long-term Hispanic residents were naturalised between 1992 and 1996 enabling them, for the first time, to cast a vote. More significantly, Republican Party backing for propositions put to the California electorate withdrawing state benefits from illegal immigrants and ending affirmative action programmes created a widely shared feeling that the GOP was anti-Hispanic. Even Asians, who Republicans had regarded as the 'model minority', because of their commitment to conservative values and the entrepreneurial ethos, joined the swing to the Democrats. In 1992, 31 per cent supported Bill Clinton's candidature. By 1996, the figure was 43 per cent (Pomper 1997: 183). In 1998, relatively high levels of turnout among minorities helped the Democrats defy predictions of electoral losses. In Georgia, for example, blacks represented 29 per cent of the total turnout compared with only 16 per cent in 1994.

2 There is a *gender gap*. Increasingly, although men have been drawn to the Republicans, women are becoming a Democratic constituency. In 1996, women were much more likely to support the re-election of President Clinton than men. Fifty-four per cent of women backed Clinton. However, he attracted the votes of only 44 per cent of men. Gerald M. Pomper emphasises that the gender gap 'remained stable among blacks and whites, among all age groups and in suburbs, and across levels of education and income' (1997: 183–4). Nor is the gender gap confined to presidential elections. The Democrats had an 8 per cent lead among women in the 1994 Congressional elections. There are a number of explanations for this:

• There is particular support for the Democrats among women who have a degree of personal independence either because they are unmarried or because they are in paid employment. They may regard the Republicans – who are associated with a commitment to 'family values' – as a party that believes women should remain within the domestic sphere.

- Although the ideological differences between the parties should not be exaggerated, the Democrats have often emphasised the protective aspects of government. They stress the positive role that government can play in protecting the citizen through, for example, the provision of health care, assistance for children and the elderly, and schooling. This appears to correspond with women's opinions. As Pomper notes: 'Clinton's emphasis on these issues, and his perceived concern for their solution, brought him the unusual degree of support from women' (1997: 185).
- Since the 1970s, large numbers of white men have switched to the Republican Party. The shift appears to have been a response to the Democrats' growing association with 'tax and spend' policies, affirmative action programmes, and the expansion of welfare provision. From the perspective of many white men, the Democrats appeared to have abandoned their interests.

The scale of the gap should not, however, be overestimated. Although there are voting differences between men and women, they are not entirely consistent and have fluctuated considerably. The gap was only 3 per cent in 1992 and six points in the 1998 mid-term elections (*New York Times* 1996; *USA Today* 1998). Second, other gaps are significantly larger than the gender gap. There are bigger gulfs between urban and rural voters, higher and lower income groups, and the different races (Ashford 1996: 66).

There is a further problem with the claim that realignment has taken place and that the Republicans are establishing themselves as the dominant party. Although there were defections from the Democratic Party, the GOP only brought some of these groupings into its ranks. The Republican core vote is now white, male, educated, Protestant, drawn from the higher-income groups, and southern. Others have lost much of their former faith in the Democrats, but have not been absorbed into the Republican camp. In other words, there has been a process of *dealignment*. As Chapter 9 noted, a growing proportion of voters have split their ticket and backed candidates representing both parties at the same elections. The proportion of the electorate calling itself 'independent' has grown from 19 per cent in 1958 to 32 per cent in 1996 (Flanigan and Zingale 1998: 61). At times, there appears to have been a positive embrace of divided government in which the White House and Congress are under the control of different parties. Political behaviour is increasingly characterised by pragmatism and volatility.

Some of the reasons for dealignment can be discerned. The mass media have become more candidate-centred. Parties are given little attention. Many newspapers have, for example, abandoned the practice of endorsing party slates (Wattenberg 1996: 91). Furthermore:

> The reaction to Vietnam and Watergate, to the credibility gaps and political abuses of the so-called imperial presidents, generated feelings of mistrust and

hostility that were directed at politicians. Those who became eligible to vote during this period were less willing to identify with a political party. Moreover, the salience of social and cultural issues rendered the traditional partisan alliances, which had been built on economic ties, much less relevant. (Wayne 1992: 70)

There are further reasons for dealignment. Many manual – or *blue-collar* – workers have lost their traditional affiliation with the Democratic Party. Deindustrialisation and the growth of the service sector led to a decline in trade-union membership. In the mid-1950s, over 30 per cent of the American workforce belonged to a union. By 1996, the figure had fallen to 14.5 per cent (Bureau of the Census 1997: 440). This weakened an important *conduit* between the worker and the Democratic Party. At the same time, many manual workers were drawn towards Republican candidates by promises of tax reductions, welfare reform, cultural traditionalism, and an assertive foreign policy. A significant proportion, known as 'Reagan Democrats', voted Republican in 1980 and 1984. Although the Democrats maintained a lead among trade unionists and their families, it narrowed to 7 per cent in 1980 and 4 per cent in 1984. Although the Party lost the 1988 presidential election, it did re-establish its dominance among trade unionists. Sixty-three per cent voted for Michael Dukakis, the Democratic candidate. Only 37 per cent supported George Bush (Pomper 1997: 75).

Stephen J. Wayne has noted the net consequences of growing voter pragmatism and volatility. The performance of politicians, issues, campaign strategy and other short-term factors assume much more importance:

> While class, religion, and geography are still related to party identification and voting behaviour, they are not as strongly related as they were in the past. Voters are less influenced by group cues. They exercise a more independent judgement on election day, a judgement that is less predictable and more subject to be influenced by the campaign itself. (Wayne 1992: 77)

Short-term factors

Campaigns are structured around images, issues, policies and events. Some observers portray the electorate as 'consumers' who will 'shop around' for policies that correspond to their interests and switch their vote when they are dissatisfied. The process is partly retrospective. People make a rational assessment of a party or candidate's record in office. As Morris Fiorina argues, voters keep 'a running tally of retrospective evaluations of party promises and performance' (quoted in Wayne 1992: 67).

However, the electorate looks forward as well as backwards. Although a significant proportion see little difference between them, most voters believe that the parties have different strengths and weaknesses. In 1992, for example, many more felt that the Democrats were better than the Republicans at managing the economy. For their part, the Republicans were believed to be much more competent in handling foreign policy matters.

Table 10.1 *Results of national election studies, 1992 (%)*

	No difference/ Don't know	Democrats	Republicans
Handling the nation's economy	43	37	20
Handling foreign affairs	33	22	45
Solving the problem of poverty	38	51	11
Making health care more affordable	34	54	12
Keeping out of war	62	20	18

Source: Wattenberg 1996: 192.

Particular issues therefore 'pull' voters towards either the Democrats or the Republicans. The end result of this 'tug-of-war' will depend upon the importance – or *salience* – of the issues. An individual who is primarily concerned with foreign policy questions will, for example, be drawn towards the GOP.

However, in both the 1992 and 1996 presidential elections, foreign policy was of only peripheral relevance. In 1992, a mere 8 per cent of voters said that foreign policy mattered most in determining the way in which they cast their vote. By contrast, 20 per cent identified health care as a crucial issue, and 43 per cent identified the economy and employment (Bennett 1993: 33). Four years later, in 1996, the economy was still the single most salient issue. Only 4 per cent of those asked said that foreign policy was the most important question facing the country (Bennett 1997: 28).

Economic factors are, then, generally pivotal in determining election outcomes. This is because income levels and employment opportunities personally affect almost every household. In 1992, the US had begun to grow again after a period of recession. Nevertheless, median household income had fallen by over $2,248 between 1989 and 1992 (Alsop 1997: 175). Of the total labour force, 7.5 per cent were unemployed. An estimated twenty-five million people were unemployed at some point during 1991 (Ashbee 1993: 159). In these circumstances, George Bush, who had been president since 1989, failed to gain a second term.

Economic performance was also important in 1996. However, there were differences between 1996 and 1992. By 1996, the economy was growing at 2.8 per cent. Unemployment had fallen back to 5.4 per cent (Alsop 1997: 157). A budget surplus was in sight. More importantly, perceptions had shifted. The Consumer Confidence Index (1985 = 100) was at 61.6 in 1992. By 1996, it had risen to 104.6 (Alsop 1997: 173). Well over half of the voters who were questioned believed that the economy was in good or excellent condition (Bennett 1997: 28). This time around, the incumbent president gained, and the 'feelgood factor' ensured Bill Clinton's re-election.

However, the assessments that voters make may not always be clinically rational appraisals of a candidate's economic record, overall performance or policy commitments. The campaign strategy, and the images that candidates construct, also play a role. Bill Clinton's 1992 appearances on MTV and the Arsenio Hall show are said to have helped him build a youthful 'in-touch' image of himself. His strategists were also successful in developing negative images of his opponents. During the 1996 election, the Clinton campaign successfully portrayed Senator Dole as an 'extreme' conservative who would withdraw health-care provision for the elderly and cut back on funding for education. In their election advertisements, the Democrats tied Bob Dole to Newt Gingrich, the Speaker of the House of Representatives, who was already widely regarded as a far-right figure. At the same time, Clinton adopted a number of 'softer' conservative themes. He called for limited government, signed a bill cutting back on welfare, and spoke in support of tough restrictions on wayward teenagers. Although, for their part, the Republicans promised a 15 per cent tax cut, they were unable to establish either taxation or President Clinton's personal character as campaign issues.

In Congressional elections, local and state issues traditionally come to the fore. In the celebrated words of the late House Speaker, Tip O'Neill, 'all politics is local'. As Marjorie Randon Hershey notes: 'Typically, an incumbent emphasizes a record of service to the district and individual constituents and at the same time criticizes that distant institution called "Congress" whose members inexplicably waste so much public money' (1997: 206).

Although, in November 1994, only 22 per cent of voters thought that national issues would be the most important factor that would influence their vote, some national patterns are evident in Congressional elections (Owens 1995: 4). In the past, political scientists identified two such trends. Firstly, they talked of a 'coat-tails' effect in those elections when both the White House and Congress were facing the voter. Popular support for a particular presidential ticket led voters to back Congressional candidates from the same party. However, it has been of limited significance since the 1960s. Between 1968 and 1996, the same party controlled the two houses of Congress and the White House at the same time for only six years. Second, the party holding the White House tended to lose Congressional seats in the mid-term elections as the incumbent president loses some of his support. This is known as the theory of surge and decline:

> There is a surge in support for the President's party and in turnout in the presidential election, which is then followed by a decline in the mid-term elections . . . between one fifth and one quarter of those who voted in congressional elections in a presidential year failed to do so two years later. (Owens 1995: 3)

However, the 'surge' that re-elected Bill Clinton in 1996 did not lead to a subsequent 'decline' in 1998.

Nevertheless, although both the 'coat-tails effect' and the 'surge and decline' theories of Congressional voting have flaws, the Congressional elections of the 1990s have undoubtedly had a partially national character. Two developments have, in particular, had a 'nationalising' effect:

1 Across the country, voters appear increasingly less ready to draw a distinction between their own member of Congress and Congress as a collective institution. In November 1994, they voted against thirty-four incumbent House Democrats and established the Republicans as the majority party in both houses. It was, at least in part, a protest against sitting members of Congress. They were seen as an unrepresentative and self-interested elite.
2 The Republican leadership in the House of Representatives pursued a national strategy. In 1994, the GOP candidates for the House adopted the *Contract with America* as a national platform (Ashford 1998).

However, the influence of issues, campaigns and candidates and the degree to which voters have the opportunity to make a rational choice between them should not be overemphasised. For example, a pre-election survey suggested that 71 per cent of those asked had not heard of the *Contract with America* (Hershey 1997: 108). Furthermore, if issues are to have an influence in determining an election outcome, three conditions must be fulfilled. First, the voter must have a clear position on an issue. Second, the issue has to be sufficiently important – or salient – to affect his or her voting behaviour. Third, there must be a clear distinction between rival candidates on the issue.

Often, these conditions are not present. So as to maximise their potential vote, candidates frequently blur their beliefs and arguments. They adopt purely symbolic political stands that have few substantive policy implications. There will, for example, be declarations that education is important or that criminals should be punished more severely. President Clinton's electoral success can, in large part, be attributed to his ability to portray himself as someone with empathy towards the values and concerns of voters. However, at the same time, he offers few commitments or pledges that have a firm policy content.

Conclusion

The road to the White House and Congress is long, uncertain and arduous. It has, within recent years, become inextricably tied to large-scale funding, much of which evades the limits imposed by the election laws. It compels public officials to devote much of their time to campaigning, and allocate correspondingly less time to the process of governing. As Anthony King notes, this makes 'it harder than it would be otherwise be for the American system as a whole to deal with some of America's most pressing problems' (1997: 3–4). Nevertheless, although many of the states will continue to jostle each other so as to secure a place at the beginning of the primary season, a lack of consensus about alternatives, and the constraints imposed by the Constitution, make fundamental reform an unlikely prospect.

References and further reading

Alsop, R. J. (ed.) (1997), *The Wall Street Journal Almanac 1998*, New York, Ballantine Books.

Ashbee, E. (1993), 'The great conservative crack-up: The Republican Party and the 1992 presidential election', *Talking Politics*, 5:3, Summer, 152–60.

Ashford, N. (1990), 'The conservative agenda and the Reagan presidency', in J. Hogan, *The Reagan Years*, Manchester, Manchester University Press.

Ashford, N. (1996), 'Angry white males', *Talking Politics*, 9:1, Autumn, 64–8.

Ashford, N. (1998), 'The Republican Party agenda and the conservative movement', in D. McSweeney and J. Owens, *The Republican Takeover of Congress*, London, Macmillan, 96–116.

Bennett, A. J. (1990), *American Government and Politics 1990*, Godalming.

Bennett, A. J. (1993), *American Government and Politics 1993*, Godalming.

Bennett, A. J. (1997), *American Government and Politics 1997*, Godalming.

Brubaker, S. C. (1998), 'The limits of campaign spending limits', *The Public Interest*, 133, Fall, 33–54.

Bureau of the Census (1997), *Statistical Abstract of the United States*, Washington, DC, US Department of Commerce.

Committee for the Study of the American Electorate (1998a), *Primary Turnout Reaching Record Lows*, <http://tap.epn.org/csae/cgans.html> 29 June, (accessed 12 December 1998).

Committee for the Study of the American Electorate (1998b), *Turnout Dips to a 56–Year Low*, <http://tap.epn.org/csae/cgans4.html> 6 November, (accessed 12 December 1998).

Congressional Quarterly (1997), *Selecting the President: From 1789 to 1996*, Washington, DC, CQ Press.

Durham, M. (1996), 'The fall and rise of the Christian right in America', *Politics Review*, 5:4, April, 26–8.

Flanigan, W. H. and N. H. Zingale (1998), *Political Behavior of the American Electorate*, Washington, DC, CQ Press.

Graber, D. A. (1997), *Mass Media and American Politics*, Washington, DC, CQ Press.

Grant, A. (1995), 'Financing American elections', *Politics Review*, 5:2, November, 9–12.

Grant, A. (1997), 'The 1996 elections and campaign finance in the United States', *Talking Politics*, 10:1, Autumn, 56–61.

Hershey, M. R. (1997), 'The Congressional elections', in G. M. Pomper *et al.*, *The Election of 1996: Reports and Interpretations*, Chatham, Chatham House, 205–39.

Jacobson, G. (1996), *The Politics of Congressional Elections*, New York, Longman.

King, A. (1997), *Running Scared: Why Politicians Spend More Time Governing than Campaigning*, New York, Free Press.

Kirksey, J. F. (1998), 'Campaign-finance reform', in G. Peele, C. J. Bailey, B. Cain and B. Guy Peters, *Developments in American Politics 3*, Basingstoke, Macmillan.

Kuttner, R. (1996), 'Why Americans don't vote', in B. Stinebrickner, *American Government 96/97*, Guilford, Dushkin Publishing Group, 164–6.

Ladd, E. C. (1996), 'The 1994 Congressional elections: the postindustrial realignment continues', in B. Stinebrickner, *American Government 96/97*, Guilford, Dushkin Publishing Group, 167–80.

Maidment, R. and M. Dawson (1994), *The United States in the Twentieth Century: Key Documents*, London, Hodder & Stoughton in association with the Open University.

Miroff, B., R. Seidelman, and T. Swanstrom (1998), *The Democratic Debate: An Introduction to American Politics*, Boston, Houghton Mifflin.

New York Times (1996), 10 November.

New York Times (1998), 3 November.

Owens, J. (1995), 'The 1994 US mid-term elections', *Politics Review*, 4:4, April, 2–6.

Polsby, N. W. and A. Wildavsky (1996), *Presidential Elections: Strategies and Structures in American Politics*, Chatham, Chatham House.

Pomper, G. M. (1997),'The presidential election', in G.M. Pomper, *The Elections of 1996: Reports and Interpretations*, Chatham, Chatham House, 173–204.

USA Today (1998), 6–8 November.

Wattenberg, M. P. (1991), *The Rise of Candidate-Centered Politics*, Cambridge, Harvard University Press.

Wattenberg, M. P. (1996), *The Decline of American Political Parties 1952–1994*, Cambridge, Harvard UP

Wayne, S. J. (1992), *The Road to the White House 1992: The Politics of Presidential Selection*, New York, St Martin's Press.

Wayne, S. J. (1996), *The Road to the White House 1996: The Politics of Presidential Selection*, New York, St Martin's Press.

11

Interest groups

Interest groups are the basis of the 'persuasion industry'. They 'lobby' – or attempt to persuade – decision makers to adopt a particular course of action. In contrast to political parties, they generally do not seek to win elected office.

Voluntary associations have always been a characteristic feature of American politics. As early as the 1830s, Alexis de Tocqueville was struck by them. 'In no country in the world', he asserted, 'has the principle of association been more successfully used, or applied to a greater multitude of objects, than in America' (1984: 95). Over the past century, interest groups have developed alongside the religious and civic groupings that Tocqueville described, and within recent years, there has been a proliferation of both organised groups and lobbying organisations. In 1991, *National Journal* identified 328 groups, 98 think-tanks, 288 trade and professional associations, and 682 company head-quarters in Washington, DC (Judis 1995b: 257). In 1997, an estimated $1.2 billion was spent by those seeking to influence the federal government (Abramson 1998). Washington, DC's K Street is now synonymous with the lobbying industry.

Why are there so many interest groups in the US? The principal reason is that the American system of government is particularly open to external influence, and this encourages the creation of organised interests. There are large numbers of access points – or openings – that enable groups to reach decision makers. These include the three branches of government in Washington, DC, as well as the different tiers of state and local government. At the same time, the use of primaries to determine the parties' candidates, and the system of election finance, present countless opportunities that enable organisations to advance their arguments and interests. Furthermore, since the turn of the century, commerce and industry have been subject to increasing regulatory control by the federal government. Companies and 'producer groups' have, as a consequence, sought to influence those in Congress and the federal bureaucracy who shape the business environment.

This chapter considers the work of interest groups. It outlines different types of interest group, assesses the methods that they employ, and asks two questions. To what extent do groups influence decision-makers? Do they play a negative or positive role in the political process?

Types of interest groups

Although the dividing lines are sometimes blurred, interest groups can be classified in terms of *issue* and *protective* groups. Issue groups are organisations that lobby on behalf of others or campaign for a broad political or social cause. The Children's Defense Fund works on behalf of children facing abuse or danger. The Sierra Club campaigns for the preservation of the natural habitat. The Family Research Council promotes a traditionalist approach towards family life.

Three features of issue group activity should be noted. In the first place, there has been a growth in the number of *single-issue* groups. For example, US Term Limits campaigns to impose restrictions on the length of time that individuals can serve in Congress. The National Tax Limitation Committee seeks to minimise taxation levels. There are 'pro-life' and 'pro-choice' campaigns. The activities of these organisations have provoked criticism. Some observers have argued that attempts to focus on one issue alone can distort the political process.

Second, organisations claiming to represent the 'public interest' have come to the fore. Public interest groups address questions traditionally underrepresented by interest groups. The most well known is Common Cause. Founded in August 1970, it was set up to challenge the hold that 'special interests' appeared to maintain over the workings of government. It has, for example, campaigned for the imposition of further spending limits in elections and the introduction of tighter controls on lobbyists. Common Cause has also called for more environmental and urban legislation.

Third, 'think-tanks' have played an increasingly visible and influential role in the process of policy initiation. These are research organisations that publish in-depth reports surveying the rationale behind, and the implications of, particular policy options. Although the tax-exempt status that many groups have gained prevents them from lobbying or campaigning directly, many are politically aligned, and their work structures the activities of legislators. The Progressive Policy Institute is broadly liberal in its orientation. The Heritage Foundation and the American Enterprise Institute are conservative.

Protective groupings advance and defend their own interests and those of their membership. They can be divided into a number of categories:

1 There are business groups. Companies such as Microsoft and General Motors attempt to influence the decision-making process. They might, for example, be seeking federal government contracts. Other companies are

---

African-American interest groups

Black politics were dominated for much of the century by organisations such as the National Association for the Advancement of Colored People (NAACP) and the National Urban League (NUL). The NAACP was formed in 1909. Its strategy rested on lobbying and the bringing of appropriate cases before the courts. It won some important, but inevitably limited early victories that extended black voting and property rights. Founded in 1911, the NUL drew together moderate African-Americans, social workers and wealthy white philanthropists. It sought to improve living conditions in the cities. While the NAACP and the NUL concentrated on winning modest, incremental reforms, the civil rights protests of the 1950s and 1960s encouraged the formation of other organisations, most notably the Southern Christian Leadership Conference which was led by Dr Martin Luther King Jr. They used direct action – such as marches and sit-ins – to protest against segregation.

However, the civil rights organisations have, at times, been challenged by more militant, black nationalist groups. In the early 1920s, Marcus Garvey led a 'back to Africa' movement. In the late 1960s, there were calls for 'black power'. In recent years, the Nation of Islam (NoI) has been prominent. Under the leadership of Louis Farrakhan, it established the committees that organised the *Million Man March* in October 1995. The NoI calls for separate black territory within the US and demands reparations for the years of slavery.

---

affected by antitrust legislation, which imposes restrictions on monopolies. Companies are not only represented directly. About fourteen thousand are members of the National Association of Manufacturers.

2 The trade – or labour – unions are brought together by the AFL-CIO (the American Federation of Labour – Congress of Industrial Organisations). Although they do play a role in American industrial life, they are significantly weaker in the US than in Europe. In 1996, only 14.5 per cent of workers were union members. Within the private sector, the proportion was, at 10 per cent, even lower (Bureau of the Census 1997: 440). The unions were badly hit by the recessions in the early 1980s and 1990s. They were also affected by the long-term process of *de-industrialisation* – the decline of the manufacturing sector where the unions traditionally had a strong hold.

3 There are professional associations, such as the American Medical Association (AMA) representing doctors, and the American Bar Association (ABA), which puts forward the interests of lawyers. The ABA has an institutionalised role in the selection of federal judges. It awards 'ratings' to nominees prior to consideration by the Senate Judiciary Committee.

4 State and local governments also act as pressure groups. As Chapter 8 established, although some of the individual states have offices in Washington,

DC, they are also represented through organisations such as the National Governors' Association, the Council of State Governments, and the National League of Cities.

As well as issue and protective groupings, there are also some *hybrid* organisations that can be placed somewhere between the two ideal types. They work on behalf of their membership, but also campaign for others beyond their own ranks. For example, the National Rifle Association (NRA) protects the rights of gun owners, but it also campaigns, more broadly, to uphold the right to 'bear arms'.

Methods of influence

The methods of influence used by an interest group are tied to the *access points* – openings to the decision makers – that are available to it. If an organisation resorts to mass action – such as demonstrations or symbolic protests – this can be because access points have been closed off. It could therefore be argued that the success of the October 1995 Million Man March – a mass protest of black men in Washington, DC – reflected the political weakness of black political organisations rather than their strength. More influential interest groups seek to influence the political process by working through established channels. They direct their efforts towards all three branches of the federal government, state governments and the localities.

The legislative branch

The US Congress has long been open to interest group influence. This is because party loyalties have traditionally been weak. Voting decisions in Congress are much more a matter of individual choice than in the European legislatures, where more rigid forms of party discipline are imposed. Members of Congress are therefore responsive to external pressures and interests. As Chapter 5 noted, a lobbying 'industry' has grown up around Capitol Hill.

Elections to Congress offer particular opportunities for interest group intervention. Groups may endorse a candidate. For example, although the trade unions have associations with the Democratic Party, they have begun to endorse some Republican candidates so as to 'reward' those who have been sympathetic towards organised labour. In 1996, they backed twenty-seven GOP House candidates (*International Herald Tribune* 1998). Groups will also publicise a candidate's record and opinions in ways that are designed either to assist or damage that candidate's electoral prospects. Some publish 'ratings' of Congressional candidates, based upon their voting record. They seek to highlight his or her attitude towards the issues they see as pivotal. For example, the Christian Coalition regularly produces 'voter guides'. These emphasise the different candidates' attitudes towards issues such as abortion, school prayer and capital punishment. In 1998, they prepared forty-five million such guides for distribution in churches two days before the elections (Greenblatt 1998: 2880). Other organisations concentrate their activities in particular districts and states. In the 1996 elections, the Sierra Club, a long-established environmental organisation, devoted over $6 million to fifteen House and eight Senate contests. Its 'issue-ads' promote the records of some candidates and attack those of others (*New York Times* 1998).

Interest groups also use finance to 'reward' and 'punish' particular candidates. As noted in Chapter 10, they work through Political Action Committees (PACs), which offer the only legal channel through which groups can donate funds to presidential or Congressional candidates. The funds are then used by candidates to cover the costs of campaigning. They pay for radio and TV commercials, staff salaries, and travel. Large sums are involved: in 1993–94, 4,618 PACs gave a total of $189 million (Grant 1995: 11).

The executive branch

Successive presidents and their aides have been accused of having too close an association with particular interests or organisations. However, in practice, although they are screened by the Office of Management and Budget (OMB), many executive branch decisions – particularly the issuing of regulations – are taken by the departments, agencies and commissions rather than the administration. Interest groups therefore seek to establish a close relationship with sections of the federal bureaucracy. These ties have been subject to considerable criticism, and some observers argue that the personnel working within the government apparatus have, in effect, been 'captured' by powerful interest groups (see Chapter 7).

Interest groups and the Internet

An extensive listing of think-tanks and issue-advocacy groups – with links – can be found at:

http://www.policy.com

The judicial branch

In contrast with the UK, the courts are open to some forms of lobbying. Interest groups can submit *amicus curiae* ('friend of the court') briefings to the Supreme Court. These are put forward between the Court's decision to consider a particular case and the date on which it hears oral submissions. Particularly controversial cases attract large numbers of *amicus* briefs. In 1989, seventy-eight were submitted to the Court before it considered *Webster v. Reproductive Health*

Services. Of these, forty-seven were put forward by pro-life groups, and thirty-one by pro-choice organisations (McKeever 1997: 109).

In practice, some interest groups have more influence on the Court's deliberations than others. Evidence given by specialist and expert organisations is likely to carry greater weight than arguments submitted by campaigns and ideological groupings.

Interest groups can also 'sponsor' a litigant by providing funding and the services of lawyers when cases are brought to the courts. There are some celebrated examples. In 1925, the American Civil Liberties Union (ACLU) and a Tennessee teacher, John Scopes, invited prosecution and a subsequent court battle by teaching Darwin's theory of evolution in defiance of state law. Tennessee legislators still insisted upon the veracity of the account of creation given in the Book of Genesis. Almost thirty years later, in 1954, the National Association for the Advancement of Colored People (NAACP) 'sponsored' a number of school desegregration cases. In the most celebrated of these, *Brown v. Board of Education (Topeka, Kansas)* (1954), the NAACP backed the case of Oliver Brown, who was seeking to ensure that his daughter could attend a nearby school rather than a 'colored school' some distance away.

Interest groups also play a role in the appointment process. Supreme Court Justices are nominated by the president, but are subject to confirmation by the Senate. Some recent appointments have attracted particular controversy. In 1987, Judge Robert Bork was attacked by critics both inside and outside the Senate. The ACLU charged that he was 'unfit' to serve. People for the American Way, an organisation established to challenge the claims of the Christian Right, launched a $2 million media campaign opposing the nomination (Hinkson Craig and O'Brien 1993: 180–2). If appointed to the Court, Bork would, it was alleged, oppose rulings such as *Roe v. Wade* (1973), thereby undermining the concept of abortion as a constitutional right.

State governments

In a federal system of government, many decisions are made at a state rather than a national level. Interest groups therefore have a presence in the different state capitals as well as Washington, DC.

According to Thad L. Beyle, business groups predominate at state level (1995: 43). This is confirmed by other studies. In 1981, Sarah McCally Morehouse found that 70 per cent of the 352 interest groups that were powerful at a state level represented business interests (Bingham 1986: 111). Companies are able to employ the most effective lobbyists, such as those who previously served as agency heads, or former legislators and governors. Three aspects of interest group activity at state level should be noted.

1 There is a relationship between pressure group influence and the character of the state economy. Pressure groups, McAlly Morehouse asserts, are

weakest in the Northeast, mid-Atlantic and Great Lakes regions. The states are the most economically diversified and industrialised.

2 The character of the party system is also significant. There is an inverse relationship between the strength of the parties and the role of pressure groups. For example, Michigan has a relatively strong party system. Issues affecting the car industry are therefore decided within the parties rather than through the interplay of interest groups.

The gun lobby

Originally formed in 1871, the National Rifle Association (NRA) is one of the most influential single-issue interest groups in the US. It now has a membership of about 2.8 million.

The NRA upholds a conservative understanding of the Second Amendment to the US Constitution. It defends the right of the citizen to 'bear arms' and seeks to counter gun-control laws put forward at federal, state or local level. The NRA believes that if law-abiding individuals are armed, they can defend themselves against the criminal, and that individual gun ownership offers a final safeguard against an over-powerful and oppressive government.

In 1975, the NRA established the Institute for Legislative Action (ILA) as its lobbying arm. It employs over seventy members of staff and has seven full-time lobbyists working on Capitol Hill. It claims a number of legislative successes, including the 1986 Firearms Owners' Protection Act. The ILA also distributes over a million leaflets and pamphlets annually offering information about the right to own a gun, firearms safety and crime-fighting measures.

The National Rifle Association has also set up a Political Action Committee – the NRA Political Victory Fund (PVF). In the 1996 mid-term elections, the PVF spent an estimated $3.6 million on contributions to different candidates' 'war chests' and on independent campaigning. Their leaflets rank candidates on the basis of their sympathy with the NRA's goals. It also endorsed more than six thousand candidates in elections to state legislatures, and twelve candidates in the state governors' races.

Although the NRA emphasises the restrictions that have been placed on gun ownership by local and state governments, it has had a considerable number of successes. In 1982, Proposition 15 in California, a measure which would have required the registration of all handguns and prevented their importation, was defeated. In 1990, in *US v. Verdugo-Urquidez*, the US Supreme Court reaffirmed that the people had the right to keep and bear firearms. In 1994, over 80 per cent of the candidates backed by the NRA-PVF were elected to the US Congress. Thirty-one states now allow sane, law-abiding citizens to carry concealed handguns.

Fortune magazine placed the NRA at number six in its 1997 league table listing the most influential pressure groups in the US.

NRA Internet site: http://www.nra.org

3 If a state legislature is highly 'professionalised' – through, for example, the payment of salaries and staff support – pressure groups will have only limited influence. In such circumstances, legislators are less reliant on interest groups for specialist information.

The impact of interest groups

What conclusions can be drawn about the overall influence of interest groups in the US political system? A number of factors are significant. A group's size undoubtedly plays a role. The American Association of Retired Persons (AARP) has grown in importance as its membership has expanded. In 1965, it had fewer than a million members. By 1980, it had risen to about twelve million. By 1994, the AARP claimed a membership of thirty-two million. On this basis, the organisation now employs 125 legislative and policy staff and has twenty-eight registered lobbyists working on its behalf (Cigler and Loomis 1995a: 12).

However, other factors – apart from numerical size – also play a part in determining a group's impact. The degree to which its goals are understood and regarded as legitimate among the general public is important. The political skills of a group's leadership and the strategy that it adopts should also be considered. The Christian Coalition, a conservative grouping committed to 'family values', gained support because it adopted a flexible approach, and sought to allay the fears of those who saw the organisation's members as religious extremists. However, US Term Limits appears to have lost supporters and allies because it was inflexible and refused to compromise. It insisted upon three two-year terms for House members, and two six-year terms for the Senate.

The influence of an interest group also rests on the degree to which it can establish a close relationship with key decision makers in the legislative branch and in the federal bureaucracy. In her account of the 104th Congress (1995–97), Elizabeth Drew records claims that lobbyists acting on behalf of 'special interests' – most especially large-scale companies – wrote legislation for Congressmen (1997: 116). It is said that a lobbyist working for the energy and petrochemical industries wrote the first draft of a bill introducing a moratorium – or 'freeze' – on the federal regulations that governed the way in which the industry operated.

There are also claims that some interest groups have established close associations with sections of the federal bureaucracy, and that 'subgovernments' or 'iron triangles' have been constructed (these were considered in Chapter 7). Some federal government programmes seem to provide particularly fertile ground for their emergence. Theodore Lowi and Benjamin Ginsberg suggest that defence spending is – at least in part – governed by an 'iron triangle'. The Senate Armed Services Committee and the House National Security Committee are bound together with government departments and agencies (such as the Department of Defense or NASA), and large contractors, most notably Boeing,

Lockheed Martin, and McDonnell Douglas (1992: 296). They collaborate so as to ensure that defence expenditure is maintained at high levels.

As Paul E. Peterson and Mark Rom note, the development of 'impact aid' was also shaped by an 'iron triangle'. The programme began during the Second World War. It initially offered federal government financial assistance to those school districts that had large concentrations of military personnel living within its area of jurisdiction. 'Impact aid' was progressively extended so as to provide additional funding for the child of every federal employee – whether military or civilian. The National Association of Impacted Districts used a strategy of 'quiet insider negotiation, partisan neutrality, and the cultivation of key influentials' (Peterson and Rom 1988: 230). Few federal legislators were willing to risk its hostility, and despite their misgivings, successive presidents agreed to the renewal of the programme.

Public choice theory and interest groups

Why do some interest groups grow, and why do others fail to attract members? Public choice theory, which employs the language, philosophy and methodology of microeconomics, and assumes that individuals are essentially *rational*, offers one answer.

In *The Logic of Collective Action*, Mancur Olson, a public choice theorist, argues that interest groups seeking advantages or benefits that would be distributed among very large numbers of people face particular difficulties. In such circumstances, individuals will generally leave commitment and action to others. They are less likely to join such a campaign, and instead become 'free riders'. For example, the National Taxpayers' Union has only been able to attract about a quarter of a million members. This represents about one in 640 taxpayers. In contrast, an interest group seeking tax concessions on behalf of a small group of companies would be much more likely to gain members and establish itself.

Further reading

Ashford, N. and S. Davies (eds) (1991), *A Dictionary of Conservative and Libertarian Thought*, London, Routledge, 214–15.

Olson, M. (1971), *Logic of Collected Action: Public Goods and the Theory of Groups*, Cambridge, Harvard University Press.

Limits and constraints

Critics of the American political system emphasise what they regard as the disproportionate influence of the most wealthy and powerful pressure groups. They point, in particular, to the role of PACs in the financing of candidates. Others stress the implications of 'iron triangles'. However, there are commentators who suggest that these claims are exaggerated. In a study of organisations representing the farming industry, William P. Browne suggests that Congressmen prefer to work with trusted 'confidants' in their home districts or states rather than Washington-based interest groups (1995: 281). There are a number of reasons why the role of interest groups may, in practice, be limited:

1   The evidence suggesting that candidates can be 'bought' with financial contributions is open to argument. At the end of 1997, *Fortune* magazine conducted a survey that asked 2,200 insiders to rank the most influential interest groups. Only three among the top ten – the Association of Trial Lawyers of America, the American Israel Public Affairs Committee and the American Medical Association – owed their influence to substantial campaign contributions. The others, *Fortune* concluded, gained their position by mobilising their grass-roots supporters, winning support in a Congressman's district, and building a relationship with a politician's staff members.
2   Many pressure groups are faced by an 'equal and opposite reaction'. This reins in their influence. People for Ethical Treatment of Animals (PETA) was founded in 1980, and by 1994, claimed 370,000 members. It campaigns for an end to experimentation on animals. PETA's efforts have, however, been countered by Putting People First (PPF), which insists that human interests should be considered above those of animals. Similarly, the National Rifle Association (NRA) is matched by Handgun Control. Furthermore, although there are large numbers of 'pro-life' groupings – including single-issue organisations such as the National Right to Life Committee – they are opposed by counter-organisations such as the National Abortion and Reproductive Rights League (NARAL) and Planned Parenthood. The trade unions – represented through the American Federation of Labour – Congress of Industrial Organisations (AFL-CIO) – face counter-pressures from business organisations such as the National Association of Manufacturers.
3   Some of the interest groups that became entrenched within the government machine – through the development of 'iron triangles' – lost their grip during the 1980s. The Reagan administration and Congress worked together in cutting federal government spending. Within this framework, budget proposals put forward by government agencies, which had been regarded as inviolable, became subject to close scrutiny by the Office of Management and Budget (OMB), Congressional committees, and party leaders. Furthermore, in 1986, Congress removed tax concessions from a number of organisations. Peterson and Rom claim that these moves reflect the decline of the 'iron triangle'. Both the president and Congress demonstrated that they had the ability 'to make fairly radical policy changes and are not captive to forces limiting them to minor, incremental adjustments' (Peterson and Rom 1988: 233).

4 It would be a mistake to generalise about the influence of interest groups. Influence can take different forms. In the US political system – based around a separation of powers – decision making requires the assent and cooperation of different institutions. As a consequence, it is much easier to *block* a policy initiative than to introduce change. In 1993–94, interest groups could prevent the Clinton health-care plan being adopted. The National Federation of Independent Businesses feared the costs that would be imposed by universal coverage. Others were concerned that reform might increase the availability of abortion. The Health Insurance Association of America ran a series of TV advertisements (based around the fictional characters of 'Harry and Louise') asserting that the Clinton plan would deny people the right to choose their own form of health insurance (Cigler and Loomis 1995b: 401–3). Interest groups did not, however, have the ability to agree upon and ensure the passage of an alternative plan.

Criticisms of interest-group activity

Should interest-group activity be seen in negative or positive terms? The 'persuasion industry' has been subject to intense criticism in recent years. Some of these criticisms – such as the role of the 'iron triangle' – have already been noted. There are, however, other reasons why interest groups and lobbyists are regarded by some observers with a degree of disdain.

1 The lobbying process has become institutionalised and professionalised. Many of the more wealthy interest groups utilise the services of a lobbying firm. Lobbyists have been described as 'hired guns'. They serve as 'go-betweens' working on behalf of those they have been paid to represent.

   Some lobbyists are the children, wives or siblings of lawmakers. Others are former Congressmen or staffers. Although the law prevents former public officials becoming lobbyists for a year after they leave their positions, many do become professional persuaders. They exploit their knowledge of the machinery of government and their acquaintance with legislators, members of the administration and bureaucrats so as to advance the interests of their clients. A 1998 survey revealed that at least 128 former members of Congress were working as lobbyists. Twenty-three per cent of those leaving Congress join the lobbying industry (Abramson 1998).

   This, critics assert, should be regarded as an abuse of public service. Former officials should not make large sums by utilising the connections they established while they were serving the public. Furthermore, some observers charge, the process of persuasion creates a climate in which institutionalised corruption can thrive. They assert that attempts to control the lobbying process – such as the 1946 Federal Regulation of Lobbying Act, which required lobbyists to register with the secretary of the Senate and the clerk of the House and file quarterly financial reports – have been ineffective. Michael Parenti alleges that:

> Along with the slick brochures, expert testimonies and technical reports, corporate lobbyists still have the slush fund, the kickback, the stock award, the high-paying job offer in private industry, the lavish parties and prostitutes, the meals, transportation, housing and vacation accommodations and the many other hustling enticements of money. (1980: 214)

2 Jonathan Rauch (1995) regards the entire lobbying 'industry' as parasitical. The realities of modern politics, he argues, compel companies and organisations to hire an army of public relations specialists, lawyers and persuaders to act on their behalf. This represents a diversion of resources. Rauch refers to 'the whirlpool in Washington, sucking up investment capital, talent, energy'. Inevitably, the American economy pays a price. Furthermore, Rauch argues, legislators have sought to appease a number of interest groups by offering federal government subsidies. Although less than 2 per cent of the American population live on farms, the farming lobby has been particularly successful in gaining subsidies and 'price supports'. He alleges that the subsidies are enough to buy each full-time farmer a Mercedes-Benz every year. Such policies are justified on the grounds that they protect employment within a threatened industry. However, subsidies require the imposition of taxes on other sectors of the economy.

3 The conservative critique of interest-group activity rests on the concept of 'producer capture'. This means that particular groups have used their political influence to secure and maintain a privileged economic position for themselves. This, they assert, happens at a federal, state and local level. For example, in 1937, the New York City taxi drivers persuaded the city authorities to impose a limit on the number of licensed cabs that were allowed to operate. Restrictions such as this prevent would-be competitors entering the market and offering cheaper fares than those charged by the established taxis. Although the taxi driver gains from this, both the passenger and 'outsiders' seeking employment in the New York taxi trade are placed at a disadvantage.

4 Theorists associated with the Left draw attention to what they regard as the disproportionate influence of large-scale corporate interests. Their starting point is President Eisenhower's warnings about the growth of the 'military–industrial complex'. Cold War defence spending brought the armaments companies together with the most senior sections of the armed forces so as to form an all-powerful, largely hidden, subgovernment that few legislators or presidents have felt able to challenge. This is a theme that has influenced academic studies such as C. Wright Mills's book, *The Power Elite* (1977), and informed the conspiracy theories that underpin the films of Oliver Stone, most notably *Nixon* and *JFK* (see also Chapter 6, p. 100).

5 Some issue groups have come under fire – particularly from the Left – for adopting *covert* tactics. In particular, there have been criticisms of the organisations associated with the Christian Right. They have, it is said, stood candidates to local boards of education as 'concerned parents' or independents. Once elected, they have used their positions to argue for the teaching of 'creationism'. This is the belief that the human race owes its origins to divine creation rather than the process of evolution.

6 Interest groups are – as a whole – unrepresentative of the public. Companies dominate the lobbying process and other groups are also elite-based. As John B. Judis observes, many do not have an active membership. Their boards of directors are self-appointed. Those groupings that do have an open, democratic structure are dominated by the most affluent sections of American society. Even those groups that champion the interests of the poor are dominated by college students and recent graduates (1995a: 22). As a consequence, it is charged, the mass of the population is marginalised. Kevin Phillips – a political analyst – argues that Washington, DC is now a 'capital so privileged and incestuous in its dealings, that ordinary citizens believe it is no longer accessible to the general public' (Abramson 1998).

7 There have been claims that foreign companies – or their subsidiaries – have used the lobbying process so as to gain a competitive advantage. There have, in particular, been allegations that Japanese businesses have 'bought' influence on Capitol Hill. In 1993, it was estimated that 125 law and public relations firms were working on behalf of Japanese interests (Hrebenar and Thomas 1995: 359).

8 Political Action Committees (PACs) have been subject to particular criticism. As Chapter 10 outlined, although PAC contributions to a candidate are limited under the Federal Election Campaign Act (FECA) of 1974, there are many ways in which the Act can be evaded.

Some observers make a further criticism. They suggest that successful candidates are beholden to the PACs that have financed their campaigns. This cuts across and detracts from their responsibilities to those who they represent. It can also distort the policy-making process. In 1990, there were over eighty PACs supporting the state of Israel. They gave financial support to almost all members of Congress, including $1.2 million to those who served on the Senate Foreign Relations Committee (Uslaner 1995: 386). This, critics allege, tilted US foreign policy in the Middle East.

PACs are said to distort the political process in two other ways. They have also played a role in undermining the political parties. Fund-raising was one of the parties' traditional functions, and part of their *raison d'être*. PACs now represent a primary source of finance for election candidates. They also reinforce *incumbency*. They distribute most of their funds to sitting members. These are the legislators who are already occupying a position, and are seeking re-election. Incumbents already have a built-in advantage – because they attract media

---

Social movements

The concept of an interest group extends to social movements. These are broad-based networks of groups and individuals. They seek radical change, and generally have a cultural as well as a political identity. They may, for example, try to develop alternative lifestyles that break with orthodox ways of living. Social movements also often resort to non-institutional methods of campaigning that go beyond formal political channels, including, for example, organised assertions of identity such as street protests. Although some social movements have a long history, most either emerged or were restructured by the events and cultural changes of the 1960s and 1970s.

The women's movement is an example of a social movement. It has had a significant impact on US politics since the 1970s. Feminist texts such as Simone de Beauvoir's *The Second Sex* and Betty Friedan's *The Feminine Mystique* created an atmosphere in which traditional cultural and sexual attitudes were challenged. Groupings such as the National Organisation for Women campaigned, albeit unsuccessfully, for an Equal Rights Amendment (ERA) to the US Constitution. The movement called for the free availability of abortion, equal pay, an opening up of traditionally male occupations, and new attitudes towards domestic labour. Hillary Rodham Clinton's remarks during the 1992 election campaign, stating that she would not be simply standing 'by my man' or staying at home and 'baking cookies', reflects the change in attitudes that the movement engendered.

The gay movement also took shape during this period. In 1969, in a now celebrated incident, the New York police raided the Stonewall bar in Greenwich Village, providing the impetus for the creation of an organised movement. It now has a cultural existence – New York's annual Gay Pride parade is now an important event in the city calendar – and it also constitutes a significant lobbying network, particularly within the Democratic Party.

---

attention and are able to deliver 'rewards' and benefits to those they represent – and their chances of winning re-election are therefore disproportionately high. PACs will wish to support likely winners. However, by allocating a very large proportion of their funds to incumbents, they thereby make it even more likely that the incumbent will be re-elected.

Traditionally, PAC enthusiasm for incumbents meant that Democrats were the winners in the battle for funding. However, following Republican successes in the 1994 elections, the pattern changed. In the first six months of 1995, House Republican members received a total of $28.1 million, more than double the amount they had received two years previously.

Because of criticisms such as these, PACs have been increasingly discredited. When former California Governor, Jerry Brown, made a bid for the Democratic Party's presidential nomination in 1992, he refused to accept PAC funds, and relied instead upon contributions from individuals.

However, the women's and gay movements have not gone unchallenged. Their growing strength contributed to the emergence of *counter-movements*. Conservative critics of feminism such as Phyllis Schlafly asserted that the ERA would undermine the traditional role of women, force women into combat units in the armed forces, and that the proposal put forward by the gay movement for same-sex marriage would destroy family life.

Conservative activists were joined by many of the churches. There are about 336,000 individual churches scattered across the US. Many have an evangelical character. Until the 1970s, they tended to shun the political process, and concentrated instead on spiritual concerns. However, the Supreme Court's 1973 ruling, *Roe v. Wade*, established abortion as a constitutional right. For many Christians, the forcible termination of a pregnancy constituted murder. At about the same time, the Internal Revenue Service (IRS) revoked the tax-exempt status of Christian schools and colleges, charging that they discriminated against black students. These events, and the apparent threat to family life posed by both feminism and the gay movement, led many evangelical Christians to join forces – in the political arena – with conservatives.

They came together in the New Christian Right. It took a number of organisational forms. In the 1980s, the Reverend Jerry Falwell's Moral Majority sought – with relatively little success – to influence the policies adopted by the Reagan administration. In the 1990s, the Christian Coalition – led for most of its existence by the Reverend Pat Robertson and Ralph Reed – adopted more developed lobbying techniques. It has had some success in shaping the Republican Party's presidential election platform.

Further reading

Durham, M. (1996), 'The Fall and Rise of the Christian Right in America', *Politics Review*, April, 26–8.

Positive features

These criticisms of interest-group activity are, however, countered by those who argue that they play a positive role in American politics. First, they note that interest groups provide legislators with specialist information. Although Congressmen have their own 'staffers', groups can offer detailed or technical knowledge that they would otherwise lack. There have, however, been suggestions that the proliferation of interest groups within recent years has led to a decline in their usefulness as sources of information. William P. Browne has argued that Congressmen are increasingly uncertain about which group has credibility and deserves attention (1995: 284).

Interest groups can also be used as a 'sounding board' by decision makers at the *policy formulation* stage of the legislative process. President Lyndon Johnson consulted George Meany, head of the trade-union confederation, the AFL-CIO, so as to gauge opinion on his proposals for anti-poverty measures. At the same time, organisations offer opportunities for political participation. There is considerable public hostility towards the decision makers in Washington, DC, and group activity can bridge the gap between the electorate and those 'inside the Beltway'.

Furthermore, the widely accepted claim that particular interest groups occupy a monopoly position in terms of political power is open to challenge. *Pluralist* theorists suggest that power is widely dispersed across society. No single group or interest holds a disproportionately powerful position for a sustained period of time or across a range of different policy areas. Political power ebbs and flows. An influential organisation will therefore be soon displaced by another grouping if it becomes unrepresentative or if other groups are more representative of public opinion. Amid all of this, the apparatus of government – the federal and state bureaucracies – play a more or less neutral role.

Conclusion

The US is 'a nation of interest groups' insofar as they play a pivotal role within the political process. They attempt to influence all three branches of the federal government as well as the states and the localities. As has been seen, pluralist theorists stress the positive features of interest-group activity. The picture they offer has become more credible in recent years. Although, as David McKay argues, a relatively small number of powerful economic groups – business, labour and agriculture – had 'captured' the decision-making process up until the 1970s, a new form of politics has emerged. There has been a large-scale growth in issue or promotional groups. No single organisation is predominant. Government has become much more open and receptive to a range of interests (1992: 24–5).

References and further reading

Abramson, J. (1998), 'The business of persuasion thrives in nation's capitol', *New York Times*, 29 September.

Berry, J. M. and K. E. Portney (1995), 'Centralizing regulatory control and interest group access: the Quayle Council on Competitiveness', in A. J. Cigler and B. A. Loomis, *Interest Group Politics*, Washington, DC, Congressional Quarterly, 319–47.

Beyle, T. L. (1995), 'Introduction – politics: parties, interest groups, and PACS', in T. L. Beyle, *State Government: CQ's Guide to Current Issues and Activities 1995–96*, Washington, DC, Congressional Quarterly, 41–5.

Bingham R. D. (1986), *State and Local Government in an Urban Society*, New York, Random House.

Browne, W. P. (1995), 'Organized interests, grassroots confidants, and Congress', in A. J. Cigler and B. A. Loomis (1995), *Interest Group Politics*, Washington, DC, Congressional Quarterly, 281–97.

Bureau of the Census (1997), *Statistical Abstract of the United States*, Washington, DC, Bureau of the Census.

Cigler, A. J. and B. A. Loomis (1995a), 'Introduction: the changing nature of interest group politics', in A. J. Cigler and B. A. Loomis, *Interest Group Politics*, Washington, DC, Congressional Quarterly, 1–31.

Cigler, A. J. and B. A. Loomis (1995b), 'Contemporary interest group politics: more than "more of the same"', in A. J. Cigler and B. A. Loomis, *Interest Group Politics*, Washington, DC, Congressional Quarterly, 393–406.

Drew, E. (1997), *Showdown: The Struggle Between the Gingrich Congress and the Clinton White House*, New York, Touchstone.

Friedman, M. and R. Friedman (1984), *Tyranny of the Status Quo*, London, Secker & Warburg.

Grant, A. (1995), 'Financing American elections', *Politics Review*, 5:2, November, 9–12.

Greenblatt, A. (1998), 'The disengaging voter', *Congressional Quarterly Weekly Report*, 24 October, 2880–1.

Hinkson Craig, B. and D. M. O'Brien (1993), *Abortion and American Politics*, Chatham, Chatham House.

Hrebenar, R. J. and C. S. Thomas (1995), 'The Japanese lobby in Washington. How different is it?' in A. J. Cigler and B. A. Loomis, *Interest Group Politics*, Washington, DC, Congressional Quarterly, 349–67.

International Herald Tribune (1998), 26 October.

Judis, J. B. (1995a), 'The contract with K Street', *The New Republic*, 4 December, 18–25.

Judis, J. B. (1995b), 'The pressure elite: inside the narrow world of advocacy group politics', in W. D. Burnham, *The American Prospect: Reader in American Politics*, Chatham, Chatham House, 256–75.

Lowi, T. J., and B. Ginsberg (1992), *American Government: Freedom and Power*, New York, W. W. Norton.

McKay, D. (1992), 'Interest group politics in the United States', *Politics Review*, April, 24–5.

McKeever, R. J. (1997), *The United States Supreme Court: A Political and Legal Analysis*, Manchester, Manchester University Press.

Mills, C. Wright (1977), *The Power Elite*, New York, Oxford University Press.

Mitchell, A. (1998), 'A new form of lobbying puts public face on private interest', *New York Times*, 30 September.

New York Times (1998), 24 October.

Parenti, M. (1980), *Democracy for the Few*, New York, St Martin's Press.

Peterson, P. E. and M. Rom (1988), 'Lower taxes, more spending, and budget deficits', in C. O. Jones (ed.), *The Reagan Legacy: Promise and Performance*, Chatham, Chatham House, 213–40.

Rauch, J. (1995), *Demosclerosis*, New York, Times Books.

Tocqueville, A. de (1984), *Democracy in America*, New York, Mentor.

Uslaner, E. M. (1995), 'All politics are global: interest groups and the making of foreign policy', in A. J. Cigler and B. A. Loomis, *Interest Group Politics*, Washington, DC, Congressional Quarterly, 369–91.

Appendices

I

The US since 1789: a brief chronology

1789	George Washington takes office as the first US president.
1791	The first ten amendments – the Bill of Rights – are added to the Constitution.
1803	The acquisition of lands from France – the 'Louisiana Purchase' – doubles the size of US territory.
1812–15	War with Britain.
1820	The Missouri Compromise.
1845	Texas is annexed.
1857	*Dred Scott v. Sandford.* The Supreme Court rules that slaves are mere property, and Congress has no power to forbid slavery in the newly established western territories.
1860	The US is becoming an industrial nation. 30,000 miles of railway track are in place. Abraham Lincoln (Republican) is elected president.
1861–65	The Civil War. 618,000 are killed by enemy fire, typhoid and dysentery. Following their defeat, the southern states are placed under military occupation.
1868	President Andrew Johnson is impeached and acquitted.
1869	The transcontinental railroad is completed, linking the east and west coasts.
1896	The Supreme Court rules, in *Plessy v. Ferguson,* that – under the 'separate but equal' doctrine – segregation is constitutional.
1910	The National Association for the Advancement of Colored People is founded.
1917	The US enters the First World War.
1919–20	The Treaty of Versailles fails to gain a two-thirds majority in the Senate and is therefore defeated.

1919	The Eighteenth Amendment to the Constitution introduces Prohibition.
1921–24	Immigration is severely restricted.
1929	The Wall Street crash ushers in a period of mass unemployment and economic depression.
1933	Franklin D. Roosevelt becomes president. He introduces the Emergency Banking Relief Act and other measures ushering in the New Deal. The federal government becomes much more involved in economic and social affairs.
1937	Roosevelt's 'court-packing' plan.
1941	Following the Japanese attack on the US naval base at Pearl Harbor, the US joins the Second World War.
1945	The Second World War comes to an end with the defeat of Germany (May) and Japan (August). The Japanese surrender follows US atom-bomb attacks on the cities of Hiroshima and Nagasaki.
1947	The US commits itself – in the Truman doctrine – to a policy of containment. It will support 'free people' across the world. The countries of western Europe begin to receive large-scale financial assistance from the US through Marshall Aid.
1948	Alger Hiss, a former State Department official, is accused of spying. Over the next few years, there is a sustained drive against alleged Soviet agents and communist sympathisers, known as McCarthyism.
1950	North Korean forces attack the non-communist south. Together with some other UN member states, US forces fight a three-year war.
1954	In *Brown v. Board of Education (Topeka, Kansas)*, the Supreme Court rules that segregation in public schools is unconstitutional. It later calls for desegegration 'with all deliberate speed'.
1955	The bus boycott in Montgomery, Alabama, marks the beginning of the civil rights movement's struggle against segregation in the southern states.
1961	President Eisenhower warns, in his valedictory address, of the dangers posed by the 'military–industrial complex'.
1962	The USSR installs nuclear missiles in Cuba. The US 'quarantines' the island. Following a tense stand-off, the USSR removes the missiles.
1963	In an address to civil rights protesters at the Lincoln Memorial in Washington, DC, Martin Luther King Jr proclaims: 'I have a dream my four little children will one day live in a nation where they will not be judged by the color of their skin but by the content of their character.'
	President John F. Kennedy is assassinated.
1964	Following an apparent attack on a US vessel in the Gulf of Tonkin, US intervention in Vietnam escalates. Both air and land forces are committed.

President Lyndon Johnson announces the War on Poverty. 'Our aim is not only to relieve the symptom of poverty, but to cure it and, above all, to prevent it.' The role of the federal government is expanded again.

1965   The Voting Rights Act and the 1964 Civil Rights Act bring segregation and the Jim Crow laws to an end in the southern states.

1969   Woodstock Festival.

1970   Four students at Kent State University protesting against the Vietnam War are shot dead by the Ohio National Guard.

1972   In an abrupt reversal of US foreign policy, President Nixon visits Communist China.

1973   In *Roe v. Wade*, the Supreme Court rules that abortion – within the first three months of a pregnancy – is an absolute constitutional right.

1974   President Richard M. Nixon resigns once it becomes clear that he will be impeached for his role in the Watergate cover-up.

1975   The National Liberation Front (Vietcong) and the North Vietnamese defeat the US-backed south. Vietnam is reunited under communist rule.

1979–81   The US Embassy in Teheran is seized by Iranian government-backed militants. The Embassy staff are held as hostages for over a year. In April 1980, a military rescue attempt fails and the Carter presidency loses its credibility.

1983   The US invasion of Grenada.

1985   Mikhail Gorbachev becomes Soviet leader. His radical reforms lead to an easing of Cold War tensions.

1986   A US bombing raid on Libya follows alleged Libyan involvement in a terrorist bomb attack on American servicemen.

The 'Iran–Contra' affair becomes public, although its overall impact on the Reagan presidency is limited.

1989   The Berlin Wall is demolished, signalling the collapse of the communist system. The conflict between the West and the Soviet bloc – the Cold War – comes to an end.

1991   Following the Iraqi invasion of Kuwait in August 1990, the US and other members of the UN coalition launch Operation Desert Storm. Iraqi forces are driven out of Kuwait.

1994   The Republican Party wins majorities in both houses of Congress. Most House Republicans are signatories to the *Contract with America*. Newt Gingrich becomes House Speaker.

1996   Bill Clinton becomes the first Democratic president to win a second term since President Franklin Roosevelt. He just fails to gain 50 per cent of the popular vote.

1998   The Clinton presidency is thrown into crisis by allegations of perjury and obstruction of justice.

             Although the Republicans maintain control of Congress, their majority in the House is reduced in the mid-term elections. Newt Gingrich resigns. The President is impeached.

1999   President Clinton is acquitted by the Senate on the impeachment charges.

             US and other NATO forces take military action against Serbia.

II

The US Constitution

We the people of the United States, in order to form a more perfect Union, establish Justice, insure domestic Tranquility, provide for the common defence, promote the general Welfare, and secure the Blessing of Liberty to ourselves and our Posterity, do ordain and establish this CONSTITUTION for the United States of America.

Article I

Section 1.   All legislative Powers herein granted shall be vested in a Congress of the United States, which shall consist of a Senate and House of Representatives.

Section 2.   The House of Representatives shall be composed of Members chosen every second Year by the People of the several States, and the Electors in each State shall have the Qualifications requisite for Electors of the most numerous Branch of the State Legislature.

No Person shall be a Representative who shall not have attained the Age of twenty-five Years, and been seven Years a Citizen of the United States, and who shall not, when elected, be an Inhabitant of that State in which he shall be chosen.

[Representatives and direct Taxes shall be apportioned among the several States which may be included within this Union, according to their respective Numbers, which shall be determined by adding to the whole Number of free Persons, including those bound to Service for a Term of Years, and excluding Indians not taxed, three-fifths of all other persons.][1] The actual Enumeration shall be made within three Years after the first Meeting of the Congress of the United States, and within every subsequent Term of ten Years, in such Manner as they shall be Law direct. The Number of Representatives shall not exceed one for every thirty thousand, but each State shall have at Least one Representative; and until such enumeration shall be made, the State of New Hampshire shall be entitled to chuse three, Massachusetts eight, Rhode Island and Providence Plantations one, Connecticut five, New York six, New Jersey four, Pennsylvania eight, Delaware one, Maryland six, Virginia ten, North Carolina five, South Carolina five, and Georgia three.

---

[1] This provision was modified by the Sixteenth Amendment. The three-fifths reference to slaves was rendered obsolete by the Thirteenth and Fourteenth Amendments.

When vacancies happen in the Representation from any State, the Executive Authority thereof shall issue Writs of Election to fill such Vacancies.

The House of Representatives shall chuse their Speaker and other Officers; and shall have the sole Power of Impeachment.

Section 3. The Senate of the United States shall be composed of two Senators from each State, chosen by the Legislature thereof,[1] for six Years; and each Senator shall have one Vote.

Immediately after they shall be assembled in Consequence of the first Election, they shall be divided as equally as may be into three Classes. The Seats of the Senators of the first Class shall be vacated at the Expiration of the second Year, of the Second Class at the Expiration of the fourth Year, and the third class at the Expiration of the sixth Year, so that one-third may be chosen every second Year; and if Vacancies happen by Resignation, or otherwise, during the Recess of the Legislature of any State, the Executive thereof may make temporary Appointments until the next Meeting of the Legislature, which shall then fill such Vacancies.

No Person shall be a Senator who shall not have attained to the Age of thirty Years, and been nine Years a Citizen of the United States, and who shall not, when elected, be an Inhabitant of that State for which he shall be chosen.

The Vice President of the United States shall be President of the Senate, but shall have no Vote, unless they be equally divided.

The Senate shall chuse their Officers, and also a President pro tempore, in the absence of the Vice President, or when he shall exercise the Office of President of the United States.

The Senate shall have the sole Power to try all Impeachments. When sitting for that Purpose, they shall be on Oath or Affirmation. When the President of the United States is tried, the Chief Justice shall preside; And no Person shall be convicted without the Concurrence of two-thirds of the Members present.

Judgment in Cases of Impeachment shall not extend further than to removal from Office, and disqualification to hold and enjoy any Office of honor, Trust or Profit under the United States; but the Party convicted shall nevertheless be liable and subject to Indictment, Trial, Judgment and Punishment, according to Law.

Section 4. The Times, Places and Manner of holding Elections for Senators and Representatives, shall be prescribed in each State by the Legislature thereof; but the Congress may at any time by Law make or alter such Regulations, except as to the Places of chusing Senators.

The Congress shall assemble at least once in every Year, and such Meeting shall be on the first Monday in December, unless they shall by Law appoint a different Day.[2]

Section 5. Each House shall be the Judge of the Elections, Returns and Qualifications of its own Members, and a Majority of each shall constitute a Quorum to do Business; but a smaller Number may adjourn from day to day, and may be authorized to compel the Attendance of absent Members, in such Manner, and under such Penalties as each House may provide.

Each House may determine the Rules of its Proceedings, punish its Members for disorderly Behavior, and, with the Concurrence of two-thirds, expel a Member.

Each House shall keep a Journal of its Proceedings and from time to time publish the same, excepting such Parts as may in their Judgment require Secrecy; and the Yeas and

[1] See the Seventeenth Amendment.
[2] See the Twentieth Amendment.

Nays of the Members of either House on any question shall, at the Desire of one-fifth of those Present, be entered on the Journal.

Neither House, during the Session of Congress, shall without the Consent of the other, adjourn for more than three days, nor to any other Place than that in which the two Houses shall be sitting.

Section 6.   The Senators and Representatives shall receive a Compensation for their Services, to be ascertained by Law, and paid out of the Treasury of the United States. They shall in all Cases, except Treason, Felony, and Breach of the peace, be privileged from Arrest during their Attendance at the Session of their respective Houses, and in going to and returning from the same; and for any Speech or Debate in either House, they shall not be questioned in any other Place.

No Senator or Representative shall, during the Time for which he was elected, be appointed to any civil Office under the Authority of the United States, which shall have been created, or the Emoluments whereof shall have been encreased during such time; and no Person holding any Office under the United States, shall be a Member of either House during his Continuance in Office.

Section 7.   All Bills for raising Revenue shall originate in the House of Representatives; but the Senate may propose or concur with Amendments as on other Bills.

Every Bill which shall have passed the House of Representatives and the Senate, shall, before it become a Law, be presented to the President of the United States; If he approve he shall sign it, but if not he shall return it, with his Objections to that House in which it shall have originated, who shall enter the at large on their Journal, and proceed to reconsider it. If after such Reconsideration two-thirds of that House shall agree to pass the Bill it shall be sent, together with the Objections, to the other House, by which it shall likewise to be reconsidered, and if approved by two-thirds of that House, it shall become a Law. But in all such Cases the Votes of both Houses shall be determined by Yeas and Nays, and the Names of the Persons voting to and against the Bill shall be entered on the Journal of each House respectively. If any Bill shall not be returned by the President within ten Days (Sunday excepted) after it shall have been presented to him, the Same shall be a Law, in like Manner as if he had signed it, unless the Congress by their Adjournment prevent its Return, in which Case it shall not be a Law.

Every Order, Resolution, or Vote to which the Concurrence of the Senate and House of Representatives may be necessary (except on a question of Adjournment) shall be presented to the President of the United States; and before the Same shall take Effect, shall be approved by him, or being disapproved by him, shall be repassed by two-thirds of the Senate and House of Representatives, according to the Rule and Limitations prescribed in the Case of a Bill.

Section 8.   The Congress shall have Power To lay and collect Taxes, Duties, Imposts and Excises, to pay the Debts and provide for the common Defence and general Welfare of the United States; but all Duties, Imposts and Excises shall be uniform throughout the United States;

To borrow money on the Credit of the United States;

To regulate Commerce with foreign Nations, and among the several States, and with the Indian Tribes;

To establish an uniform Rule of Naturalization, and uniform Laws on the subject of Bankruptcies throughout the United States.

To coin Money, regulate the Value thereof, and of foreign Coin, and fix the Standard of Weights and Measures;

To provide for the Punishment of counterfeiting the Securities and current Coin of the United States;

To establish Post Offices and post Roads;

To promote the Progress of Science and useful arts, by securing for limited Times to Authors and Inventors the exclusive Right to their respective Writings and Discoveries;

To constitute Tribunals inferior to the supreme Court;

To define and punish Piracies and Felonies committed on the high Seas, and Offenses against the Law of Nations;

To declare War, grant Letters of Marque and Reprisal, and make Rules concerning Captures on Land and Water;

To raise and support Armies, but no Appropriation of Money to that Use shall be for a longer Term than two Years;

To provide and maintain a Navy;

To make Rules for the Government and Regulation of the land and naval Forces;

To provide for calling forth the Militia to execute the Laws of the Union, suppress Insurrections and repel Invasions;

To provide for organizing, arming, and disciplining the Militia, and for governing such Part of them as may be employed in the Service of the United States, reserving to the States respectively, the Appointment of the Officers, and the Authority of training the Militia according to the discipline prescribed by Congress;

To exercise exclusive Legislation in all Cases whatsoever, over such District (not exceeding ten Miles square) as may, by Cession of particular States, and the acceptance of Congress become the Seat of the Government of the United States, and to exercise like Authority over all Places purchased by the Consent of the Legislature of the State in which the Same shall be, for the Erection of Forts, Magazines, Arsenals, dock-Yards, and other needful Buildings; – And

To make all Laws which shall be necessary and proper for carrying into Execution the foregoing Powers, and all other Powers vested by this Constitution in the Government of the United States, or in any Department or Office thereof.

Section 9.   The Migration or Importation of such Persons as any of the States now existing shall think proper to admit, shall not be prohibited by the Congress prior to the Year one thousand eight hundred and eight, but a tax or duty may be imposed on such importation, not exceeding ten dollars for each Person.

The privilege of the Writ of Habeas Corpus shall not be suspended, unless when in Cases of Rebellion or Invasion the public Safety may require it.

No Bill of Attainder or ex post facto Law shall be passed.

No capitation, or other direct Tax shall be laid, unless in Proportion to the Census or Enumeration herein before directed to be taken.[1]

No Tax or Duty shall be laid on Articles exported from any State.

No Preference shall be given by an Regulation of Commerce or Revenue to the Ports of one State over those of another; nor shall Vessels bound to, or from one State, be obliged to enter, clear, or pay Duties in another.

No Money shall be drawn from the Treasury, but in Consequence of Appropriations made by Law; and a regular Statement and Account of the Receipts and Expenditures of all public Money shall be published from time to time.

No Title of Nobility shall be granted by the United States: And no Person holding any

---

[1] See the Sixteenth Amendment.

Office of Profit or Trust under them, shall, without the Consent of the Congress, accept of any present, Emolument, Office, or Title, of any kind whatever, from any King, Prince, or foreign State.

Section 10.   No State shall enter into any Treaty, Alliance, or Confederation; grant Letters of Marque and Reprisal; coin Money; emit Bills of Credit; make any Thing but gold and silver Coin a Tender in Payment of Debts; pass any Bill of Attainder, ex post facto Law, or Law impairing the Obligation of Contracts, or grant any Title of Nobility.

No State shall, without the Consent of the Congress, lay any Imposts or Duties on Imports or Exports, except what may be absolutely necessary for executing its inspection Laws; and the net Product of all Duties and Imposts, laid by any State on Imports or Exports, shall be for the Use of the Treasury of the United States and all such Laws shall be subject to the Revision and Controul of the Congress.

No State shall, without the Consent of Congress, lay any duty of Tonnage, keep Troops, or Ships of War in time of Peace, enter into any Agreement or Compact with another State, or with a foreign Power, or engage in War, unless actually invaded, or in such imminent Danger as will not admit of delay.

Article II

Section 1.   The executive Power shall be vested in a President of the United States of America. He shall hold his Office during the Term of four Years, and, together with the Vice President, chosen for the same Term, be elected, as follows

Each State shall appoint, in such Manner as the Legislature thereof may direct, a Number of Electors, equal to the whole number of Senators and Representatives to which the State may be entitled in the Congress; but no Senator or Representative or Person holding an Office of Trust or Profit under the United States shall be appointed an Elector.

The Electors shall meet in their respective States, and vote by Ballot for two persons, of whom one at least shall not be an Inhabitant of the same State with themselves. And they shall make a List of all Persons voted for, and of the Number of Votes for each; which List they shall sign and certify, and transmit sealed to the Seat of the Government of the United States, directed to the President of the Senate. The President of the Senate shall, in the Presence of the Senate and House of Representatives, open all the Certificates, and the Votes shall then be counted. The Person having the greatest Number of Votes shall be the President, if such Number be a Majority of the whole Number of Electors appointed; and if there be more than one who have such Majority, and have an Equal Number of Votes, then the House of Representatives shall immediately chuse by Ballot one of them for President; and if no Person have a Majority, then from the five highest on the List the said House shall in like Manner chuse the President, but in chusing the President, the Votes shall be taken by States, the Representation from each State having one Vote; A quorum for this Purpose shall consist of a Member or Members from two-thirds of the States, and a Majority of all the States shall be necessary to a Choice. In every Case, after the Choice of the President, the Person having the greatest Number of Votes of the Electors shall be the Vice-President. But if there should remain two or more who have equal votes, the Senate shall chuse from them by Ballot the Vice President.[1]

---

[1] This paragraph was superseded by the Twelfth Amendment.

The Congress may determine the Time of chusing the Electors, and the Day on which they shall give their Vote; which Day shall be the same throughout the United States.

No person except a natural born Citizen, or a Citizen of the United States, at the time of the Adoption of this Constitution, shall be eligible to the Office of President; neither shall any Person be eligible to that Office who shall not have attained the Age of thirty-five Years, and been fourteen Years a Resident within the United States.

In Case of the Removal of the President from Office, or of his Death, Resignation, or Inability to discharge the Powers and Duties of the said office, the same shall devolve on the Vice President, and the congress may by Law provide for the Case of Removal, Death, Resignation or Inability, both the President and Vice President, declaring what Officer shall then act as President, and such Officer shall act accordingly, until the Disability be removed, or a President shall be elected.

The President shall, at stated Times, receive for his Services, a Compensation, which shall neither be encreased nor diminished during the Period for which he shall have been elected, and he shall not receive within that Period any other Emolument from the United States, or any of them.

Before he enters on the Execution of his Office, he shall take the following Oath or Affirmation: – 'I do solemnly swear (or affirm) that I will faithfully execute the Office of President of the United States, and will to the best of my Ability, preserve, protect and defend the Constitution of the United States.'

Section 2.   The President shall be Commander in Chief of the Army and Navy of the United States, and of the Militia of the several States, when called into the actual Service of the United States; he may require the Opinion in writing, of the principal officer in each of the executive Departments, upon any subject relating to the Duties of their respective Offices, and he shall have Power to Grant Reprieves and Pardons for Offenses against the United States, except in Cases of Impeachment.

He shall have Power, by and with the Advice and Consent of the Senate, to make Treaties, provided two-thirds of the Senators present concur; and he shall nominate, and by and with the Advice and Consent of the Senate, shall appoint Ambassadors, other public Ministers and Consuls, Judges of the supreme Court, and all other Officers of the United States, whose Appointments are not herein otherwise provided for, and which shall be established by Law: but the Congress may by Law vest the Appointment of such inferior Offices, as they think proper, in the President alone, in the Courts of Law, or in the Heads of Departments.

The President shall have Power to fill up all Vacancies that may happen during the Recess of the Senate by granting Commissions which shall expire at the End of their next Session.

Section 3.   He shall from time to time give to the Congress Information of the State of the Union, and recommend to their Consideration such Measures as he shall judge necessary and expedient; he may, on extraordinary Occasions, convene both Houses, or either of them, and in Cases of Disagreement between them, with Respect to the Time of Adjournment, he may adjourn them to such Time as he shall think proper; he shall receive Ambassadors and other public Ministers; he shall take Care that the Laws be faithfully executed, and shall Commission all of the Officers of the United States.

Section 4.   The President, Vice President and all civil Officers of the United States, shall be removed from Office on Impeachment for, and Conviction of, Treason, Bribery, or other high Crimes and Misdemeanors.

Article III

Section 1.   The judicial Power of the United States shall be vested in one supreme Court, and in such inferior Courts as the Congress may from time to time ordain and establish. The judges, both of the supreme and inferior Courts, shall hold their offices during good Behavior, and shall, at stated Times, receive for the Services a Compensation which shall not be diminished during their Continuance in Office.

Section 2.   The judicial Power shall extend to all Cases, in Law and Equity, arising under this Constitution, the Laws of the United States and Treaties made, or which shall be made, under the Authority; – to all Cases affecting Ambassadors, other public Ministers and Consuls; – to all Cases of admiralty and maritime Jurisdiction; – to Controversies to which the United States shall be a Party; – to Controversies between two or more States; – between a State and Citizens of another State;[1] – Between Citizens of different States; – between Citizens of the same State claiming Lands under Grants of different States, and between a State, or the Citizens thereof, and foreign States, Citizens or Subjects.

In all Cases affecting Ambassadors, other public Ministers and Consuls, and those in which a State shall be a Party, the supreme Court shall have original Jurisdiction. In all the other Cases before mentioned, the supreme Court shall have appellate Jurisdiction, both as to Law and Fact, with such Exceptions, and under such Regulations as the Congress shall make.

The trial of all Crimes, except in Cases of Impeachment, shall be by Jury, and such Trial shall be held in the State where the said Crimes shall have been committed; but when not committed within any State, the Trial shall be at such Place or Places as the Congress may by Law have directed.

Section 3.   Treason against the United States, shall consist only in levying War against them, or in adhering to their Enemies, giving them Aid and Comfort. No Person shall be convicted of Treason unless on the Testimony of two Witnesses to the same overt Act, or on Confession in open Court.

The Congress shall have power to declare the Punishment of Treason, but no Attainder of Treason shall work Corruption of Blood, or Forfeiture except during the Life of the Person attainted.

Article IV

Section 1.   Full Faith and Credit shall be given in each State to the public acts, Records, and judicial Proceedings of every other State. And the Congress may by general Laws prescribe the Manner in which such Acts, Records and Proceedings shall be proved, and the Effect thereof.

Section 2.   The Citizens of each State shall be entitled to all Privileges and Immunities of Citizens in the several States.

A Person charged in any State with Treason, Felony, or other Crime, who shall flee from Justice, and be found in another State, shall on demand of the executive Authority of the State from which he fled, be delivered up, to be removed to the State having Jurisdiction of the Crime.

---

[1] See the Eleventh Amendment.

No Person held to Service or Labour in one State, under the Laws thereof, escaping into another, shall in Consequence of any Law or Regulation therein, be discharged from such Service or Labour, but shall be delivered up on Claim of the Party to whom such Service or Labour may be due.[1]

Section 3. New States may be admitted by the Congress into this Union; but no new States shall be formed or erected within the Jurisdiction of any other State; nor any State be formed by the Junction of two or more States, or parts of States, without the Consent of the Legislatures of the States concerned as well as of the Congress.

The Congress shall have Power to dispose of and make all needful Rules and Regulations respecting the Territory or other Property belonging to the United States; and nothing in this Constitution shall be so constructed as to Prejudice any Claims of the United States, or of any particular State.

Section 4. The United States shall guarantee to every State in this Union of Republican Form of Government, and shall protect each of them against Invasion; and on Application of the Legislature, or of the Executive (when the Legislature cannot be convened) against domestic Violence.

Article V

The Congress whenever two-thirds of both houses shall deem it necessary, shall propose Amendments to this Constitution, or, on the Application of the Legislatures of two-thirds of the several States, shall call a Convention for proposing Amendments, which, in either Case, shall be valid to all Intents and Purposes, as part of this Constitution, when ratified by the Legislature of three-fourths of the several States, or by Conventions in three-fourths thereof, as the one or the other Mode of Ratification may be proposed by the Congress; Provided that no Amendment which may be made prior to the Year One thousand eight hundred and eight shall in any Manner affect the first and fourth Clauses in the Ninth Section of the first Article; and that no State, without its Consent, shall be deprived of its equal Suffrage in the Senate.

Article VI

All Debts contracted and Engagements entered into, before the Adoption of this Constitution, shall be as valid against the United States under this Constitution, as under the Confederation.

This Constitution, and the Laws of the United States which shall be make in Purusance thereof; and all Treaties made, or which shall be made, under the Authority of the United States, shall be the supreme Law of the Land; and the Judges in every State shall be bound thereby, any Thing in the Constitution of Laws of any State to the Contrary notwithstanding.

The Senators and Representatives before mentioned, and the Members of the several State Legislatures, and all executive and judicial Officers, both of the United States and of the several States, shall be bound by Oath or Affirmation, to support this Constitution;

---

[1] Obsolete. See the Thirteenth Amendment.

but no religious Test shall ever be required as a Qualification to any Office or public Trust under the United States.

Article VII

The Ratification of the Conventions of nine States shall be sufficient for the Establishment of this Constitution between the States so ratifying the Same. Done in Convention by the Unanimous Consent of the States Present the Seventeenth Day of September in the Year of our Lord one thousand seven hundred and Eighty seven and of the Independence of the United States of America the Twelfth. In Witness whereof We have hereunto subscribed our Names.

Go. Washington
Presid't and deputy from Virginia

Delaware
Geo: Read
John Dickinson
Jaco: Broom
Gunning Bedford jun
Richard Bassett

Maryland
James McHenry
Danl Carroll
Dan: of St. Thos Jenifer

South Carolina
J. Rutledge
Charles Pinckney
Charles Cotesworth Pinckney
Pierce Butler

Georgia
William Few
Abr Baldwin

Virginia
John Blair
James Madison, Jr.

North Carolina
Wm Blount
Hu Williamson
Richd Dobbs Spaight

Pennsylvania
B. Franklin

New York
Alexander Hamilton

New Jersey
Wil: Livingston
David Brearley
Wm. Paterson
Jona: Dayton

New Hampshire
John Langdon
Nicholas Gilman

Massachusetts
Nathaniel Gorham
Rufus King

Connecticut
Wm. Saml Johnson
Roger Sherman
Robt. Morris

Thos. Fitzsimmons
James Wilson
Thomas Mifflin
Geo. Clymer
Jared Ingersoll
Gouv Morris

Attest:
William Jackson, Secretary

Amendments[1]

Amendment I

Congress shall make no law respecting an establishment of religion, or prohibiting the free exercise thereof; or abridging the freedom of speech, or of the press; or the right of the people peaceably to assemble, and to petition the Government for a redress of grievances.

Amendment II

A well regulated Militia, being necessary to the security of a free State, the right of the people to keep and bear Arms, shall not be infringed.

Amendment III

No Soldier shall, in time of peace be quartered in any house, without the consent of the Owner, nor in time of war, but in a manner to be prescribed by law.

Amendment IV

The right of the people to be secure in their persons, houses, papers, and effects, against unreasonable searches and seizures, shall not be violated, and no Warrants shall issue, but upon probable cause, supported by Oath or affirmation, and particularly describing the place to be searched, and the persons or things to be seized.

Amendment V

No person shall be held to answer for a capital, or otherwise infamous crime, unless on a presentation or indictment of a Grand Jury, except in cases arising in the land or naval forces, or in the Militia, when in actual service in time of War or public danger; nor shall any person be subject for the same offense to be twice put in jeopardy of life or limb, nor shall be compelled in any criminal case to be a witness against himself, nor be deprived of life, liberty, or property, without due process of law; nor shall private property be taken for public use, without just compensation.

Amendment VI

In all criminal prosecutions, the accused shall enjoy the right to a speedy and public trial, by an impartial jury of the State and district wherein the crime shall have been committed, which district shall have been previously ascertained by law, and to be informed of the nature and the cause of the accusation; to be confronted with the witnesses against him; to have the compulsory process for obtaining witnesses in his favor, and to have the Assistance of Counsel for his defense.

[1] The first ten Amendments were adopted in 1791.

Amendment VII

In suits at common law, where the value in controversy shall exceed twenty dollars, the right of trial by jury shall be preserved, and no fact by a jury, shall be otherwise reexamined in any Court of the United States, than according to the rules of the common law.

Amendment VIII

Excessive bail shall not be required, nor excessive fines imposed, nor cruel and unusual punishments inflicted.

Amendment IX

The enumeration in the Constitution, of certain rights shall not be construed to deny or disparge others retained by the people.

Amendment X

The powers not delegated to the United States by the Constitution, nor prohibited by it to the States, are reserved to the States respectively, or to the people.

Amendment XI[1]

The Judicial power of the United States shall not be construed to extend to any suit in law or equity, commenced or prosecuted against one of the United States by Citizens of another State, or by Citizens or Subjects of any Foreign States.

Amendment XII[2]

The Electors shall meet in their respective states and vote by ballot for President and Vice President, one of whom, at least, shall not be inhabitant of the same state with themselves; they shall name in their ballots the person voted for as President and in distinct ballots the person voted for as Vice President, and they shall make distinct lists of all persons voted for as President, and of all persons voted for as Vice President, and of the number of votes for each, which lists they shall sign and certify, and transmit sealed to the seat of the government of the United States, directed to the President of the Senate; – The President of the Senate shall, in the presence of the Senate and House of Representatives, open all the certificates and the votes shall then be counted; – The person having the greatest number of votes for President, shall be the President, if such number be a majority of the whole number of Electors appointed; and if no person have such majority, then from the persons having the highest numbers not exceeding three on the list of those voted for as President, the House of Representatives shall choose immediately, by ballot, the President. But in choosing the President, the votes shall be taken by states, the representation from each state having one vote; a quorum for this purpose shall consist of a member or members from two-thirds of the states, and a

[1] Adopted in 1798.
[2] Adopted in 1804.

majority of all the states shall be necessary to a choice. And if the House of Representatives shall not choose a President whenever the right of choice shall devolve upon them, before the fourth day of March next following, then the Vice President shall act as President, as in the case of the death or other constitutional disability of the President. – The person having the greatest number of votes as Vice President, shall be the Vice President, if such number be a majority of the whole number of Electors appointed, and if no person have a majority, then from the two highest numbers on the list, the Senate shall choose the Vice President; a quorum for the purpose shall consist of two-thirds of the whole number of Senators, and a majority of the whole number shall be necessary to a choice. But no person constitutionally ineligible to the office of President shall be eligible to that of Vice President of the United States.

Amendment XIII[1]

Section 1.   Neither slavery nor involuntary servitude, except as a punishment for crime whereof the party shall have been duly convicted, shall exist within the United States, or any place subject to their jurisdiction.

Section 2.   Congress shall have power to enforce this article by appropriate legislation.

Amendment XIV[2]

Section 1.   All persons born or naturalized in the United States and subject to the jurisdiction thereof, are citizens of the United States and of the State wherein they reside. No State shall make or enforce any law which shall abridge the privileges or immunities of citizens of the United States; nor shall any State deprive any person of life, liberty, or property, without the due process of law; nor deny to any person within its jurisdiction the equal protection of the laws.

Section 2.   Representatives shall be apportioned among the several States according to their respective numbers, counting the whole number of persons in each State, excluding Indians not taxed. But when the right to vote at any election for the choice of electors for President and Vice President of the United States, Representatives in Congress, the Executive and Judicial Officers of a State, or the members of the Legislature thereof, is denied to any of the male inhabitants of such State, being twenty-one years of age, and citizens of the United States, or in any way abridged, except for participation in rebellion, or other crime, the basis of representation therein shall be reduced in the proportion which the number of such male citizens shall bear to the whole number of male citizens twenty-one years of age in such State.

Section 3.   No person shall be Senator or Representative in Congress, or elector of President and Vice President, or hold any office, civil or military, under the United States, or under any State, who, having previously taken an oath, as a member of Congress, or as an officer of the United States, or as a member of any State legislature, or as an executive or judicial officer of any State, to support the Constitution of the United States, shall have engaged in insurrection or rebellion against the same, or given aid or comfort to the enemies thereof. But Congress may by a vote of two-thirds of each House, remove such disability.

---

[1] Adopted in 1865.
[2] Adopted in 1868.

Section 4. The validity of the public debt of the United States, authorized by law, including debts incurred for payment of pensions and bounties for services in suppressing insurrection or rebellion, shall not be questioned. But neither the United States nor any State shall assume or pay any debt or obligation incurred in aid or insurrection of rebellion against the United States, or any claim for the loss or emancipation of any slave; but all such debts, obligations and claims shall be held illegal and void.

Section 5. The Congress shall have power to enforce, by appropriate legislation, the provisions of this article.

Amendment XV[1]

Section 1. The right of citizens of the United States to vote shall not be denied or abridged by the United States or by any State on account of race, color, or previous condition of servitude.

Section 2. The Congress shall have power to enforce this article by appropriate legislation.

Amendment XVI[2]

The Congress shall have power to lay and collect taxes on incomes, from whatever source derived, without apportionment among the several States, and without regard to any census or enumeration.

Amendment XVII[3]

The Senate of the United States shall be composed of two Senators from each State, elected by the people thereof, for six years, and each Senator shall have one vote. The electors in each state shall have the qualifications requisite for electors of the most numerous branch of the state legislatures.

When vacancies happen in the representation of any State in the Senate, the executive authority of such State shall issue writs of election to fill such vacancies: Provided, That the legislature of any State may empower the executive thereof to make temporary appointments until the people fill the vacancies by election as the legislature may direct.

This amendment shall not be so construed as to affect the election of term of any Senator chosen before it becomes valid as part of the Constitution.

Amendment XVIII[4]

Section 1. After one year from the ratification of this article the manufacture, sale, or transportation in intoxicating liquors within, the importation thereof into, or the exportation thereof from the United States and all territory subject to the jurisdiction thereof for beverage purposes is hereby prohibited.

Section 2. The Congress and the several States shall have concurrent power to enforce this article by appropriate legislation.

[1] Adopted in 1870.
[2] Adopted in 1913.
[3] Adopted in 1913.
[4] Adopted in 1919. Repealed by the Twenty-first Amendment.

Section 3. This article shall be inoperative unless it shall have been ratified as an amendment to the Constitution by the legislatures of the several States, as provided in the Constitution, within seven years from the date of the submission hereof to the States by the Congress.

Amendment XIX[1]

The right of Citizens of the United States to vote shall not be denied or abridged by the United States or by any State on account of sex.

Congress shall have power to enforce this article by appropriate legislation.

Amendment XX[2]

Section 1. The terms of the President and Vice President shall end at noon on the 20th day of January, and the terms of Senators and Representatives at noon on the 3d day of January, of the years in which such terms would have ended if this article had not been ratified; and the terms of their successors shall then begin.

Section 2. The Congress shall assemble at least once in every year, and such meeting shall begin at noon on the 3d day of January, unless they shall by law appoint a different day.

Section 3. If, at the time fixed for the beginning of the term of the President, the President elect shall have died, the Vice President elect shall become President. If a President shall not have been chosen before the time fixed for the beginning of his term, or if the President elect shall have failed to qualify, then the Vice President elect shall act as President until a President shall have qualified; and the Congress may by law provide for the case wherein neither a President elect nor a Vice President elect shall have qualified, declaring who shall then act as President, or the manner in which one who is to act shall be selected, and such person shall act accordingly until President or Vice President shall have qualified.

Section 4. The Congress may by law provide for the case of the death of any of the persons from whom the House of Representatives may choose a President whenever the right of choice shall have devolved upon them, and for the case of the death of any of the persons from whom the Senate may choose a Vice President whenever the right of choice shall have devolved upon them.

Section 5. Sections 1 and 2 shall take effect on the 15th day of October following the ratification of this article.

Section 6. This article shall be inoperative unless it shall have been ratified as an amendment to the Constitution by the legislatures of three-fourths of the several States within seven years from the date of its submission.

Amendment XXI[3]

Section 1. The eighteenth article of amendment to the Constitution of the United States is hereby repealed.

---

[1] Adopted in 1920.
[2] Adopted in 1933.
[3] Adopted in 1933.

Section 2. The transportation or importation into any State, Territory, or possession of the United States for delivery or use therein of intoxicating liquors, in violation of the laws thereof, is hereby prohibited.

Section 3. This article shall be inoperative unless it shall have been ratified as an amendment to the Constitution by conventions in the several States, as provided in the Constitution, within seven years from the date of the submission hereof to the States by the Congress.

Amendment XXII[1]

Section 1. No person shall be elected to the office of the President more than twice, and no person who has held the office of President, or acted as President, for more than two years of a term to which some other person was elected President shall be elected to the office of the President more than once. But this Article shall not apply to any person holding the office of President when this Article was proposed by the Congress, and shall not prevent any person who may be holding the office of President, or acting as President, during the term within which this Article becomes operative from holding the office of President or acting as President during the remainder of such term.

Section 2. This article shall be inoperative unless it shall have been ratified as an amendment to the Constitution by the Legislatures of three-fourths of the several States within seven years from the date of its submission to the States by the Congress.

Amendment XXIII[2]

Section 1. The District constituting the seat of Government of the United States shall appoint in such manner as the Congress may direct:

A number of electors of President and Vice President equal to the whole number of Senators and Representatives in Congress to which the District would be entitled if it were a State, but in no event more than the least populous State; they shall be in addition to those appointed by the States; but they shall be considered, for the purposes of the election of President and Vice President, to be electors appointed by a State; and they shall meet in the District and perform such duties as provided by the twelfth article of amendment.

Section 2. The Congress shall have power to enforce this article by appropriate legislation.

Amendment XXIV[3]

Section 1. The right of citizens of the United States to vote in any primary or other election for the President or Vice President, for electors for President or Vice President, or for Senator or Representative in Congress, shall not be denied or abridged by the United States or any State by reason of failure to pay any poll tax or other tax.

Section 2. The Congress shall have power to enforce this article by appropriate legislation.

---

[1] Adopted in 1951.
[2] Adopted in 1961.
[3] Adopted in 1964.

Amendment XXV[1]

Section 1.   In case of the removal of the President from office or his death or resignation, the Vice President shall become President.

Section 2.   Whenever there is a vacancy in the office of the Vice President, the President shall nominate a Vice President who shall take the office upon confirmation by a majority vote of both houses of Congress.

Section 3.   Whenever the President transmits to the President pro tempore of the Senate and the Speaker of the House of Representatives his written declaration that he is unable to discharge the powers and duties of his office, and until he transmits to them a written declaration to the contrary, such powers and duties shall be discharged by the Vice President as Acting President.

Section 4.   Whenever the Vice President and a majority of either the principal officers of the executive departments or of such other body as Congress may by law provide, transmit to the President pro tempore of the Senate and the Speaker of the House of Representatives their written declaration that the President is unable to discharge the powers and duties of his office, the Vice President shall immediately assume the powers and duties of the office as Acting President.

Thereafter, when the President transmits to the President pro tempore of the Senate and the Speaker of the House of Representatives, his written declaration that no inability exists, he shall resume the powers and duties of his office unless the Vice President and a majority of either the principal officers of the executive department or of such other body as Congress may by law provide, transmit within four days to the President pro tempore of the Senate and the Speaker of the House of Representatives their written declaration that the President is unable to discharge the powers and duties of his office. Thereupon Congress shall decide the issue, assembling within 48 hours for that purpose if not in session. If the Congress, within 21 days after receipt of the latter written declaration, or, if Congress is not in session, with 21 days after Congress is required to assemble, determines by two-thirds vote of both houses that the President is unable to discharge the powers and duties of his office, the Vice President shall continue to discharge the same as Acting President; otherwise, the President shall resume the powers and duties of his office.

Amendment XXVI[2]

Section 1.   The Right to Citizens of the United States, who are eighteen years of age or older, to vote shall not be denied or abridged by the United States or by any State on account of age.

Section 2.   The Congress shall have power to enforce this article by appropriate legislation.

Amendment XXVII[3]

No law, varying the compensation for the services of the Senators and Representatives, shall take effect, until an election of Representatives shall have intervened.

---

[1] Adopted in 1967.
[2] Adopted in 1971.
[3] Adopted in 1992.

Index